Columba

Columba

Tim Clarkson

First published in Great Britain in 2012 by
John Donald, an imprint of Birlinn Ltd

West Newington House
10 Newington Road
Edinburgh
EH9 1QS

www.birlinn.co.uk

ISBN: 978 0 85976 711 8

British Library Cataloguing-in-Publication Data
A catalogue record for this book is available
on request from the British Library

Typeset and designed by Mark Blackadder

Printed and bound in Britain by Bell and Bain Ltd, Glasgow

Contents

List of Plates

List of Maps

Genealogical Tables

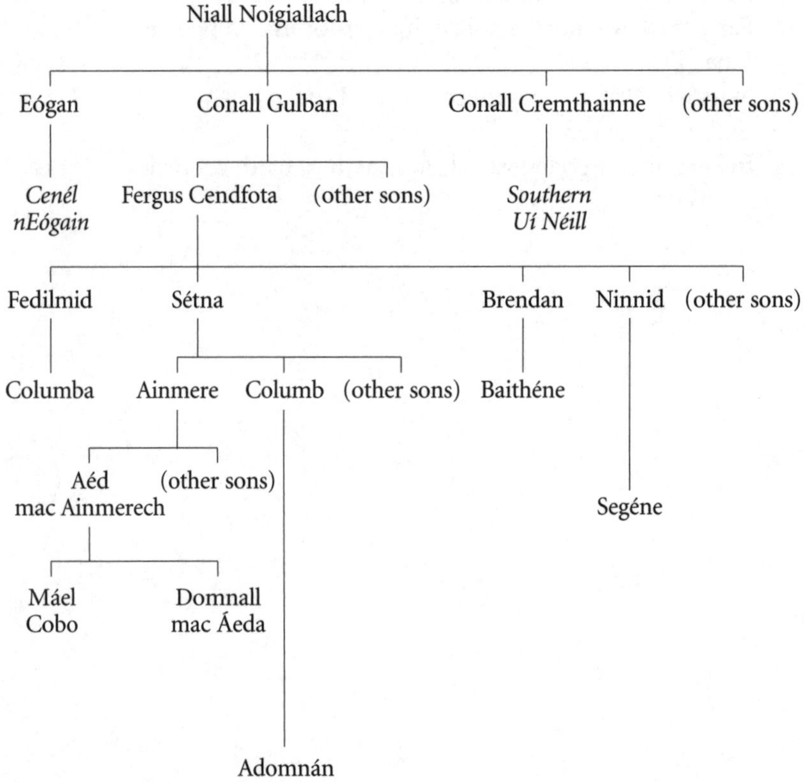

CENÉL CONAILL

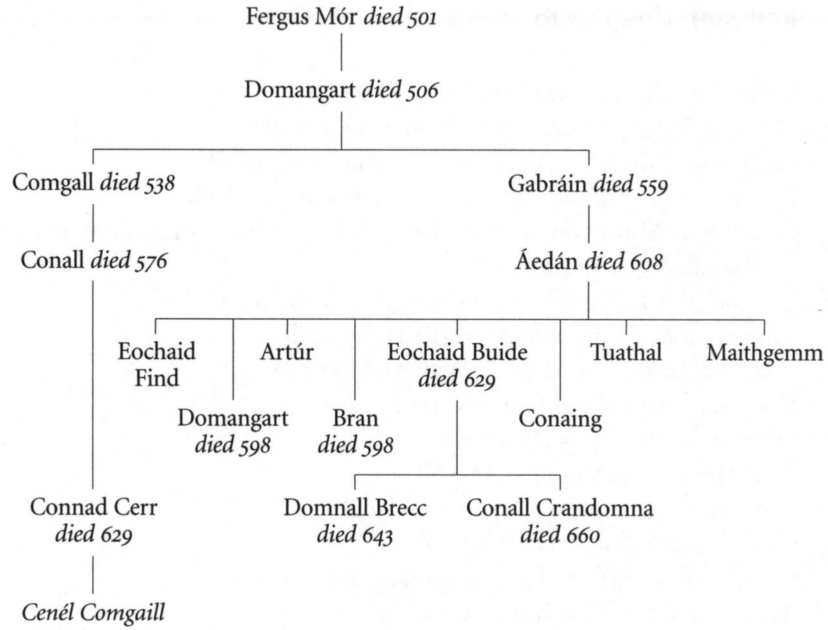

CENÉL nGABRÁIN

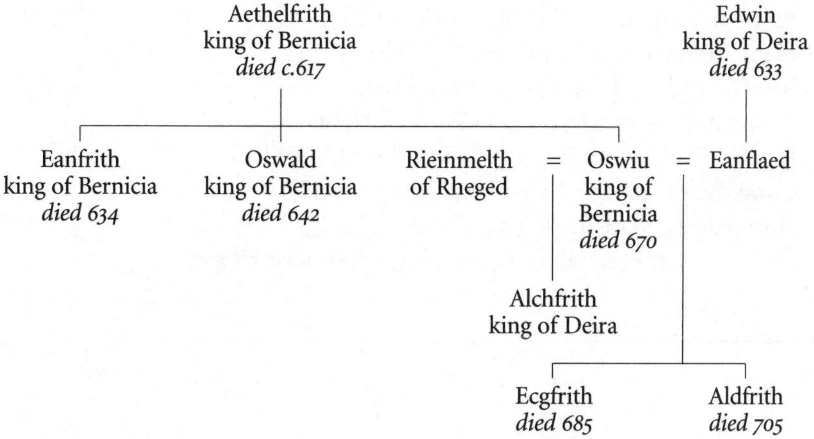

SEVENTH-CENTURY KINGS OF NORTHUMBRIA

Kings of Tara, c.540–1000

Tuathal Maelgarb, d.544 (Southern Uí Néill)
Diarmait mac Cerbaill, d.565 (Southern Uí Néill)
Forgus mac Muirchertaig, d.566? (Northern Uí Néill)
Domnall mac Muirchertaig, d.566? (Northern Uí Néill)
Báetán mac Muirchertaig, d.572 (Northern Uí Néill) or Báetán mac Cairill, d.579 (Dál Fiatach)
Eochaid mac Domnaill, d.572 (Northern Uí Néill)
Ainmere mac Sétnai, d.569 (Northern Uí Néill)
Áed mac Ainmerech, d.598 (Northern Uí Néill)
Fiachna Lurgan, d.626 (Dál nAraidi)
Colmán Rímid, d.604 (Northern Uí Néill)
Áed Sláine, d.604 (Southern Uí Néill)
Áed Uaridnach, d.612 (Northern Uí Néill)
Congal Cáech, d.637 (Dál nAraidi)
Cathal mac Finguine, d.742 (Eoganachta of Munster)
Áed Allán, d.743 (Northern Uí Néill)
Donnchad Midi, d.797 (Southern Uí Néill)
Áed Oirdnide, d.819 (Northern Uí Néill)
Conchobar mac Donnchada, d.833 (Southern Uí Néill)
Niall Caille, d.846 (Northern Uí Néill)
Máel Sechnaill, d.862 (Southern Uí Néill)
Áed Findliath, d.879 (Northern Uí Néill)
Flann Sinna, d.916 (Southern Uí Néill)
Niall Glúndub, d.919 (Northern Uí Néill)
Donnchad Donn, d.944 (Southern Uí Néill)
Ruaidrí Ua Canannáin, d.950 (Northern Uí Néill)
Congalach Cnogba, d.956 (Southern Uí Néill)
Domnall ua Néill, d.980 (Northern Uí Néill)
Máel Sechnaill mac Domnaill, d.1022 (Southern Uí Néill)

Introduction: Finding Columba

Christianity arrived in Britain during the Roman period. It was one of many foreign cults and, at first, attracted only a small number of followers. Not until the early fourth century AD, when Constantine the Great became a high-profile convert, did Christianity gain wider popularity throughout the Roman Empire. Even then, its progress in Britain remained slow. The native Britons and their Roman masters were reluctant to abandon their old beliefs. By c.400, when the Roman occupation of Britain was drawing to a close, much of the population still worshipped pagan gods. This was especially true of northern areas beyond the imperial frontier, in what is now Scotland, and also in neighbouring Ireland which had never been part of the Empire. During the fifth century, however, considerable headway was made by Christian missionaries labouring in what had once been the Roman part of Britain, roughly a large swathe of territory between the English Channel and the Forth–Clyde isthmus. In this region churches and monasteries were founded, priests were ordained and bishops were appointed. An ecclesiastical hierarchy arose, its personnel acknowledging the authority of the Pope in Rome. Before the end of the fifth century, missionaries from Britain had already crossed over to Ireland and were establishing churches there. Others perhaps ventured into the far north of their own land, into regions beyond the Forth–Clyde line, to bring the Word of God to the heathen Picts.

By the middle of the sixth century, the erstwhile Roman areas of Britain had been largely Christianised. In contemporary Ireland, too, the new religion was overtaking paganism as the preferred package of spiritual beliefs. It was around this time that St Columba came to prominence on both sides of the Irish Sea, as a key player in political as well as in ecclesiastical affairs. In life he achieved much as a holy man of great energy and charisma. In death he was venerated as the patron saint of numerous churches in Britain and Ireland, some of which claimed him – rightly or wrongly – as their founder. Today he is primarily associated with the tiny Scottish isle of Iona, the site of his most famous monastery, but his story begins in Ireland, the country of his birth. In medieval times, many Irish churches claimed to have been founded by him, even when their true origins belong to much later periods. Some claims are, nevertheless, likely to be genuine, as we shall see in the following chapters.

The main aim of this book is to tell the story of Columba as both living man and venerated saint. It is not, however, a straightforward biography. While there is no doubt that Columba existed, and that we know more about him than about any of his contemporaries, a complete biographical portrait is beyond reach. This is because the sources of information are not themselves biographical by any modern definition of the term. What they offer instead is an idealised picture of a renowned holy man whose eligibility for sainthood was evident as much to his companions in life as to later generations of followers. More is said on this topic in Chapter 1, but here we can briefly mention the most valuable of the early sources: *Vita Sancti Columbae*, the Life of St Columba, written by Abbot Adomnán of Iona. Adomnán was himself elevated to sainthood in recognition of his achievements and was one of the great churchmen of his age. He wrote the *Vita* at the end of the seventh century, about a hundred years after Columba's death. He is not only our main source of information on Columba's life and career, but also played a major role in promoting the cult of Columba the saint. In the following pages it will become evident that parts of the present study are as much about Adomnán as about Columba himself.

Three broad themes form the principal threads of this book. One is the story of Columba from his birth in Ireland c.521 to his death on Iona in 597. This constitutes the biographical element and is the main topic of Chapters 2 to 6. It runs parallel with a second thread, a study of Adomnán in his role as author of *Vita Sancti Columbae*. The third thread is the posthumous cult of Columba that arose in the wake of his death. A visible manifestation of this cult was the growth of a federation or *paruchia* of churches and monasteries acknowledging the spiritual leadership of his successors in the abbacy of Iona. Chapters 7 and 8 trace the story of this federation from its origins in the saint's lifetime to its decline in the twelfth century. The human elements of the *paruchia* – the monks, nuns and lay people who dwelt at the various sites within it – comprised the Columban *familia* or 'family'. Their story, too, will be told in this book. A look at modern perceptions of Columba forms the basis of the final chapter which serves as an epilogue to his life and achievements.

Most of the 'history' mentioned in this book took place in the early medieval period, a span of roughly seven hundred years from c.400 to c.1100. It was a time of profound changes across the British Isles, not the least of which was the triumph of Christianity over paganism. Other significant developments were political rather than spiritual and included the rise of new 'ethnic' identities and the disappearance of old ones. Thus, in the first half of the book, we encounter the native Picts of ancient Scotland, but they play no part in the narrative after we pass the beginning of the tenth century. The disappearance of a recognisable Pictish identity coincides with, and was to some extent a direct result of, the birth of Alba, a kingdom that eventually became the great medieval realm of Scotland. Alba's principal language was Gaelic, the main language of Ireland and the native speech of both Columba and Adomnán. Gaelic had long been spoken by the people we usually call 'Scots' whose ancestral territory comprised much of Argyll and many Hebridean isles as well as parts of northern Ireland. The Picts originally spoke a different language, a tongue related more closely to Welsh, until they too adopted Gaelic when they merged with the Scots in the ninth century. Both Irish and Scottish Gaelic, together with Welsh and Pictish, belong to the Celtic group of languages. The origins of all four lie in the indigenous tongues of the British Isles that were spoken in prehistoric, pre-Roman times. These Celtic languages are thus quite distinct from English, which was introduced to Britain by Angles, Saxons and other Germanic immigrants in the fourth and fifth centuries. The various groups of 'Anglo-Saxons' eventually conquered nearly all the southern half of Britain, assimilating or expelling the native Britons and establishing kingdoms of their own. By c.1000 the individual Anglo-Saxon realms had been replaced by a single, unified kingdom which we now call England.

Columba's story begins long before the terms 'England' and 'Scotland' entered the vocabulary of political geography. He lived in an age when Britain and Ireland were divided among numerous small kingdoms whose rulers frequently engaged in warfare with one another. As we shall see, he was born into a prominent noble family and was himself a direct descendant of kings. His ancestry placed him in the highest tier of Irish society, a status that gave him certain advantages in dealings with powerful people. It is worth keeping this in mind when we begin to look for the 'real' Columba, the historical figure behind the saintly image drawn so eloquently by Adomnán. The real Columba was both aristocrat and abbot, an heir of kings as well as a virtuous man of God. This dual aspect of his character – the prince and the priest – will become apparent in the following pages.

CHAPTER 1
The Sources

Vita Columbae

Our main source of information on Columba was produced a hundred years after his death. Its author, Adomnán, was one of the foremost ecclesiastical figures of the early medieval period. He succeeded to the abbacy of Iona in 679 and oversaw the monastery until his passing in 704. A man of great learning, he had already written *De Locis Sanctis*, a major study of the Holy Places, before turning his scholarly attention to Iona's founder. His book about Columba was written in the closing years of the seventh century, at a time when stories and legends of the monastery's beginnings were circulating among the brethren. Some of these existed in written form, but most were oral tales passed down through generations of monks. From this large body of tradition Adomnán selected the raw data for his best-known literary work: *Vita Sancti Columbae*, 'Life of Saint Columba' (hereafter *Vita Columbae*).

The *Vita* is rightly regarded as a rich storehouse of information on Columba and his times. It is not a work of biography in the modern sense. Its main purpose was not to present a factual narrative of Columba's life and career, but rather to explain why he deserved the mantle of sainthood, and why his followers were right to revere him a hundred years later. Additional objectives of the *Vita* included the promotion of Iona as the premier religious centre of the Gaelic world and as the mother-church of a federation of satellite monasteries in Ireland and Britain. The book also gave its author an opportunity to disseminate his views on a number of issues that were important in his own era. Indeed, only by recognising Adomnán's motives in writing the *Vita* can we begin to understand what he says about Columba and his reasons for saying it. This is a crucial point, and one that needs to be kept in mind by any modern reader. None of us should approach *Vita Columbae* without a measure of caution. To fully appreciate its contents we need to understand not only why Adomnán wrote it, but for whom it was written and what the first generation of readers – his contemporaries on Iona and elsewhere – expected to find in its pages.

Vita Columbae belongs to a literary genre called 'hagiography', this being an umbrella term for biographical writings about saints. The word derives from Greek *hagios*, 'holy', which, when used in a Christian context, can also mean 'saint'. Adomnán was familiar with this genre long before making his own contribution to it. His extensive study of religious texts had brought him into contact with the best examples of Continental hagiography, such as the fourth-century Latin *vita* or 'Life' of Saint Martin of Tours by Sulpicius Severus. Copies of this and other influential *vitae* were housed in the great monastic libraries of Western Christendom, including those at major sites in Britain and Ireland. Adomnán no doubt became acquainted with many of these works in his youth, during his clerical education, and clearly had detailed knowledge of them when he commenced his Life of Columba. He used the earlier *vitae* as templates for his book, knowing that their influence on the structure of his narrative would be recognised and appreciated by his readers. By drawing on techniques employed by esteemed Christian writers of the past, Adomnán was not so much seeking to boost his own literary credentials as demonstrating that Columba deserved the literary treatment bestowed upon Martin and other famous saints.[1]

All hagiographers in early medieval times were members of the clergy. So, too, were the overwhelming majority of their readers. In an era when literacy was the preserve of ecclesiastical personnel and of a few members of the secular elite, the intended audience for the Life of a saint was highly exclusive. *Vita Columbae* was written primarily for the brethren of Iona and for the wider community of holy men and women in the Columban family of churches. These folk were accustomed to reading and studying religious texts as part of their daily routine. Many were accomplished scholars and teachers, or expert copyists of manuscripts, or well-known authorities on aspects of Christian doctrine. They were interested in history, just as we are today, but their interpretation of past events differed from ours. To a monk or nun in early medieval times, history was not so much a record of human progress as clear evidence of the unfolding of God's Will. Proof that this was the case could be found in the Bible, where the events of the Old Testament hinted at what was to come in the New. History, then, was not simply a record of the past, but a guide to the future. More specifically, it provided lessons from bygone times that enabled folk in the present to be better-equipped for troubles that might lie ahead. This was the sort of message that a medieval hagiographer was expected to offer in the pages of a *vita*. Thus, while Adomnán's readers wanted to learn about Columba's career as a holy man in the sixth century, they also hoped to gain useful insights into their own lives. They wanted the book to have contemporary relevance. What this means for today's historian is that *Vita Columbae* is as much a primary source for Adomnán's time as for Columba's.[2]

The structure of Vita Columbae

Four *vitae*, in particular, had a profound influence on Adomnán. One, the Life of St Martin by Sulpicius Severus, has already been mentioned. The others were the Life of St Antony, written in Greek by Athanasius of Alexandria, the Life of St Germanus by Constantius of Lyon and the Life of St Benedict, the latter incorporated by Pope Gregory the Great in his *Dialogues*. Traces of all four are discernible in *Vita Columbae*, with the influence of Sulpicius and Gregory being especially evident.[3] The most obvious similarity between the *vitae* of Columba, Martin and Benedict is their tripartite structure, a feature not uncommon in hagiography. Although its origins lie in Classical Greek biographical writing, this threefold division had special appeal to Christian authors, not least because it enabled them to reflect the Holy Trinity in the arrangement of their narratives. By dividing his work into three sections or 'books', Adomnán replicated an arrangement employed by Sulpicius in the fifth century and used with good effect by Gregory in the sixth.[4] Likewise, Adomnán borrowed the idea of two prefaces from Sulpicius, who had in turn borrowed the same from the *vita* of Antony by Athanasius. This particular device did not originate with Athanasius, who wrote only one preface, but with a Latin translation of *Vita Antonii* by Evagrius of Antioch who added a preface of his own to an existing one.[5] Adomnán's familiarity with the Evagrius edition is confirmed by his word-for-word borrowing from it, especially in the account of Columba's final days. He saw little need to acknowledge this and other literary debts, knowing that the influence of earlier hagiographers would be recognised by his monastic readers. Far from being derided as plagiarism, as they would surely be today, these deliberate and obvious imitations would have met with the approval of his peers.

The first preface of *Vita Columbae* is too brief to give a detailed introduction to the overall structure, but the second is more illuminating. Here, Adomnán tells us that the first section of the work contains Columba's 'prophetic revelations', the second 'divine miracles worked through him', while the third describes 'angelic apparitions and certain phenomena of heavenly light'. Scholars have noted the close parallel with the second preface of Sulpicius, which likewise gives a synopsis of the three-part division. In his own second preface, Adomnán included themes and portions of text borrowed from the Life of Martin. His assurance that 'no one should think I would write anything false about this remarkable man [Columba], nor even anything doubtful or uncertain' is an echo of words used by Sulpicius.[6] Similarly, near the end of the second preface, Adomnán relates that Columba 'could not let even an hour pass without giving himself to praying or reading or writing or some other task', again paraphrasing a comment originally attached by Sulpicius to Martin.[7]

One aspect of *Vita Columbae* that clearly sets it apart from modern biographical writing is a jumbled chronology. Episodes in Columba's life are not described in the order in which they happened. Instead, the reader is carried backwards and forwards across the saint's career. Adomnán makes no apology for rejecting a strict linear timeline in favour of a less rigid, thematic approach. In the first chapter of Book One, he informs his readers that the ensuing prophecies of Columba are to be presented *praepostero ordine*, 'out of their proper order'.[8] A prime example is the story of Columba's pregnant mother Eithne being visited by an angel who announced that her unborn son had a great destiny. Although we might have expected such a tale to appear near the beginning of a saintly *vita*, we do not encounter it until fairly late in Book Three. This does not mean that *Vita Columbae* has a random or haphazard structure. On the contrary, Adomnán had already indicated, via the second preface, that he preferred to group what he regarded as the key events of Columba's life, the saintly miracles, by category rather than by chronology. His choice of categories – prophecies, miracles of power and apparitions of angels or of heavenly light – finds its closest parallel in Gregory's *Dialogues*, where miracles associated with St Benedict are grouped in an almost identical way.[9] Not every miraculous event fitted neatly into Adomnán's threefold arrangement. Some fitted into more than one category, an issue of which he himself was fully aware.[10] In Book Two, for instance, supposedly a collection of Columba's miracles of power, he placed the story of a monk called Librán. Although largely concerned with prophecy and therefore appearing to belong more correctly with the theme of Book One, this particular tale conformed to Adomnán's ideas about certain prophecies providing evidence of miraculous power. We therefore encounter it in Book Two.[11]

Book Three demonstrates how Columba, a person selected by God for a special destiny, became doubly worthy of sainthood through good deeds and unselfish living. The key miraculous theme here is the appearance of angels and heavenly light, usually via dreams or visions, to various individuals including the saint himself. These apparitions served an important hagiographical purpose in confirming Columba's special connection with the Divine, a point emphasised by Adomnán when he stressed that such things were revealed as clear, complete visions to Columba alone. Other folk, being not specially chosen by God, saw only part of an apparition rather than the whole.[12] The visions of angels seen by Columba usually came at the moment of a person's death when the celestial emissaries arrived to carry away the soul of the deceased. Angelic visions received by other people include the one mentioned above, in which an angel appeared to Eithne while she was pregnant with Columba, together with instances where angels were seen walking alongside the saint. The moment of Columba's own death, when his ascension to Heaven was accompanied by an ethereal host, was also claimed to have been witnessed by contemporaries.

Adomnán's sources

Vita Columbae is now more than thirteen centuries old. It is a uniquely valuable work and we should consider ourselves fortunate that it has survived into our time. Not only has no Columba-related hagiography of similar quality been preserved, it is likely that nothing comparable to Adomnán's text was ever written. He was, in any case, the ideal person to take on such a task. His intellectual and literary talents gave him the necessary qualifications to write a Life worthy of Iona's founder, while his high reputation in lands far beyond the monastery guaranteed that his work would be well received. He realised, nonetheless, that his authorship alone was not enough to ensure widespread acceptance and approval. Unconfirmed, uncorroborated testimony is always vulnerable to challenge or doubt. This was true even in early medieval times when belief in saintly miracles and other supernatural phenomena was normal. Adomnán knew this, of course, and was careful to acknowledge that any statement of alleged 'fact' requires supporting testimony and citation of a reliable source. His diligence in crediting his sources is admirable. He remains, nonetheless, a hagiographer rather than a historian. In the context of his chosen genre he was a master of his craft.[13]

There is no bibliography in *Vita Columbae*, no footnotes or endnotes referring the reader to written sources consulted and verified by the author. If Adomnán had chosen to pepper his text with a modern citation system, we would be confronted today by numerous instances of 'pers. comm.' but few bibliographical references. He states that his information came chiefly from the oral testimony of *experti*, 'learned men', *seniores*, 'elders', and other individuals whom he describes as 'trustworthy men who knew the facts'. In many cases, an informant reported to Adomnán what had been told by an older contemporary who had in turn heard a story about Columba from some long-dead witness of a miracle. Although Adomnán occasionally describes how such information reached him through several stages of transmission, it hardly needs stating that his referencing method would be regarded by modern historians as wholly insufficient. Old traditions passed via word of mouth to a medieval author are, of course, impossible to verify, regardless of whether or not the author identified his informants by name. Needless to say, Adomnán and his peers took a different view. It was enough for them to know that a particular story had been 'handed down to us by learned men'.[14]

We thus come to an important difference between ancient and modern readers of hagiography. Today, we are instinctively sceptical of any medieval author who regarded old tales of supernatural events as reliable evidence. Such scepticism was far less common in Adomnán's time. He and his contemporaries inhabited a world where the boundaries between natural and supernatural occurrences were blurred, a world in which unexplained happenings were commonly attributed to Otherworld powers. Among Christian communities the greatest of these powers was God, whose potency had no limit. Equally limitless was the power manifested by God in the special human beings whom He chose for a Divine purpose. It was believed that such individuals were capable of achieving whatever God wished them to achieve and, by definition, their powers were limited only by whatever boundaries God chose to apply. With an unwavering belief in such principles, Adomnán had no reason to doubt that everything he had been told about Columba's miraculous powers was true.[15] To doubt the existence of such powers was to challenge God's authority. The ease with which some modern readers of the *Vita* dismiss as superstitious nonsense its carefully crafted miracle-stories would have profoundly bemused and distressed its author.

Although the bulk of Adomnán's information about Columba was supplied by oral tradition he does indicate that some of it came 'from what I could find already in writing'.[16] He does not say what these written sources were. There can be little doubt that they included transcriptions of stories that were otherwise orally preserved. Indeed, Adomnán refers to one story, an account of a celestial vision seen by an elderly priest at the moment of Columba's death, that he encountered in both written and spoken forms. It was reported at first-hand to Fergnae, an Irish hermit, who in turn relayed it to monks from Iona. Many years later, when these same brethren were in their twilight years, they described the miracle to Adomnán. 'This vision,' he explained, 'we have found recorded in writing, and we have also learned it from some of those old men to whom Fergnae himself had told the story, and who repeated it without hesitation.'[17] It is unlikely to have been an isolated case. In fact, there is much to commend the suggestion that oral traditions about Columba were committed to writing as part of a systematic programme of documentation initiated within a generation of his death.[18] This is not to imply that Adomnán's written sources were more reliable than unwritten ones. Oral tradition circulating among the monks of Iona in the seventh century is likely to have preserved fairly accurate recollections of the founder alongside fictional or exaggerated reports of his deeds. Nevertheless, those stories in *Vita Columbae* that contain specific details about persons and places were probably written down while eyewitnesses still lived or soon after their passing. Total reliance on verbal transmission of detailed historical and geographical data, such as lineages and place-names, would have been viewed as unwise. Much of what was known about Columba, then, was probably written down on Iona at quite an early stage and preserved for the education of future generations of monks.

Among the literary sources that certainly existed in Adomnán's time was a collection of miracle-stories written by Abbot Cumméne who died on Iona in 669. This has not survived, but we know of its existence because the scribe of the oldest known manuscript of Adomnán's work referred to it. At the end of a passage dealing with Columba's anointing of the warrior-king Áedán mac Gabráin, Adomnán mentions that the saint 'prophesied the future of Áedán's sons and grandsons and great-grandsons'. Although Adomnán says nothing more about this prophecy, the scribe of the oldest manuscript appended a brief description prefaced by the following words:

> Cumméne the White in the book which he wrote on the miraculous powers of St Columba gives this account of St Columba's prophecy about Áedán and his descendants and his kingdom.[19]

Cumméne succeeded to the abbacy of Iona in 657, having probably been a resident of the monastery for many years. Like Columba, he belonged to the Cenél Conaill kindred of northern Ireland, as did many of Iona's early abbots. He may have arrived on Iona during the thirty-year abbacy of his uncle Ségéne (died 652). Indeed, it seems likely that this was the case, and that the book on Columba's miracles was written during this period. Historians now see Cumméne's book as the product of a formal programme of information-gathering implemented and supervised by Ségéne.[20] The latter seems to have been eager to collect the kind of oral traditions mentioned above, including eyewitness testimonies by people who had met Columba in life. We may be seeing glimpses of his project in Adomnán's narrative. In one passage, for instance, we learn of a monk called Silnan who not only witnessed one of Columba's miracles but played an active part in it. Adomnán asserts the truth of the story by adding that Silnan recounted it 'in the presence of Abbot Ségéne and other elders'.[21] In another passage, Adomnán tells of a young Irish boy called Ernéne who received Columba's blessing and upon whom the saint laid a prophecy. In later years, after becoming a famous priest in his own right, Ernéne related the tale to Ségéne and other senior monks. One of the latter was Failbe, a future abbot of Iona and Adomnán's immediate predecessor. A third example of Ségéne's desire to collect stories of the founder appears in Adomnán's opening chapter, where we learn of a miracle witnessed by the Northumbrian king Oswald on the eve of a great battle in 634. Oswald was a devotee of Columba and claimed that the saint had appeared to him in a vision, prophesying victory and a happy reign. As with the tale of Ernéne, Adomnán heard this tale from Failbe who 'swore that he had heard the story of the vision from the lips of King Oswald himself as he was relating it to Abbot Ségéne'.[22] What these episodes appear to show is a systematic effort by Ségéne to collect direct verbal testimony from people who had witnessed or experienced the effects of Columba's God-given powers. Failbe seems to have played a key role in this exercise, perhaps as note-taker, while Cumméne may have been given the task of compiling the stories into a definitive compendium.

How much use Adomnán made of Cumméne's book of miracles is hard to discern. There can be no doubt that he used it as a source, but he did not simply 'cut and paste' its contents into his own text. We know, for instance, that he omitted Cumméne's description of Columba's prophecy about the descendants of King Áedán. Moreover, it is clear that Adomnán acquired stories that were perhaps unknown to Ségéne and Cumméne and their contemporaries, an example being eyewitness testimony of a fiery pillar that rose into the sky on the night of Columba's death. This was witnessed by Ernéne moccu Fir Roide, a monk at the Irish monastery of Drumhome in Donegal, who recounted it in old age to a young Adomnán, almost certainly before the latter came to Iona.[23] The likely absence of any record of this event among the traditions gathered by Ségéne and Cumméne would not have been regarded as an oversight on their part. On the contrary, a new tale providing further proof of Columba's power would have been welcomed on Iona – as long as the source was reputable. Additional material of this sort was simply added to the existing corpus of data that confirmed Columba as a man selected by God for a special destiny. It is even possible that Adomnán regarded Cumméne's account as inadequate proof of Columba's powers and saw a need to 'beef up' the saint's image with new data that he himself acquired in Ireland. He may also have felt that Cumméne's approach to miracles did not compare favourably with how the hagiographers of other saints were handling this crucial topic.[24]

Cumméne's book was not intended solely as a record of Columba's holiness. Like Adomnán, Cumméne used stories with sixth-century settings to convey information relating to his own time. Of this we can be certain, even though only a tiny fragment of Cumméne's text survives. The fragment is actually a good example of how a fairly conventional story of Columba's prophetic abilities could become a vehicle for comment on seventh-century affairs. As it relates to the complex web of contemporary Irish politics we shall examine it more closely in Chapter 3. The manuscript containing this tiny surviving portion of Cumméne's book is discussed in the next section.

Manuscripts and editions of Vita Columbae

The early medieval history of Britain and Ireland is rarely presented by people who lived and wrote in those times. It is usually encountered indirectly, via several stages of transmission, invariably in much-altered form. This makes it all the more valuable that the two oldest surviving manuscripts of *Historia ecclesiastica gentis Anglorum*, 'The Ecclesiastical History of the English People', a work completed by the Venerable Bede at Jarrow in Northumbria, were written within a dozen years of the author's death in 735.[25] One of these was formerly, but erroneously, believed to contain his signature. We can, in fact, be sure that neither of these manuscripts was seen by Bede. Remarkably, in the case of Adomnán's *Vita Columbae*, our oldest manuscript may have been perused and handled by Adomnán himself. This volume is kept today in the public library at Schaffhausen, a town in northern Switzerland close to the border with Germany. Its scribe wrote the following words on the last page:

> Whoever reads these books of the virtues of St Columba, let him pray to the Lord for me, Dorbbéne, that after death I may possess eternal life.

Historians have identified Dorbbéne as a cleric of that name who became abbot of Iona in the early eighth century. His tenure of the abbacy was brief, lasting barely five months until his death in September 713.[26] Little is known of him, although later traditions linked his ancestry to Cenél Conaill, the Irish royal kindred to which

Columba, Ségéne, Cumméne and Adomnán all belonged. Whether Dorbbéne transcribed a copy of *Vita Columbae* during his brief period as abbot, or at an earlier point in his career, we are unable to say. It nonetheless remains a tantalising possibility that the manuscript we now possess was written before 704, in the scriptorium on Iona, and that it was inspected there by Adomnán.[27]

The manuscript's subsequent history makes quite an interesting tale. At some point it left Iona, perhaps in the early ninth century when the Columban community established a major new monastery at Kells in Ireland. It may have been kept thereafter at the Kells library, or at another Irish monastery, but we cannot be certain of this. What we do know is that the manuscript eventually came to the great abbey of Reichenau, a Benedictine foundation on Lake Constance in southern Germany. Reichenau was established in 724 under Frankish patronage and quickly gained renown as a centre of learning. Like a number of other Frankish monasteries it became a home for Irish monks who came as students and pilgrims. One of these travellers brought Dorbbéne's copy of *Vita Columbae* and gave it to the monastic library. Although we do not know when this happened, a plausible context is the 840s, during the abbacy of Walahfrid Strabo, when the Reichenau library acquired many books. Walahfrid had a special interest in Iona, having written a short *vita* of St Blathmac who was martyred on the island by Vikings in 825. Dorbbéne's book was still at Reichenau eight hundred years later, in 1621, when it was borrowed and transcribed by Father Stephen White, an Irish Jesuit and antiquarian scholar. From White's copy others were made, including one which formed the basis of the first published edition of *Vita Columbae* in 1647. Although the Dorbbéne manuscript probably came back to Reichenau after White had finished with it, its return was not permanent and, in the following century, it was discovered in the public library at Schaffhausen. For this reason it was not transferred to the state library of Baden at Karlsruhe with other literary treasures from Reichenau after the abbey's dissolution in the early 1800s. The present whereabouts of White's personal copy, transcribed by his own hand, are unknown. It may or may not have been among his possessions when he came back to Ireland in 1634.

All the standard modern editions of *Vita Columbae* have been produced from first-hand perusal of Dorbbéne's manuscript. Until fifty years ago, the most authoritative of these was produced in 1857 by the Irish cleric and antiquarian scholar William Reeves (1815–1892). This was superseded in 1961 by a magisterial edition by Alan Orr Anderson and his wife Marjorie Ogilvie Anderson. Prior to Stephen White's discovery of Dorbbéne's text, the *Vita* was known only from manuscripts of much later provenance, the earliest being a copy transcribed at Durham in the late twelfth century. From the same period or a little later comes a manuscript formerly held in the Cottonian collection at London's Ashburnham House which was tragically engulfed by fire in 1731. This volume was severely burned but is now held in the British Library alongside other survivors of the conflagration. Also at the British Library is a much later manuscript of c.1500. Neither this nor its Cottonian or Durham predecessors contain a version of *Vita Columbae* derived from Dorbbéne's. Detailed analysis shows that they were transcribed instead from another copy of the *Vita*, the text of which was slightly different. It is possible that this variant text was the one written for King Alexander I of Scotland in the first quarter of the twelfth century and mentioned in the damaged Cottonian copy. Sadly, it is now lost.[28]

Throughout the present study the Latin quotations from *Vita Columbae* are taken from the Anderson edition of 1961 with reference to a revision produced by Marjorie Anderson thirty years later. English translations of individual extracts are generally those of Richard Sharpe in the Penguin Classics edition of 1995, but, in a few instances, the Andersons' own translation has been preferred. The introductory material and notes provided by both Professor Sharpe and the Andersons are indispensable as sources of biographical data on Columba and Adomnán. Also useful in this regard is the older Latin edition by William Reeves (1857) and J. T. Fowler's revision of it (1894), together with the annotated extracts (in English) presented by Alan Orr Anderson in his magisterial *Early Sources of Scottish History* of 1922.

Amra Coluim Chille

Around the time of Columba's death, a poem was composed in commemoration of his life and deeds. This eulogy was similar to others circulating in contemporary Ireland, all belonging to a genre of 'praise poetry' which had parallels in Britain and elsewhere. *Amra*

Coluim Chille, 'The Eulogy of Columcille', is reputedly the work of Dallán Forgaill, the chief bard of Ireland, whose death occurred one year after the saint's own passing.[29] Most Irish eulogies of the time were composed in praise of warlords and other members of the aristocratic elite, and the *Amra* is no exception. It highlights Columba's membership of the Cenél Conaill of northern Ireland, a branch of the powerful Uí Néill group of royal families. From its verses we gain a glimpse of his origins and early career in Ireland, but only tantalising hints of his later activities in Britain. This is unsurprising, given that a eulogising poet's prime objective was not to offer biographical information but rather to highlight praiseworthy aspects of his subject's character. If Columba had been a mighty warlord, his courage and military skill would have formed the core of Dallán's poem and his victories would have been listed. In keeping with this format, the *Amra* concentrates on the saint's strengths – spiritual and intellectual rather than martial and physical – by praising his humility and asceticism and by noting his triumphs as scholar, teacher and missionary instead of a list of battles. Like the great warrior-princes of the Uí Néill, his own kin, Columba is described in the poem as a 'champion', his chosen battlefield being the Christian's perpetual struggle against sin and temptation.[30] On a literary level, then, *Amra Coluim Chille* appears to blend traditional Celtic praise-poetry about secular deeds with hagiography about religious ones. On a cultural level it combines themes such as ancestry and nobility, both of which were important in ancient Irish society, with overtly Christian ideas such as ascetism and scholarship. What sets the *Amra* apart from conventional hagiography is its avoidance of miracle-stories and other supernatural references. The resulting picture of Columba shows a real person who achieved his goals through virtues inherent in him from birth. It portrays him as a praiseworthy Irish nobleman who had no need of special powers conferred by God.

Despite offering minimal biographical data, the *Amra* remains an important text. Its claim, as stated in a preface, to be the authentic work of Dallán Forgaill makes it potentially our oldest source of information on Columba. It was highly regarded in early medieval Ireland and had become, by c.900, a popular text for students and scholars in Irish monasteries. It is likely that many copies were in circulation before the beginning of the eleventh century, when the preface was added. The copies that survive today are almost like workbooks, the original verses broken into sections annotated with scholarly notes. Other, later verses about Columba were included in the preface, but these add nothing to our picture of the historical figure. Their chief interest is in showing how a large body of poetry and folklore grew around him in the centuries after his death.

Our oldest copy of the *Amra* dates from c.1100, roughly a hundred years after the preface was added to the original poem. It forms part of *Lebor na hUidre*, 'Book of the Dun Cow', itself the oldest surviving text written in Irish Gaelic. The *Lebor* is an important manuscript, the contents of which include, among many other literary treasures, the earliest known version of the famous heroic tale *Táin Bó Cúailnge*, 'The Cattle Raid of Cooley'. Copies of the *Amra* are preserved in a further eight manuscripts, one of which is another compilation of ancient Irish texts written at the end of the twelfth century or at the beginning of the thirteenth.[31] All nine versions of *Amra Coluim Chille* have been studied, edited, and in some cases translated into Modern Irish or English, thus making them accessible to today's scholars. Nevertheless, any hope of unearthing useful data about Columba's life from the fragmented verses and obscure annotations is tempered by the knowledge that we are not dealing here with an unaltered source from c.600. If Adomnán's *Vita* has to be used cautiously, then a similar warning applies to the *Amra* in whichever version we choose to consult it.

The Iona Chronicle

As well as written versions of stories about Columba, the monks of Iona also maintained a record of notable or 'newsworthy' events. Historians usually refer to this long-vanished text as the Iona Chronicle. It took the form of a set of annals in which significant happenings affecting the monastery or of interest to its personnel were recorded in a year-by-year format. Although the original text in which they were written has not survived, these annals were eventually incorporated into other chronicles maintained by monasteries in Ireland which, in turn, were copied and preserved. Of the surviving texts the two principal collections are the *Annals of Ulster* and the *Annals of Tigernach*, both of which are regarded as preserving material originally written on Iona. By rigorously examining these annals historians have been able to deduce that the Iona Chronicle was maintained on the island from c.650 to c.740, with a possibility that the earlier date should be pushed back towards 600.[32] It began as a journal of important events in the life of the monastery before becoming a record of secular as well as religious events further afield. Thus, in addition to making entries for the deeds and obituaries of abbots and bishops, the monks also noted battles, sieges, royal deaths and natural disasters. Some non-ecclesiastical entries refer to people and places in Ireland or Britain, while others describe faraway events, news of which must have reached the Columban community via its extensive contacts in the wider world. It is likely, for instance, that the Chronicle provided Adomnán with information on a volcanic eruption in Italy, an event mentioned in *Vita Columbae*. In addition, the Chronicle's year-by-year entries would have enabled him to construct a chronological framework for his narrative.

The manuscripts containing the Irish annals are late, the oldest being the *Annals of Innisfallen* which survive in a copy written c.1100. Both the *Annals of Ulster* and the *Annals of Tigernach*, our main repositories for data from the Iona Chronicle, are preserved in much later manuscripts of, respectively, the fifteenth and fourteenth centuries. Their relationship to one another is complex, for they do not give identical information. Because the differences in content are most marked in the period before the tenth century, it is sometimes difficult to know which collection is accurately reporting an event originally noted in the Iona Chronicle. In some cases, both sets of annals report the same event in a broadly similar way, but, in other cases, their treatment is very different. To compound the problem, we sometimes find an event reported in one but completely absent from the other. Given the various problems – late manuscripts, inconsistent reporting and uncertain reliability – we must approach the *Annals of Ulster*, the *Annals of Tigernach* and the other Irish annals with careful steps.[33]

The Irish Life

The O'Donnell clan of Tyrconnell in north-east Ireland were the descendants of Cenél Conaill, the ancient royal kindred to which Columba himself belonged. In the early sixteenth century, the clan's most prominent leader was Manus O'Donnell, a dynamic figure whose prowess in war ran alongside interests in literature and history. Manus embarked on a major project to gather stories about Columba from every part of Ireland, his aim being to produce a definitive compendium of information on the saint whom he and his countrymen called *Columcille*. The resulting work was completed in 1532 and given the title *Betha Coluim Chille*, 'Life of Columcille'. Unlike Adomnán's *Vita Columbae*, it was written in Irish Gaelic, 'Old Irish', rather than in Latin. It was not so much a work of hagiography as a synthesis of various types of data drawn from a broad range of sources. Manus himself is credited with blending and reworking this material into a single narrative, but he probably commissioned professional scribes to write it. Although his editing skills are to be admired, the finished text of the *Betha* was not so seamless as to prevent easy identification of its sources. Among the latter was an older Gaelic *vita*, known today as the Irish Life, a work of somewhat later composition than Adomnán's work and partly derived from it. The identity of its original author is unknown.

The Irish Life is a homily or sermon intended for reading aloud. Its primary audience may have been the Columban *paruchia* of churches and monasteries, especially those in Ireland.[34] It differs from *Vita Columbae* by closely following a linear chronology which traces the saint's life from birth to death. In other respects the two works are of similar character. Each, for instance, is essentially a collection of miracle-stories presented by a competent hagiographer. At times, their respective narratives cover the same ground, yet they are not identical. Many passages in the Irish Life were clearly derived from Adomnán's text, often with additional information not provided by him, but others were not. Thus, while Adomnán devotes few words to Columba's childhood, the author of the Irish Life provides a much fuller account of these years, supplementing his narrative with details about the saint's education and early travels. The two works also differ slightly in their geographical emphasis, with a greater number of Ireland-based stories appearing in the Irish Life. Episodes occurring in Britain were of lesser interest to the author and, in some cases, receive scant attention from his pen.[35] His focus on Ireland was not due merely to his being a native of the country, for Adomnán also originated there. It stemmed rather from a desire to show Columba travelling from place to place, establishing churches and monasteries in various Irish kingdoms, and so laying the foundations of the great *paruchia* of later times. How many of these settlements were really founded by Columba was a secondary concern. Many, as we shall see, did not appear until long after the sixth century. Such considerations would not have troubled the author of the Irish Life. He achieved his primary purpose in giving the Columban federation in Ireland clear written testimony that it was an ecclesiastical network of the greatest antiquity.[36]

Historians have long puzzled over the date of the Irish Life. Some regard it as a work of the eleventh or twelfth century, while others date it as early as the ninth.[37] The oldest surviving copy is found in *Leabhar Breac*, 'Speckled Book', a fifteenth-century manuscript now preserved in the Royal Irish Academy. Linguistic features indicate that the original Life belongs to a much earlier period than the compilation of *Leabhar Breac*, while the narrative itself provides further clues. One possible indicator of date is that the manuscript describes certain Irish churches as sites actually visited by Columba. The monastery at Kells, which eventually succeeded Iona as the headquarters of the Columban federation, appears in this context.[38] As we know from other sources that Kells did not become part of the Columba federation until c.804, Columba's alleged visit there almost certainly never took place. The story of the visit is surely a fiction devised in the ninth century to make the connection between Kells and Columba seem more ancient than it really was. In literary terms the story shows that the composition of the Irish Life cannot be dated earlier than 800. We have good reason to date it much later, to the middle years of the twelfth century, when Derry replaced Kells as the primary centre of the *familia*. Justification for assigning this later date comes from a reference in the Life to the Gospel of Martin, a precious totem supposedly retrieved by Columba from the tomb of St Martin at Tours in Frankish Gaul. This was one of the most famous religious artefacts in Ireland and a priceless possession of the Derry monks. After the headship of the federation moved there from Kells around 1150, the Gospel became a key relic associated with the symbolic rank of *comarba*, 'successor', of Columba. The abbots of Derry, as the new holders of this revered title, were also the guardians of the famous Gospel. Any tale describing a visit to Martin's shrine at Tours must have been concocted in this period, to strengthen the bond between Columba and his Derry-based *comarba*. If so, then the Irish Life as a whole may belong to this period. It was most likely produced between 1150 and 1200, at Derry, whence came the copy used by Manus O'Donnell in his compilation of *Betha Coluim Chille*.[39]

Additional texts

Other sources of information on Columba include a 'Life' written at the Frankish monastery of St Gallen in present-day Switzerland. This is essentially an abridged version of Adomnán's *Vita Columbae* and seems to be derived from Dorbbéne's copy. It survives in a manuscript of the ninth century and in a number of later copies, but adds nothing new to Adomnán's portrait of Columba.[40] Rather more intriguing are entries for Columba in the old Irish calendars, the most useful of which is *Félire Óengusso*, 'Martyrology of Óengus', a chronological sequence of verses marking the death-dates of famous saints. Although the earliest surviving copy is in a manuscript of c.1410, close analysis shows the original text to be a composition of some six hundred years earlier.[41] Columba is said to have died on 9 June 597 and the *Martyrology*'s corresponding entry has several items of biographical information not given by Adomnán. The reputed author was Óengus, a monk at the monastery of Tallaght near Dublin. If the attribution is correct, Óengus may also have had a hand in the composition of a similar work produced at the same scriptorium and known today as the *Martyrology of Tallaght*. Both martyrologies are potentially useful sources for our picture of Columba, but they require cautious handling.

Inevitably, given his stature as a renowned holy man, Columba often appears in hagiography relating to other saints. Little of this material is reliable, partly because it survives in manuscripts of late date or of uncertain provenance. A few *vitae* of saints who were genuine contemporaries of Columba can be considered, however, in our search for useful biographical information. These tend to be much shorter, less eloquently written and less accurate in matters of history than *Vita Columbae*. Some incorporate outlandish elements drawn from a common storehouse of hagiographical themes and motifs. Others seem eager to describe encounters between saints who almost certainly never met in life. A small number of these minor *vitae* are cited periodically in the present study and, in one or two instances, their testimony is cautiously accepted as more or less reliable.

Our most useful source outside the texts produced on Iona is Bede's *Ecclesiastical History*, a work already mentioned in the context of the date of *Vita Columbae*. A large amount of modern scholarship continues to be devoted to this highly respected work. Bede had much to say about Columba and Adomnán, and about Iona's role as a major centre of faith and learning. As far as we know, he never saw a copy of *Vita Columbae*, but did, in all likelihood, meet its author in person. An encounter between the two probably took place when Adomnán visited the monastery at Jarrow where Bede spent almost his entire life. Bede had enormous respect for Adomnán, but, at the same time, regarded him as a representative of what some present-day observers refer to as 'Celtic Christianity'. Bede's disdain for certain religious customs practised by 'Celtic' clergy in Britain and Ireland runs like a thread through the *Ecclesiastical History* and means that his account of Columba is not objective. His biased views and strong opinions should always be borne in mind by anyone who consults his writings.

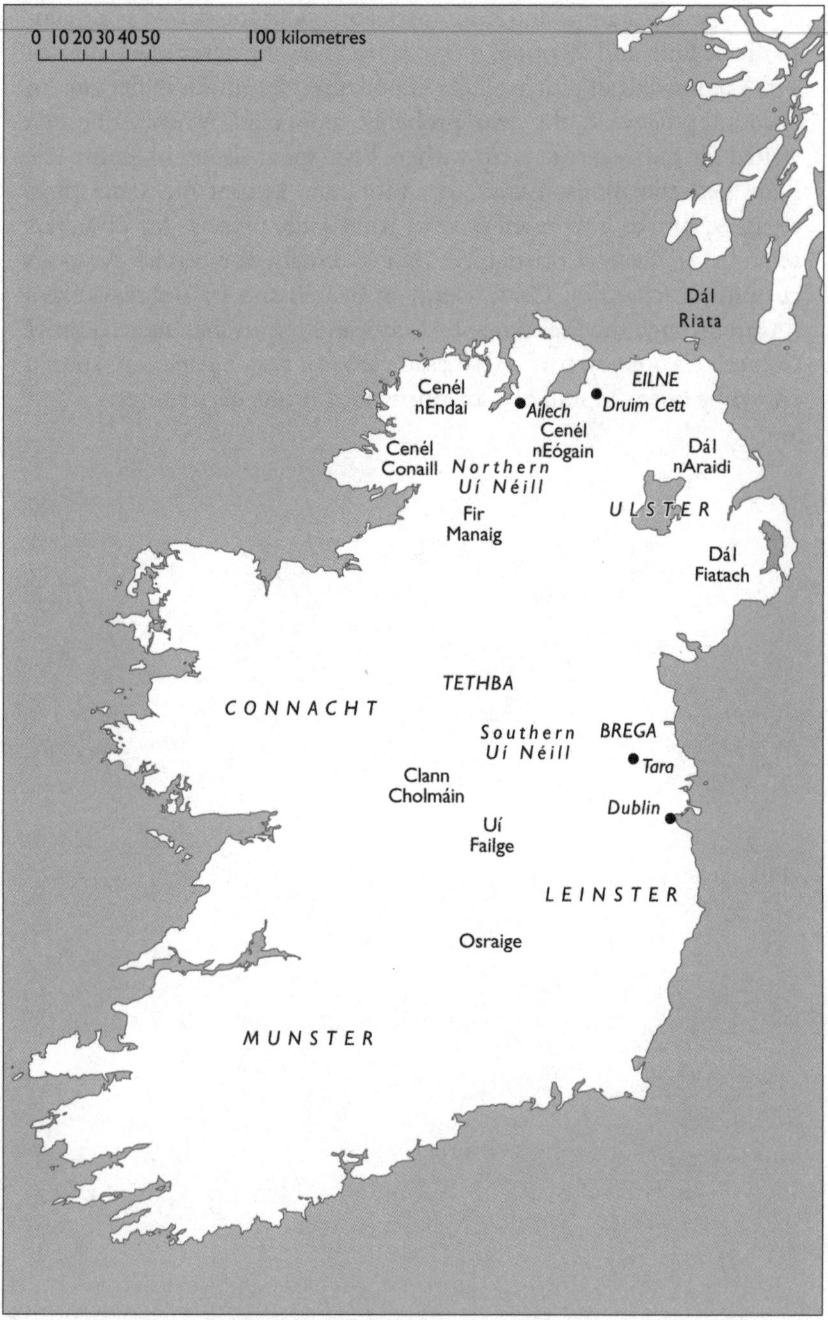

Early medieval Ireland: kingdoms and kindreds

CHAPTER 2
Ireland to Iona

Early Christian Ireland

The beginnings of Irish Christianity can be traced back to the mission of Palladius in the early fifth century. Palladius was probably a priest at Auxerre in Gaul and may have served as deacon under the renowned St Germanus. In 431, Pope Celestine made Palladius a bishop and dispatched him to Ireland as a missionary.[1] The success of the mission seems to have been rather limited, in spite of later optimistic claims by Bede and some Irish clerics. A more widespread tradition credits the conversion of Ireland to Patrick, the country's premier national saint. Patrick was a Briton who, in youth, had been taken to Ireland as a slave. After escaping to freedom, he returned to Britain where he became a priest, but captivity among the heathen Irish had left him with a desire to convert them to Christianity. At some point in the fifth century, most likely after 450, he went back to Ireland to undertake an evangelising mission. If we believe his later hagiographers, he was more successful than Palladius and gained a larger number of converts. An alternative view sees the two missions operating in different parts of the country, with Patrick concentrating on the north, while Palladius, his precursor by one or two generations, was based mainly in Leinster. Moreover, it is possible that the Pope appointed Palladius as bishop to an existing community of Irish Christians as well as missionary to their pagan neighbours. Patrick, on the other hand, may have undertaken his own evangelising labours in districts where paganism was the sole religion.

While little is known of Palladius, the early literature on Patrick is comparatively rich. We even possess Patrick's own writings in the forms of a strongly worded letter to a gang of pirates and a theological 'confession'.[2] After his death he became the focus of a saintly cult which generated a substantial body of oral folklore and written hagiography, all of which has undoubtedly magnified his achievement. In truth, he was one of a number of missionaries who came to Ireland from a Britain that was at least partly Christianised by c.450. Palladius, notwithstanding his likely connection with Gaul, seems also to have had British contacts. There are good reasons to identify the obscure Irish saints Auxilius, Iserninus and Secundinus as Britons who came to Ireland in the fifth century.[3] In fact, it would not be too wide of the mark to see the earliest phase of Irish Christianity not as a papal initiative but as a British one.

Later Irish tradition tells us that Patrick founded many churches. We can assume that he did indeed establish settlements from where his mission continued after his death, but how many is hard to judge. His impact in life was no doubt sufficient to maintain the impetus after he was gone and we should envisage his disciples consolidating his achievements in the sixth century. By c.500, the task of converting pagans was already being undertaken by native Irish priests as well as by a new generation of missionaries from Britain. Monasteries began to appear all over Ireland as more and more of the population received baptism. Young Irish converts and those born into the Faith flocked to these settlements to train as monks and nuns. Tracts of agricultural land, granted by local kings and chieftains, enabled the monasteries to sustain themselves on large estates similar to those of secular lords. An Irish ecclesiastical hierarchy appeared, as had happened in Britain a century or more earlier, in which the head of the monastery was an abbot or, more rarely, an abbess. Elsewhere in Western Christendom the senior religious figure of a district was normally the local bishop whose residence was often a cathedral church of what had formerly been a Roman city.[4] In Britain, as in Gaul, Italy and Spain, enough of the fabric of Roman urbanism survived into the fifth and sixth centuries to make this situation viable. Not so in Ireland, which had always lain outside the Roman Empire. Ireland had no cities, no walled towns, no settlements large enough to acquire an urban character. What it did possess, in early Christian times, were monasteries of great size. These, then, became quasi-urban centres and episcopal seats, but in every case the bishop of a monastery was subordinate to its abbot. Not until a much later period, when the Irish clergy began to conform to the conventions of the rest of Western Europe, was this unusual division of authority reversed.

By 521, traditionally regarded as the year of St Columba's birth, Ireland could be regarded as a Christian land. Pockets of paganism undoubtedly existed, and many communities were reluctant to abandon rituals practised by their ancestors, but the old religion was in retreat and its priesthood now lurked on the margins of society. Spiritual authority lay firmly in the hands of abbots and bishops, especially those of the largest and most influential monasteries. These powerful figures were the living saints of Columba's own lifetime. Among them were Finnian of Clonard, Ciaran of Clonmacnoise and – if she existed – Abbess Brigid of Kildare. All were members of an ecclesiastical elite that saw itself as equal in status to the secular elite. The latter's principal representatives were kings, and it was on their territory that churches and monasteries were established. The two groups interacted closely in symbiotic relationships based on patronage and mutual obligation. Baptised kings benefited from these arrangements by appearing more sophisticated and less 'barbarian' than their pagan peers. They gained access to the powerful technology of Latin documentation which preserved their edicts in a way that traditional methods of oral recording could not. In short, the adoption of Christianity enabled a king to appear more Roman and therefore more 'imperial'.

Colum Cille

Early medieval Ireland was a patchwork of small kingdoms whose rulers competed with one another for wealth, territory and supremacy. In the north-west, in what is now County Donegal, one of these kingdoms was ruled by Cenél Conaill, 'Conall's kindred', a powerful family descended from King Conall Gulban. The latter is remembered today in the place-name Tyrconnell, an Anglicised form of Gaelic *Tír Conaill*, 'Conall's Land'. He was a son of Niall Noígiallach, 'Niall of the Nine Hostages', a semi-legendary king who probably lived in the first half of the fifth century. Cenél Conaill was one of a number of families claiming Niall as forefather. Collectively these were known as the Uí Néill, 'Descendants of Niall', but they were not a unified political entity. They comprised two regional blocs, a northern and a southern division, each of which included a number of distinct *cenéla* or royal families. To the northern division belonged Cenél Conaill, Cenél nEndai and Cenél nEógain ('Eógan's Kindred'), the latter holding sway in *Tír Eóghain*, 'Eógan's Land', now County Tyrone. These three families, each headed by its own king, competed for the headship of the Northern Uí Néill. They were also involved in contests for wider supremacy, not only with neighbours in the north but with the Southern Uí Néill whose territories spanned large tracts of the Irish midlands.[5]

In the early sixth century, a Cenél Conaill prince called Fedilmid mac Fergusa married Eithne, daughter of Naue or Mac Noe, 'Son of a Ship'. One tradition identifies Mac Noe as Dimma mac Noe, a member of the Fir Manaig people of what is now County Fermanagh, while another associates him with the Corpraige of the Fannat peninsula in northern Donegal.[6] Fedilmid was a grandson of Conall Gulban and thus a great-grandson of the Uí Néill progenitor Niall Noígiallach. On 7 December 521, so the traditional story goes, at the village of Gartan in Donegal, Eithne gave birth to a son.[7] Gartan lay outside the core domains of Cenél Conaill and seems an unlikely birthplace for a scion of the kindred, but the geographical context may nonetheless be correct. We know too little about political boundaries in sixth-century Donegal to dismiss it as spurious. Folklore of the district claims that the site of the house where the boy was born is marked by a stone on the hillside above the western side of Lough Gartan. Today, a Celtic cross of modern construction marks the place.

In the absence of contrary information we have little reason to doubt the traditional version of events. This relates that the son of Fedilmid and Eithne was given the Gaelic name Crimthann, 'Fox'.[8] Like many aristocratic families in Ireland at that time, the child's parents delivered him into the care of a foster-father. It was common practice for male fosterlings to undergo military training when they reached an appropriate age and this is undoubtedly the path that Crimthann would have followed had his fosterage been with a secular household. His parents sent him instead to Cruithnechan, an elderly priest, whose church may have lain at Kilcronaghan (*Cill Chruithneacháin*) near Tobermore in County Londonderry. The choice of foster-father plainly indicates that Fedilmid and Eithne wanted their son to pursue a religious career, in spite of the fact that they themselves may have been pagans. We have no precise information on the family's religious beliefs, but Adomnán's avoidance of the issue suggests that Crimthann was born into a non-Christian household. Indeed, it is possible that some branches of the Northern Uí Néill still adhered to paganism at this time. Cruithnechan duly baptised Crimthann, bestowing upon him the name *Colum*, meaning 'dove', the Latin form of which is the more familiar *Columba*. Among the material collected by Manus O'Donnell in *Betha Coluim Chille* is a tradition that the young Columba lived with his foster-father at Kilmacrenan, a few miles north-east of Lough Gartan. This place, formerly known as *Doire-Eithne*, 'Eithne's Oakwood', may have been owned by the boy's mother. Five miles to the south stood the ancient religious site of Temple Douglas where pagan rites associated with an artificial mound had already given way to Christian mass. The ruins visible at Temple Douglas today are those of a sixteenth-century church erected on the site by Manus O'Donnell himself. Here, Columba became so immersed in learning the psalms that the local children teased him gently, calling him *Colum Cille*, 'Colum of the Church', the name by which he is still generally known in Ireland.[9]

Several tales were woven around Columba's fosterage, their purpose being to show that the miraculous powers credited to him in later life were evident in childhood. Three such stories appear in the Irish Life. In one, Columba raises Cruithnechan from the dead after the aged priest suffers a fatal fall. Another relates how a seer foretold the future extent of the Columban *paruchia* after the saint ate half a

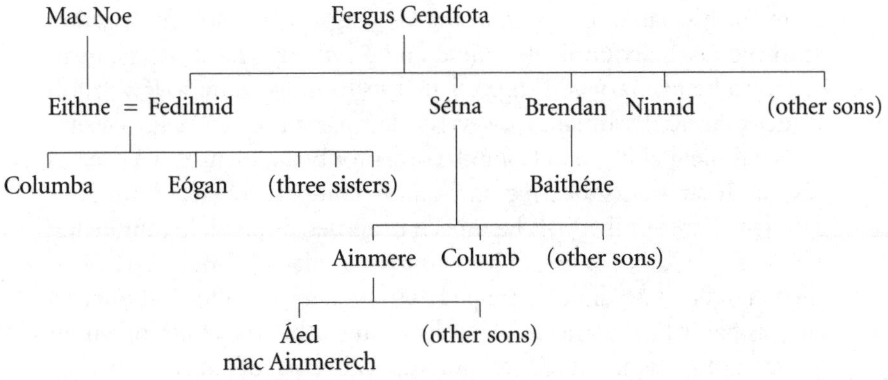

COLUMBA'S FAMILY TREE

cake 'east of the water' and the other half west of it. 'Likewise shall be the territory of this lad,' said the seer, 'half of it east of the sea, that is in Scotland, and the other half west of the sea, that is in Ireland.' A third story shows the young Columba reciting unaided a psalm he had not previously learned.[10] These three tales rely on conventional themes drawn from a common stock of hagiographical motifs and contribute little to our understanding of the saint's early years. This is a pity, for Cruithnechan surely played a significant role in Columba's boyhood and must have influenced the beginning of his career. Adomnán mentions him only once, and briefly, in the context of a miracle during Columba's childhood, but this is sufficient to confirm him as a genuine historical figure. In the Irish Life he is called *mac Cellachain*, 'Cellachan's son', but we have no idea who Cellachan was or where he lived. Thus, although Cruithnechan is still remembered in Ireland as St Crunathan or Cronaghan, founder of the old parish church at Kilcronaghan, he emerges from the hagiographical texts as little more than a foil to his miracle-working fosterling.

Deacon

Adomnán is characteristically vague on the next phase of Columba's career, when the boy became the pupil of a holy man called Bishop Uinniau. There can be no doubt that Uinniau's role in the shaping of the future saint was as influential as Cruithnechan's had been, but, unfortunately, we know just as little about him. Adomnán gives three forms of his name: *Uinniau*, in the language of the Britons, together with the Gaelic equivalents *Finnio* and *Findbarr*. The Brittonic form seems to be primary and suggests that its bearer was himself a Briton rather than an Irishman. However, Adomnán's use of Gaelic alternatives has inevitably led to Columba's mentor being identified as one of several Irish saints bearing the name Findbarr or its diminutive Finnian. Three individuals have been proposed as possible candidates: Findbarr of Cork, Finnian of Movilla and Finnian of Clonard. The first died in 623 and no doubt belonged to the generation after Columba so can probably be disregarded. This leaves the other two, both of whom seem to fit the required chronology. Finnian of Movilla, whose monastery stood at the northern end of Strangford Lough near the town of Newtownards, died in 549. His namesake, founder of Clonard in Meath, passed away in 579. This is not enough to securely identify either of them as Adomnán's Uinniau-Finnio, but it does make both worthy of consideration. The name Uinniau, as we have seen, is Brittonic, yet both Finnians were regarded in medieval tradition as natives of Ireland. From this we might reasonably conclude that the Uinniau or Finnio of *Vita Columbae* was not one of the Irish Finnians but a Briton whose main sphere of activity lay in Ireland. A compromise theory proposes that he and the two Finnians were in fact one and the same, despite Finnian of Movilla and Finnian of Clonard not sharing the same feast-day in the Christian calendar. Two different feast-days surely imply two different saints. The Irish Life does, in fact, distinguish between the Finnians by crediting each with a separate phase of Columba's religious training. Another hypothesis identifies Adomnán's Uinniau-Finnio as St Ninian or Nynia, a Briton described by Bede as founder of Whithorn in Galloway. *Ninian* is here seen as a scribal error for *Uinniau* who then becomes not only Columba's mentor but also Whithorn's founding-saint.[11] Interestingly, a story about Finnian of Movilla places him at Whithorn during his youth, at a time when the religious community there was reputedly headed by an Irish abbot called Mugint. Although this tale supports the idea of a connection between Finnian and Ninian, its authenticity cannot be verified. It may have been created at a time when Whithorn's fame as a cult-centre made it a suitable setting for stories not only about Ninian but about other saints too. If Finnian of Movilla did spend time in Galloway, his name's similarity to Brittonic Ninian and Uinniau might be no more than coincidence. In truth, then, we have no clear understanding of who Adomnán's Uinniau or Finnio really was or whether he came to Ireland from Britain. On the other hand, the sources leave us in no doubt that one bearer of the name was indeed a figure of considerable importance on both sides of the Irish Sea in the sixth century. This Uinniau wrote a penitential, a book of penances, and corresponded with the famous British writer St Gildas. We know, too, that this Uinniau was a Briton who lived in Ireland from c.540 and that he was regarded by his contemporaries as a great scholar and teacher. It is therefore possible, perhaps even probable, that he and Columba's teacher were one and the same.

Columba became a student at Uinniau's monastic school. Adomnán gives no indication of where this lay, but it was presumably a well-known destination for novice monks. Supporters of the

Uinniau=Finnian equation would identify it as Movilla, or perhaps as the monastery near Dromin in County Louth where local folklore places Finnian's education of Columba. Of Columba's time at Uinniau's school we know almost nothing beyond his attainment of the rank of deacon and an early demonstration of his God-given power. Adomnán describes this miracle, performed by Columba in the presence of Uinniau and others, as an echo of Christ's famous miracle at the wedding in Cana. In Adomnán's account we see Columba converting water from a nearby spring into wine for the mass, before modestly crediting the wondrous feat not to himself but to his mentor.[12] This is Adomnán's only reference to Columba's time with Uinniau.

We next meet the young deacon in Leinster, under the tutelage of an elderly priest called Gemman who, according to one tradition, had once been a bard. Gemman appears in only one portion of Adomnán's narrative, as an eyewitness with Columba to a particularly savage murder.[13] To Adomnán, this brutal slaying and its consequences provided a useful illustration of Columba's miraculous powers of prophecy. It occurred on a day when Columba and Gemman were out on the 'open plain', each immersed in private reading and sitting a little apart. A young girl suddenly came into view, running wildly towards them. She was being pursued by a man, 'a pitiless persecutor of innocent folk'. On reaching Gemman she sought protection by hiding behind him. Gemman summoned Columba, and together the two clerics tried to shield the terrified girl. Their efforts were not enough to save her, and a vicious spear-thrust ended her life. Distressed and enraged, Columba prophesied that the murderer would die there and then. 'That slaughterer of innocents,' wrote Adomnán, 'fell dead upon the spot.' News of the incident, and reports of Columba's power of foresight, spread swiftly throughout Ireland. From this we might infer that the tale was well-known during the saint's lifetime. Setting aside the miraculous aspect we can perhaps accept it as a true story. More importantly, it offers an insight into how Adomnán and his contemporaries viewed Columba's personality. To them, he clearly felt no qualms about demanding immediate and lethal punishment for the most heinous acts of violence. Although such ruthlessness is not normally associated with a Christian holy man, it is consistent with hints and allusions elsewhere and probably depicts his character fairly accurately. He was humble and modest, but neither meek nor fearful.

We can picture him as a forceful, quick-tempered individual who was not easily intimidated by the aggressive behaviour of armed men. Nor was the episode involving the murdered girl a lone example of his summoning of vengeance upon wrongdoers. It did, however, hold special significance for Adomnán himself. In 697, the author of *Vita Columbae* summoned the secular and religious elites of the Gaelic world to attend a great gathering in Ireland. There he promulgated the 'Law of Innocents', a piece of clerical legislation asserting the immunity of women, children and priests from the ravages of war. This was the crowning achievement of Adomnán's career, for it addressed issues of morality and behaviour that concerned him deeply. By including in *Vita Columbae* the tragic story of a young girl whom not even the mighty Columba could save from a deadly spear, Adomnán brought the plight of 'innocents' in his own time to the attention of his readers.[14]

How long Columba spent as Gemman's pupil is unknown. With the exception of the incident described above, Adomnán gives no account of this phase of Columba's life. Turning to other sources we find several tales that attempt to fill the gap, but all are of questionable validity and none can be accepted at face value. The Irish Life claims that Columba's clerical education continued with a move to Meath, to the great monastery at Clonard.[15] This was one of the premier religious houses of early medieval Ireland, its community of monks allegedly numbering several thousand. Here, under the guidance of the other St Finnian, whom we have already met as the namesake of Movilla's founder, the young Columba is said to have completed his training. In the *Martyrology of Óengus* the formal ordination of Columba as a priest is credited to Etchen, Bishop of Clonfad in Westmeath, but the origin of this information is unknown.[16] The Irish Life next shows Columba leaving Clonard for Glasnevin, a suburb of modern Dublin, where a monastic school founded by St Mobhi lay beside the River Tolka. Among the Glasnevin students at the time of Columba's arrival was a young monk called Comgall, a northern Irishman from what is now County Antrim, who later founded the great monastery of Bangor beside Belfast Lough. As we shall see, Comgall and Columba are subsequently depicted by Adomnán as like-minded friends. If this does not merely represent a seventh-century hagiographer's hope for co-operation between Bangor and Iona in his own time, the friendship between the respective founders may have been real. It might have begun at Glasnevin if, as the Irish Life asserts, both were students under Mobhi. The Irish Life suggests that Columba's sojourn there was brief. He left after Mobhi warned the monks and novices to abandon the monastery lest the *buide chonnail* or 'yellow plague' engulf them. This deadly pestilence, an outbreak of bubonic plague, ravaged Western Europe in the 540s. Its impact on the British Isles was very severe. In Wales it claimed the life of Maelgwn, king of Gwynedd, while in Ireland its high-profile victims included St Ciarán, abbot of Clonmacnoise.[17] The Irish Life shows Columba leaving Glasnevin and heading north to the realm of his Cenél Conaill kinsmen. A return to the lands of his birth does not seem implausible, but our scepticism is roused by the additional information that he founded a monastery at Derry soon afterwards. It seems far more likely that Iona was Columba's earliest foundation, and that Derry was established some years later. Here, the author of the Irish Life reverses the chronology by claiming Derry as the senior church of what would eventually become the Columban federation. In so doing, he is simply reflecting the situation of his own time, the eleventh and twelfth centuries, when Derry was the federation's headquarters.[18] A more accurate range of dates for Derry's origins and for the founding of other Columban churches mentioned in this portion of the Irish Life is discussed in Chapter 5.

The Synod of Tailtiu

St Mobhi of Glasnevin died in 545, when Columba was in his early twenties. The Irish Life describes how Columba learned of Mobhi's death from two Glasnevin monks who came to Derry. As noted above, Derry was probably not a Christian settlement at this time and therefore an unlikely setting. On the other hand, it might not have lain very far from where Columba was living. The Grianán of Ailech, the main royal stronghold of Cenél Conaill, stands only 5 miles away. Columba may have been somewhere in the vicinity of Ailech, perhaps visiting his family, when news of Mobhi's passing reached him. Adomnán is silent on the matter, his narrative saying nothing of the period between Columba's training with Gemman and Uinniau and the events of 563. In that year, so Adomnán tells us, Columba 'sailed away from Ireland to Britain, choosing to be a pilgrim for Christ'.[19]

Such a course of action would not have sparked much surprise. Overseas pilgrimages by holy men and women were regarded as displays of piety and were far from unusual. From the sixth century onwards, many Irish clerics pursued missionary labours in Britain or in Continental Europe. At first glance, Columba's departure from Ireland looks as unremarkable as similar voyages undertaken by his compatriots. It would seem, however, that his so-called 'pilgrimage' was less ordinary than most. Leaving Ireland may have been the final act in a dramatic series of events in which he became inextricably tangled. Adomnán is typically vague on the circumstances leading up to the departure and avoids a detailed explanation. He plainly felt uncomfortable with the topic and tried to brush it aside. What appears to be the crux of the drama receives only a passing mention in *Vita Columbae*, essentially a footnote to an unrelated incident from Columba's childhood:

> Many years after this, St Columba was excommunicated for some trivial and quite excusable offences by a synod that, as eventually became known, had acted wrongly.[20]

The offences are not described by Adomnán, but we can be fairly sure that the synod did not regard them as trivial. Excommunication, the most severe of all ecclesiastical sanctions, was reserved for transgressions of the utmost seriousness. Long after Columba's lifetime, a belief arose in Ireland that his pilgrimage to Britain was no voluntary venture but rather a period of exile demanded by the Irish ecclesiastical hierarchy.[21] It was said that this punishment was imposed because of his involvement in the Battle of Cúl Drebene, a savage encounter in 561 between the northern and southern branches of the Uí Néill. Although the alleged link between the battle and Columba's pilgrimage first appears c.1000, it might be based on reliable earlier traditions. Indeed, Adomnán hints that the link was known in his own time when he twice dates Columba's departure from Ireland by reference to Cúl Drebene.[22] It is possible, then, that he regarded the two events as connected, but felt reluctant to state this directly. He was undoubtedly aware of the circumstances surrounding the battle. Being himself a member of Cenél Conaill, one of the two most powerful septs of the Northern Uí Néill, he would not have been ignorant of past events that had shaped the fortunes of his kin. No doubt he could have written more about

Cúl Drebene, but chose instead to conceal his knowledge. For detailed information we must turn to the annalists, whose entry for the battle identifies the key players:

> The battle of Cuil Dreimne, in which 3000 fell, won over Diarmait son of Cerball. Forgus and Domnall, two sons of Mac Erca, i.e. two sons of Muirchertach son of Muiredach son of Eógan son of Niall, and Ainmere son of Sétna, and Ninnid son of Daui, were victors, with Áed son of Eochu Tirmcharna, king of Connacht. They prevailed through the prayers of Colum Cille.

The scribe of a later copy of the annals added a more imaginative embellishment:

> The battle of Cuil Dreimne. It was Fraechán, son of Teimnén, who made the druidic fence for Diarmait. Tuatán son of Dimán son of Sárán son of Cormac son of Eógan cast the druidic fence over them. Maglaine leaped over it and he alone was killed.

Cúl Drebene or Cuil Dreimne is now Cooldrumman on the outskirts of Carney in County Sligo. Here, on low ground below the towering heights of Ben Bulben, the Northern and Southern Uí Néill met in battle. Columba's involvement, according to lore collected by Manus O'Donnell, centred on his role as instigator of hostilities. He was said to have encouraged the northerners, two of whom were his first cousins, to make war on the southern high-king Diarmait mac Cerbaill. One curious tale identifies the source of Columba's enmity towards Diarmait as a petty dispute over a book belonging to Finnian of Movilla. In what is often quoted as the first known case of copyright infringement, Finnian is said to have become angry when Columba copied the book without permission. The matter was brought to King Diarmait, who ordered the unauthorised copy to be handed over to Finnian. Columba then sought revenge on the king by bringing about his defeat at Cúl Drebene. This, of course, is a fictional tale. A more realistic reconstruction of the circumstances might see Columba offering prayers of victory for his northern kinsmen, perhaps at a public ceremony, thus incurring the wrath of the southerners. The core of Diarmait's kingdom lay in Meath, a region whose key sites included the sacred royal centres of Tara and Tailtiu, the latter now the hillfort of Rath Dubh, 4 miles south-east of Kells. From pre-Christian times through to the early modern era Tailtiu hosted an annual gathering, known as the Teltown Fair, originally a public assembly of the Southern Uí Néill kings. From Adomnán we learn that the synod whose members demanded Columba's excommunication was also convened at Tailtiu, deep in the heartlands of Diarmait mac Cerbaill.[23] Drawing all the various strands of data together, we begin to see a plausible context for Columba's excommunication and subsequent 'pilgrimage' or exile. The sequence of events may have begun on the eve of the Battle of Cúl Drebene, with Columba seeking divine intervention on behalf of the Northern Uí Néill. Such partisan use of prayer by an ordained priest, especially one who is said to have attended monastic schools in the south, may have caused consternation among the southern clergy. Their dismay was possibly nurtured by King Diarmait, who might even have suggested that a synod be convened to discuss the issue.[24] Columba's 'sin', in the eyes of his southern peers, was perhaps a failure to set aside his northern allegiance on the eve of a bloody slaughter.[25] If so, then merely praying for Diarmait's defeat was probably not the real bone of contention. A prince in holy orders would surely have been forgiven a whispered prayer for his own kinsmen's fortunes in war. But Columba possibly overstepped the mark and let his political affiliation be known to all and sundry. He may even have openly proclaimed his support for the northern army as it mustered for war.

The Kingship of Tara

The hill of Teamhair, Anglicised as 'Tara', stands beside the River Boyne in present-day County Meath, some 20 miles north-west of Dublin. It is a rich archaeological landscape of ringforts, earthworks, barrows and other prehistoric features. The site appears to have been used as a ceremonial venue over a very long period, from as far back as the Stone Age to the early centuries AD. Although it seems to have gone out of regular use before the Christian era, it long retained iconic status as a place of ancient ritual. In early medieval times it became associated with claims of paramount kingship over the whole of Ireland. Even after the coming of Christianity, the idea of a symbolic 'kingship of Tara' was maintained, not only by the royal kindreds but by the Christian clergy who served their spiritual needs. The obvious pagan connotations of the grass-grown monuments on the hill of Teamhair were no obstacle to the monks of Ireland and, when they began to note the affairs of kings in their chronicles, they happily described the mightiest as kings of Tara. In reality, the ancient site played little more than a symbolic role after the middle of the sixth century. It is most unlikely that any early medieval monarch actually resided there for an extensive period. Most, if not all, would have made brief ceremonial visits to the hill, the first and most important being a sacred rite of inauguration. In any case, some kings who were accorded the title 'king of Tara' dwelt far away and had no close connection with the Boyne Valley or its environs. Where, then, did these nominal rulers of 'Tara' actually originate? A glance at the annals for the period c.650 to c.950 shows that the title lay almost exclusively with the Northern and Southern Uí Néill. This does not mean that it simply denoted overkingship of the various Uí Néill septs for, as the annals themselves indicate, it was occasionally held by non-Uí Néill rulers. What it does seem to mean is that the kingship of Tara – the symbolic sovereignty of all Ireland – was at times an Uí Néill monopoly.

Whether Columba's excommunication by the synod incorporated a demand that he leave Ireland we are unable to say. Adomnán's dating of the 'pilgrimage' to Britain within two years of Cul Drebene does suggest that the two events might be linked. We can tentatively assign the Synod of Tailtiu to a date between the battle and the departure, perhaps to the median year 562. Columba was either forced into exile by command of the synod or voluntarily chose to leave Ireland because fallout from the battle had made his position untenable. His departure may have been preceded by a private realisation, or even a public acknowledgement, of the dilemma faced by a man of God who was also prince of a warlike clan.[26] The pull of his instinctive allegiance to Cenél Conaill was perhaps too strong to resist as long as he remained in his homeland. We know with hindsight that his exile from Ireland was not permanent, for he made many return visits and continued to play a major role in Irish affairs. Adomnán states that the synod overturned its original verdict and withdrew the excommunication, despite one senior cleric still insisting that the penalty had been imposed 'for a good reason'.[27] It is difficult to discern from Adomnán's account whether more than one gathering was convened to discuss the matter. Some historians envisage two synods, the second overturning the first's decision, but Adomnán seems to describe a one-off meeting which simply reversed its initial decree after further discussion. To Adomnán, the crucial moment came when the esteemed St Brendan of Birr addressed the synod in forceful support of Columba. Brendan accused the southern clergy of making a grave error. He told them that he had seen Columba, 'the man of God whom you despise', being accompanied on his journey to Tailtiu by angels and by a celestial pillar of flame. 'For in no sense,' Brendan added, 'does God excommunicate him in accordance with your wrong judgement, but rather glorifies him more and more.'[28] The initial excommunication, Brendan's intervention and the synod's subsequent change of heart could all have happened at a single gathering rather than on two separate occasions. Debate may have gone on for several days, with an initial decision being overturned after further wrangling. Whatever the true course of events after Cúl Drebene, and whatever the precise timetable of pronouncements from Tailtiu, Columba went ahead and embarked on his 'pilgrimage'. In 563, accompanied by a small band of followers, he left Ireland and sailed to Britain.

King Conall

Columba's departure from his homeland, whether as enthusiastic pilgrim or penitent exile, was no voyage into the unknown. He was not the kind of man to cast himself on the open sea at the mercy of the waves, trusting in God to be washed ashore in some favourable spot. A late tale of doubtful provenance shows him making his first landfall on the Hebridean isle of Oronsay. There he was disappointed to learn that the Irish coast was still visible, so he returned to his ship and resumed

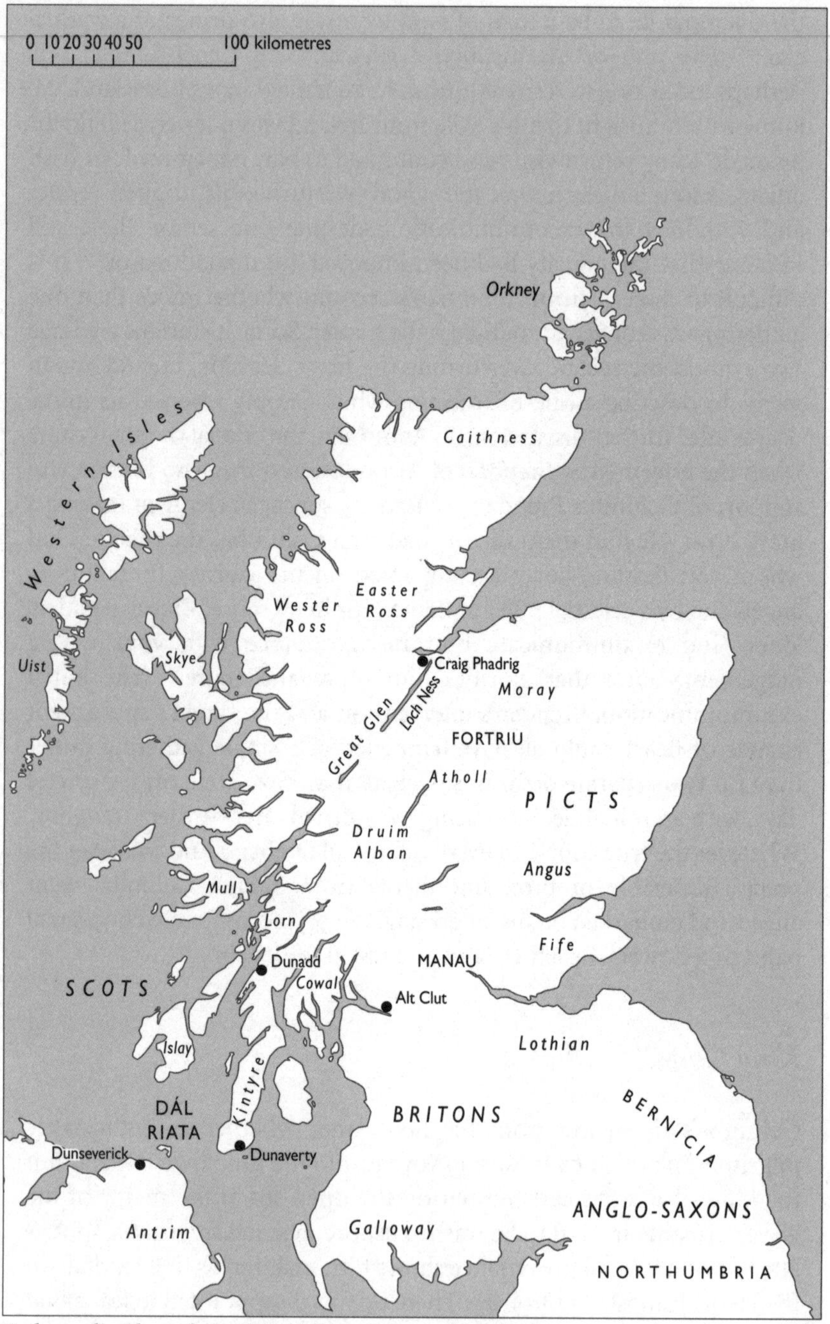

Early medieval northern Britain: kingdoms and kindreds

his journey. This is almost certainly a fictional story, but it has helped to place Columba among the 'wandering saints' of the Celtic world. It is far more likely that he set out from Ireland with a specific destination in mind, and that his arrival was carefully planned in advance. The place in question was a small island off the west coast of Mull. Adomnán calls it *Ioua insula*, using the Latinised form of an old Gaelic name, the meaning of which might be 'Isle of the Yew Trees'.[29] An erroneous transcription of *Ioua* in an eighteenth-century copy of *Vita Columbae* has given us the island's more familiar name *Iona*.

In our modern world, most habitable territory is either owned or claimed by someone, usually a person or group whose right to hold the land has real or imagined legitimacy. Likewise, most territory in Britain and Ireland in the sixth century was subject to claims of ownership. Even remote Hebridean islands were coveted and claimed, especially if their fishing-grounds were rich or their soils were capable of supporting agriculture. Iona, where Columba and his companions established their new home, was no barren rocky outpost. Like many small islands off the north-west shores of Britain its centre is a raised area of hills and moors. Surrounding this upland zone are low-lying coastal strips called 'machairs', whose sandy soil is suitable for raising crops and livestock. Machair soil draws its fertility from a high seashell content which counteracts the acidic quality of the peat further inland. With such productive tilth Iona was a viable location for a religious community seeking to establish a settlement. Moreover, the island's upland zone is not wholly unproductive: sheep can be grazed on the hills; peat can be fertilised with seaweed to enable limited inland cultivation. Iona's agricultural prospects had already been exploited long before the sixth century and people were almost certainly living there up to the time when Columba arrived. An Iron Age fort at Dun Bhuirg on the west coast was occupied in the first three centuries AD and there are other traces of prehistoric settlement. Indeed, it is hard to imagine that the Irish monks found the island completely deserted in 563. The descendants of earlier inhabitants were presumably still farming the machairs and rendering a tithe of their yield to a local lord. If the lord was not himself a resident of Iona, he may have been based on Mull, perhaps answering in turn to a ruler of higher status. Authority over these islands rested ultimately with the most powerful ruler in the region and, when Columba and his fellow travellers came to Iona, the regional overlord was Conall mac Comgaill, a king of the Scots.

Who were the Scots?

Roman writers gave the Latin name *Scotti* to a people who raided the coasts of Roman Britain. In much later times these 'Scots' were to give their name to a large part of the island, but their original abode was a smaller region centred on the northern part of the Irish Sea. They emerge into the early medieval period inhabiting territory in Britain and Ireland as a maritime people who exploited the seaways for trade and communication. Those in Britain dwelt mainly in what are now Argyll and the Inner Hebrides, but here they did not constitute a single political entity. They were rather a collection of smaller units, each ruled as a separate kingdom by one or more dominant families. Their unifying feature, in so far as they had one, was not political but linguistic: they spoke a Gaelic language. These Argyll and Hebridean Scots were thus more akin to the inhabitants of Ireland than to the native Britons and Picts with whom they shared land frontiers in north-west Britain. According to their own origin-legend they had migrated from Ireland to Britain around AD 500. Bede knew of this legend in the early eighth century and repeated it in his *Ecclesiastical History* where he stated that the first migrants had been led by a certain Reuda. By c.900, this ancestral leader had become a king called Fergus Mór whose story remained thereafter the orthodox version of Scottish origins. It was regarded as genuine history for the next thousand years, not least because it provided a rational explanation of why one of the early peoples of Britain spoke Gaelic rather than a native British, 'Brittonic' language. Not until the end of the twentieth century was this 'migrationist' scenario seriously questioned. Under close scrutiny its flaws quickly became apparent. For example, it did not sit comfortably with the archaeological data from Argyll which showed minimal Irish influence on early settlement. Moreover, the old legend known to Bede was exposed as a literary fiction devised by the Scots themselves for political reasons. What has since emerged is a new explanation, a scenario in which the Scots of north-west Britain are not immigrants from Ireland but communities of indigenous Britons who adopted Gaelic speech through close interaction with Irish neighbours. Some of these folk, at some point before c.500, went over to northern Ireland to settle there, or perhaps to seize land by force, but it was not their native country.

Conall mac Comgaill's core domain comprised the Cowal Peninsula and the neighbouring island of Bute. He and his kinsmen were the leading power in these territories and in other places around the Firth of Clyde. They later became known as *Cenél Comgaill*, 'Comgall's Kindred', after adopting Conall's father as a revered ancestor. The name Cowal, itself an Anglicisation of modern Gaelic *Comhgall*, can be interpreted as meaning 'Comgall's Land'. To the chroniclers of early times the people of Cowal and Bute were 'Scots', as also were most inhabitants of what we now call Argyll, 'the coastland of the Gael'. A more ancient name for this region was *Dál Riata*, a name of obscure origin and uncertain antiquity, the first element of which is Gaelic *dál*, 'portion' or 'share'. In Columba's time, Dál Riata was a patchwork of small kingdoms and lordships, each ruled by a dominant kin-group to whom other landowning families owed allegiance as clients. Comgall's kindred was one such ruling elite, while the family of his brother Gabrán was another. Gabrán's power-base lay in Kintyre, the long western peninsula separated from Cowal by Loch Fyne. The two brothers inherited from their father, Domangart Reti, an extensive overkingship in southern Argyll comprising Cowal, Bute, Kintyre and other territories. A power-sharing arrangement seems to have been agreed by which each branch of Domangart's family would hold the overkingship in alternating succession, to lessen the risk of dynastic rivalry and violent kin-strife. Thus, when Comgall died in 538, Gabrán succeeded him as overking, but, on Gabrán's death twenty years later, his own sons stepped aside in favour of their cousin Conall mac Comgaill. It was in the fifth year of Conall's kingship that Columba arrived on the western fringe of Argyll.

The Irish annals preserve a record of Conall's death in 576:

The death of Conall, Comgall's son, king of Dál Riata. He

> reigned sixteen years. He gave the island of Iona as an offering to Columcille.

The main annalistic compilations, as we have seen, incorporated material originally written on Iona. This record of Conall's passing surely derives from the original Iona Chronicle.[30] It shows that the monks regarded him as the secular lord who allowed Columba to settle on the island. The king 'offered' Iona as a gift, presumably via a formal transfer of landholding rights. This is likely to have been sealed with a verbal oath rather than a written document, but would have been accepted by both parties as a sworn agreement. Permission was given not only for building a monastery but also for exploiting various natural resources. Some historians suggest that Columba stayed briefly with the king at a royal residence, basing their theory on Adomnán's reference to a conversation between the two men 'two years after the battle of Cúl Drebene'.[31] This dialogue, we may assume, took place in 563, the year of Columba's arrival in Britain. If we knew that it took place at one of Conall's dwellings, rather than on Iona, we might reasonably assume that Columba was living with the king as a house-guest while the monastery was being built. Alternatively, the conversation may have occurred during a brief visit by one party to the other, in the weeks or months after Columba took up residence on Iona. Although the saint spoke 'in the presence of King Conall', the setting need not necessarily have been a royal abode rather than a monastic one. Thus, while it is possible that Columba stayed with the king before settling on Iona, it is equally possible that he did not, and that a residence on the island had already been prepared even before he embarked on his 'pilgrimage'. The saint may have received confirmation of the land-grant some months before departing from Ireland, perhaps via intermediaries passing to and fro across the sea.

The monastery on Iona had been flourishing for about a dozen years when its royal benefactor passed away. Aside from his association with Columba, Conall mac Comgaill is sometimes seen by modern observers as a weak or ineffectual king.[32] This view is based on a particular interpretation of certain textual references, none of which has a close connection with the sixth century. One of the main planks of the 'weak Conall' theory is the title *rig Dál Riada*, 'king of Dál Riata', bestowed upon him in the annal entry on his death. His three immediate predecessors – brother, father and grandfather – are each called *ri Alban*, 'king of Alba', in their respective obituary notices. Since the term *Alba* is usually equated with 'Scotland' as a whole, it is generally seen as encompassing a much larger area than just Dál Riata. Conall, as merely *rig Dál Riada*, has thus been seen as a less successful monarch than his predecessors and a vassal of powerful neighbours. The hypothesis collapses when we note that Alba belongs to the political terminology of the ninth, tenth and eleventh centuries.[33] It was a name borne by the extensive realm that preceded the kingdom of Scotland, but it was not used in this sense by the annalists prior to an entry for 900. Where it appears in genuine earlier entries it usually denotes the whole island of Britain. The obituary notices for the trio of kings 'of Alba' who preceded Conall are therefore late additions to the annals. They were inserted retrospectively, perhaps in the tenth century, at a time when Dál Riata was indeed part of Alba. The latter kingdom also included the heartlands of the Picts in what are now Perthshire and Fife, and possibly extended to Moray. We can be fairly certain that Conall's predecessors had no authority in these eastern districts. If they ever held sway beyond their ancestral domains, their overlordship was probably confined to Argyll. None of the three is likely to have ruled the huge area corresponding to tenth-century Alba. They may have ruled as successive overkings of Dál Riata, but, if so, they were surely no more powerful than Conall himself.

Another vague piece of data is Conall's description as *taoiseach*, 'chieftain', rather than *ri*, 'king', in two of the Irish annalistic texts. These are late compilations, respectively of the twelfth and seventeenth centuries, drawn from various sources. Their testimony has been used to suggest that Conall's status was downgraded from *ri* to *taoiseach* in his own time.[34] It hardly needs stating that an Irish chronicler of the twelfth or seventeenth century was unlikely to have had unique and accurate information about the rank of a king who died in Britain in 576. Nor does it seem wise or necessary to draw specific inferences about sixth-century political history from non-specific Gaelic terminology. Even if *taoiseach* was applied to Conall by a genuinely ancient source, its meaning is too vague to sustain a specific interpretation. As well as 'chieftain' the term can also mean 'sub-king' or simply 'leader'. It need not be taken as an indicator of diminished status and certainly cannot be used as evidence that Conall was forced into submission by a powerful adversary. The Pictish king Bridei, son of Maelchon, has sometimes been mentioned in this context. The two men were certainly contemporaries, and both had direct contact with Columba, but there is no warrant for seeing Conall as Bridei's vassal. More will be said of Maelchon's son in Chapter 6.

The same late traditions that call Conall *taoiseach* also say that he ruled *gan roinn*, a phrase whose possible meanings include 'without dissension', 'without division (of territory)' or 'without a verse (of praise poetry)'. Although we cannot verify the reliability of these traditions we may note that any king whose reign was not marred by dissent or loss of territory was surely a strong ruler and a competent warlord. Conall's political interests and territorial ambitions probably extended to Ireland, in which case the welcome he gave to Columba may be viewed in the context of his dynasty's Irish interests. That he was concerned with political events in Ireland is suggested by an episode in *Vita Columbae*. The hagiographical context is a miracle performed by Columba in Conall's presence, but the background may be an actual historical incident. According to Adomnán, Columba's special powers enabled him to give his royal patron a detailed account of an Irish battle, naming the chief protagonists and foreseeing the outcome, even as it was being fought far away. Adomnán's contemporaries on Iona and in Ireland would no doubt have been familiar with the event in question, which was fought at Moin Daire Lothair, an unidentified *moin*, 'bog'. The name was given by the annalists to a site that Adomnán refers to as *Ondemmone* (perhaps 'Stone of the bog'). On both sides the chief protagonists were the Cruithin, a people of Ulster, with one faction being aided by the Northern Uí Néill whose powerful support was enough to secure victory. A poem appended to the annal implies that Ainmere mac Setnai, king of Cenél Conaill, gained territory in the aftermath of the battle. The main interest for Adomnán and his readers lay in the miraculous real-time report of the fighting, this being further proof of Columba's supernatural powers. For us, the key point is that the report was given in the presence of Conall mac Comgaill. We may infer that it was specifically intended for his ears, and that the outcome of the battle concerned him because it directly affected his interests in northern Ireland. Columba was presumably in a position to give a detailed account not because of a miraculous power of foresight but because he had already received tidings of the battle from his Irish contacts. Conall would not have listened to the news had he not requested it for some specific reason, such as his holding of territory in Ireland as well as in Britain. With this in mind there is no reason to believe that he was a king of lesser stature than those who fought at Moin Daire Lothair.

A starting-point for an assessment of Conall's reign is his obituary notice in the annals, an entry almost certainly written on Iona within a hundred years of his passing. The title *rig Dál Riada* shows that the Columban monks regarded him as overking of all Argyll, not merely as king of Cowal and Kintyre. Neither they nor Adomnán offer support for the idea that he was an ineffectual ruler. In addition to noting his death, the Irish annals have the following entry six years earlier:

> 570 A campaign in Iardoman by Colmán Bec mac Diarmata and Conall mac Comgaill[35]

We cannot be sure that this information comes from Iona. Its placing of Colmán Bec, an Irish king, before Conall of Dál Riata suggests that it originated in Ireland. Whatever its provenance, it shows the existence of a belief that Conall waged war outside his core territory. Historians usually identify *Iardoman* as the Inner Hebrides, stretching from Skye in the north to Islay in the south. Later Irish tradition pinpointed Islay and Seil as key targets of the campaign, but other places may have been involved, especially if the main objective was plunder. The military context, then, could have been a major raid by two seafaring powers acting in unison. On a political level, Conall perhaps hoped to bring certain Hebridean territories under his authority. If so, this might explain why he was in a position to grant Iona to a group of religious pilgrims: an earlier campaign among the seaways of Iardoman might have subjected the island to his rule.[36] Colmán Bec, 'Young Colmán', was a son of Diarmait mac Cerbaill, the king whose defeat at Cúl Drebene in 561 had possibly led to Columba's excommunication. Like his father, Colmán was a contender for the Southern Uí Néill overkingship and a warlord of high ambition. His participation in the Iardoman campaign alongside Conall suggests that the latter's status remained undiminished. There is no hint whatsoever that Conall was the junior partner in the alliance. More controversial is the wider political setting implied by co-operation between the patron of a Cenél Conaill abbot and the son of a king who had once counted the same abbot among his bitterest foes. If we accept that the Iardoman campaign really happened, and that its context was correctly described by the annalists, we should probably imagine the two chief participants as long-term foes who briefly suspended their political differences to indulge in a bout of seaborne looting.

As a postscript to this brief discussion of Conall we may ask why he agreed to allow a group of Irish monks to settle in his territory. In other words, what did he seek to gain from their arrival? The answer is unlikely to lie in the spiritual aspect of their coming to Argyll. Secular factors surely played a greater role, with Conall envisaging political advantage from his generous gift of land. He knew, for instance, that the monks were no ordinary band of pilgrims. They were led by a senior prince of the Northern Uí Néill, a man who might have come to Dál Riata as a visiting monarch had his parents chosen a different path for him. As recent events in Ireland had already shown, Columba found it hard to disentangle his religious vocation from his loyalty to powerful kinsmen in Donegal. He might therefore have been perceived by Conall not so much as a holy pilgrim as an ambassador representing his family's political interests. It is even possible that Columba himself adopted this guise in early dealings with the Cowal king, and that the latter's granting of Iona sealed a political accord with Cenél Conaill. If so, then Columba's kin back home must have expected collateral benefits to come their way from the Dál Riatan namesake of their eponymous ancestor. Such benefits probably lay in Ireland rather than in Britain. As we shall see in the next chapter, the sixth-century rulers of southern Argyll had a major stake in territory close to the heartlands of the Northern Uí Néill. Perhaps Conall mac Comgaill and the lords of Ailech saw advantages in forging closer ties with one another in 563? In that year, the Cenél Conaill king Ainmere mac Setnai participated alongside other Uí Néill warlords in the victory at Moin Daire Lothair. New political friendships might have been sought after the great battle, especially by Ainmere whose domains were greatly increased by it. Conall mac Comgaill may have been approached around this time as a potential ally against the Cruithin, unless Conall himself made the initial contact through fear of Cruithin encroachment on his own Irish interests. In such a scenario, it is easy to see the granting of a small Hebridean island to Columba and his fellow pilgrims as a condition of some agreement between Ainmere and Conall. We may note, in passing, that both Columba and his chief deputy Baithéne were Ainmere's first cousins.

CHAPTER 3
King Áedán

The anointing of Áedán

The death of Conall mac Comgaill in 576 led to an outbreak of hostilities involving his kinsmen. The key event in this conflict was a battle in which one of his sons was slain:

> The Battle of Teloch in Kintyre, and in it Donnchad, son of Conall mac Comgaill, and many others of the *socii* ['allies'] of the sons of Gabrán fell.[1]

Kintyre was the chief domain of the family of Gabrán, Conall's paternal uncle. Gabrán had preceded Conall in the overkingship of their family's ancestral territory in southern Argyll. During Conall's tenure of this regional sovereignty Gabrán's sons may have continued to rule Kintyre as under-kings. If, as seems likely, the two branches of the family acknowledged a rotating overkingship, Conall's rightful successor should have been a scion of Gabrán's line. This arrangement does appear to have been maintained after Conall's death, for the kingship was earmarked for his cousin Eógan or Eóganán, a son of Gabrán. Adomnán implies that Columba was by then regarded by both branches as a royal high priest whose responsibilities included anointing a new monarch. He adds that Columba expected to perform this role at Eóganán's coronation but was persuaded instead to anoint Áedán, another of Gabrán's sons, as Conall's successor. Adomnán attributes the change of heart to Divine intervention, presenting the fanciful image of an angel flogging Columba until he complied with God's demand that Áedán should be the next king.[2] Little of this curious episode in *Vita Columbae* is factual. It may have originated long after Columba's time, perhaps during Adomnán's abbacy in the late seventh century, to explain or justify Iona's continuing support for Gabrán's kindred. Adomnán possibly fabricated it to curry favour with Eóganán's descendants – or with Áedán's – in the late 690s. Alternatively, he may have found it in the book of miracles written by Cumméne, who might in fact be the real inventor of the story. A further possibility is that the entire tale was concocted by Columba himself, especially if his rejection of Eóganán's candidacy required a convincing explanation at the time. Reporting to his contemporaries that an aggressive angel had swayed his allegiance might have answered those who questioned his sudden change of heart. The support he subsequently gave to Áedán throughout his reign certainly appears to have been genuine. If, however, we choose to dismiss the anointing episode as fiction devised in the late 600s, we have no reason to assign Columba any influence on the royal succession. He may simply have accepted the outcome of a dynastic crisis in which he played no active role. Like other high-status individuals whose positions were affected by Conall's death, the abbot of Iona perhaps did little more than passively observe from the sidelines. Our attention thus returns to the Battle of Teloch, and to the likelihood that it was fought between rivals for the regional overkingship.[3] If the context was not rather a combined response by Cowal and Kintyre to some external threat, then the battle was most likely a contest between Domangart's descendants. A son of Conall perished, as did various *socii* of Gabrán's kin, but the annalists do not say who was fighting whom, nor do they identify the victor. It is a strong possibility that the latter was Áedán, and that his victory obliged the elites of southern Argyll to pledge allegiance to him. The position of his brother Eóganán at this time is unknown but he was not a casualty of the battle and lived a further twenty-five years. He was no doubt pushed aside and given a subordinate role within the kingdom.

The anointing of Áedán is one of the most controversial episodes in *Vita Columbae*. If we dismiss Adomnán's references to Eóganán being Columba's first choice, we begin to feel sceptical about other parts of the story. In the manner described by Adomnán (perhaps originally by Cumméne) the anointing ceremony would, in any case, have been unprecedented. Inauguration of kings in the British Isles in the sixth century is likely to have remained deeply rooted in the ancient past. Few royal rituals would have acquired an overtly Christian aspect at this time. A sacred element undoubtedly featured, but, in most cases, the accompanying oaths and rites would have been conducted in what was essentially a pagan setting. Elsewhere in *Vita Columbae* we learn that heathen priests, rather than Christian ones, still played key roles in the affairs of kings in some parts of northern Britain. Even in Ireland, where Christianity was certainly flourishing by c.550, residual pagan elements still lingered in the repertoire of royal ritual. The annalists tell that the traditional inauguration rite of the 'kingship of Tara', the symbolic overkingship of Ireland, was performed for the last time in 560, its recipient being Diarmait mac Cerbaill of the Southern Uí Néill. What this surely means is that Diarmait's was the last full-blooded heathen inauguration, a final manifestation of the ancient *Feis Temrach*, 'Feast of Tara', by which a new high-king forged a sacred bond with the goddess Medb, 'Maeve'.[4] In 576, when Áedán succeeded to the kingship of southern Argyll, Christianity already had a foothold among his people. The monastery on Iona, by then in its twelfth year, was spreading its influence across the region. Missionary ventures by Columba's monks and, in all likelihood, by others operating independently of Iona were bringing the Scots into the Christian fold. But the process was gradual. We cannot even be sure that the list of Christian converts in 576 included Áedán himself, or anyone in his immediate family. The story of Columba's involvement in Áedán's inauguration must therefore rouse our suspicions on religious grounds alone. Anointing of kings by Christian clergy seems to appear in the eighth century, not the sixth, and even then in Continental Europe rather than in Britain and Ireland. Although the abandonment of the Feast of Tara shows the increasing power of the Irish churches, we may note that its final flourish in 560, some hundred years after St Patrick's mission, looks remarkably late. If pagan rites were still a major component of Irish royal inauguration at this time, we may assume that their abandonment was similarly slow in northern Britain. The idea of an overtly Christian king-making ceremony being performed in Dál Riata in 576 seems unlikely.

As a partial compromise we might cautiously accept parts of Adomnán's story by envisaging Columba's anointing of Áedán as a token Christian element in a longer sequence of traditional pagan rites. Adomnán locates the anointing or 'ordination' on Iona, to which Áedán had supposedly travelled for this very purpose. Columba arrived later, having come from an island called Hinba where his monks maintained a satellite monastery. Writing that the saint 'laid his hand on Áedán's head in ordination and blessed him', Adomnán drew on well-known biblical imagery, specifically the anointing of Saul, king of Israel, by the prophet Samuel.[5] In borrowing from the Old Testament to present a particular view of kingship Adomnán was not alone: his contemporaries, most notably Bede, frequently did the same. What is more uncertain is whether or not the laying-on of Columba's hand really happened. It is not unfeasible that it did, for Columba was well-versed in Scripture and may have deliberately chosen to imitate the Israelite anointing ritual when Áedán stepped forward to receive his blessing. Less plausible is the implied notion that this was the only such ritual required by the customs of sixth-century Dál Riata.[6] If it happened at all, it may have been regarded by contemporaries as a brief nod to Christianity at the end of a traditional pagan ceremony. We can probably imagine the main event taking place at a site steeped in ancient ritual where the aura of mighty ancestors was keenly felt. One possible venue is a rocky outcrop near Keil Point, at the southern tip of the Kintyre peninsula, where a carved footprint may have been used in inaugurations. Similar footprints elsewhere in the Gaelic world were still being used for this purpose to the end of the medieval era by lords and chieftains in both Scotland and Ireland.[7] Perhaps the Kintyre footprint played a role in king-making rituals for the descendants of Domangart Reti? At this site a nearby spring and well would have provided water for sacred anointings by pagan high priests and, in time, by their Christian successors. In the distance looms the distinctive bulk of Dunaverty, known to the Iona annalists as *Aberte*, a mighty coastal stronghold of Gabrán's kindred. Although the footprint is now associated with the adjacent St Columba's Chapel, it was almost certainly carved long before the saint's arrival in Argyll. He would have recognised it for what it was: a relic of heathen customs and a reminder of spiritual beliefs that he constantly strove to overturn. It might have been here, rather than on Iona, that Áedán's royal anointing occurred. If so, it was no doubt a largely pagan ceremony in which Columba played little or no part.

The king and his high priest

Áedán is renowned as one of the greatest of early Scottish kings. During his long reign of more than thirty years he undertook military campaigns far beyond his core domains in Kintyre, leading his warriors to many victories and laying distant lands under tribute. At the height of his power his authority was acknowledged across a broad swathe of territory stretching east from the Hebridean isles to the mouth of the River Forth. Like his predecessor Conall mac Comgaill, he secured not only the overkingship of southern Argyll but also a wider hegemony extending north through the Hebridean zone. He became, like Conall, a paramount ruler among the Scots, holding sovereignty over many kindreds. His authority was also acknowledged in Ireland, where his family held sway over part of what is now County Antrim. This Irish offshoot, roughly corresponding to the modern districts of Moyle and Ballymoney, shared the name of the Hebridean lands of the Scots: *Dál Riata*. Its chief centre of power was *Dún Sobhairce*, a coastal promontory fort on the rocky headland where the medieval ruins of Dunseverick Castle stand today. In the annals and other early records it is frequently difficult for the modern reader to identify whether 'Scottish' or 'Irish' Dál Riata is being referred to at any one time. The simplest solution is to acknowledge that we are not dealing here with two separate territories but with a single maritime realm whose people were not so much divided by the sea as connected by it. We may note in this context that the east coast of Antrim is sundered from Kintyre by only 12 miles of water.

Adomnán frequently casts Columba in the role of 'high priest' to Áedán's monarch. Templates for this already existed in the Old Testament where Hebrew patriarchs offered medieval hagiographers suitable models. One biblical example of an idealised relationship between priest and king was the bond between the prophet Samuel and the Israelite ruler Saul. This provided Christian writers with an example of how 'church-state' relations ought to be conducted. Transposing such a model to early medieval times, and persuading a king of its benefits, was an altogether different prospect. Columba may have relished such a challenge in his dealings with Áedán. As a scholar well-versed in the Scriptures he was familiar with biblical templates for his own role within Áedán's kingdom. Whether he consciously borrowed them as mantles to be worn by himself we have no way of knowing. Setting aside this hagiographical image of spiritual adviser to a mighty king, we have little reason to doubt that Columba was regarded by Áedán as chief cleric of the realm. The pagan priests who had preceded the earliest Christian missionaries to Dál Riata would surely have taken on this role had not their positions of power and influence been usurped by abbots and bishops. Adomnán, of course, was eager to depict Columba as Áedán's spiritual mentor. It was an image that, to some extent, might have reflected reality. How much influence Columba wielded in secular, *non-spiritual* affairs is an entirely different question.

At some point in his life, if not indeed in infancy, Áedán received Christian baptism. The event is not mentioned by Adomnán so we may assume that the rite was not performed by Columba. Another priest, perhaps an earlier missionary from Ireland, presumably baptised Áedán before Columba's arrival in Argyll. One passage in *Vita Columbae* seems to confirm that Áedán's children were Christians from a young age, but it gives no hint that any of them were baptised on Iona. The passage in question shows a seated Columba asking Áedán which of his three elder sons will succeed him, a question to which the king has no immediate answer. Columba then prophesies that none of this trio will ascend the throne. 'They will all be slaughtered by enemies and fall in battle,' he adds ominously, before requesting that the younger sons be brought to him. 'The one whom the Lord has chosen,' he prophesies, 'will run directly to my arms.' When the boys appear, the first to run to the saint is Eochaid Buide, 'Yellow Eochaid', who snuggles against him. Columba then turns to Áedán and says: 'This one will survive to be king after you, and his sons will be kings after him.'[8] Needless to say, the prophecy was fulfilled: two of the older princes died in battle with a people called Miathi, while the third perished at the hands of Anglo-Saxon foes. Eochaid Buide eventually succeeded his father and was followed in the kingship by his own sons and grandsons. All of this was easy hagiography for Adomnán, or for Cumméne, one of whom borrowed the episode from the Old Testament and matched it to events that had already happened. In the biblical episode we see the prophet Samuel identifying the child David as a future king of the Israelites, despite David having older brothers. The seventh-century version is essentially a direct copy and its prophetic element can therefore be set aside as hagiographical fiction. Nonetheless, we cannot dismiss the entire scene so lightly. When the biblical allusions are peeled away, we may be witnessing a real incident, a visit to Iona by Áedán and his offspring, during which the king and his high priest talked about the succession and other dynastic issues.[9] Such discussion would surely have lain outside the usual remit of an abbot, unless he held special status as a royal counsellor in secular as well as spiritual matters. We can go no further than this. If we accept the bare bones of the passage as historical, we might feel tempted to see Columba as a Gaelic Samuel to Áedán's Saul. If we reject the entire tale as seventh-century fiction, we have no reason to assign Columba any role in the choice of Áedán's heir. Similarly, we can choose to accept or reject the cameo of little Eochaid running forward to receive the saint's blessing. On the related issue of Áedán's personal religious affiliation, the story would leave us in little doubt that he and his children were Christians *if* we could be certain that it was based on a real event.

On another occasion Columba is said to have foretold the fortunes of King Áedán's dynasty. The precise details of this prophecy were omitted by Adomnán, but we know what they were because they appear in Dorbbéne's copy of *Vita Columbae*. They had previously been described by Cumméne and were inserted by Dorbbéne in his transcript of the *Vita*. What this additional material shows us is Columba warning Áedán that disaster will befall his descendants if they ever harm the saint's relatives in Ireland. 'This prophecy was fulfilled in our own time,' wrote Cumméne, 'at the battle of Mag Roth, when Áedán's grandson Domnall Brecc laid waste the territory of the saint's kinsman Domnall Ua Ainmerech.' The battle in question took place in 639 at Moira in County Down. It was essentially a contest for overlordship between two alliances of Irish kings, one of which was led by Domnall mac Áeda, a grandson of Columba's cousin King Ainmere. Domnall's foes in 639 included his namesake, Áedán's grandson Domnall Brecc, whose military career was a litany of spectacular failures. The defeat at Mag Roth had very severe consequences for Áedán's dynasty, which may have lost territory as well as political influence in north-east Ireland as a direct consequence. A catastrophe of similar proportions occurred four years later at Strathcarron, near Falkirk in Stirlingshire, where Domnall Brecc was defeated and slain by an army of Britons from the Clyde. It was most likely this latter battle, rather than Mag Roth, that Cumméne had in mind when he wrote that 'from that day to this the family of Áedán is held in subjection by strangers, a fact which brings sighs of sorrow to the breast'. He did not identify the 'strangers', but they were probably the victorious Clyde Britons of 643. The prophecy placed in the mouth of Columba was therefore retrospective. Far from being an example of sixth-century foresight it was actually Cumméne's assessment of seventh-century military events. It was Iona's way of telling Áedán's descendants that the monastery disapproved of Domnall Brecc's alignment with the enemies of the Northern Uí Néill. Domnall mac Áeda, the victor at Mag Roth, was a member of Cenél Conaill, the kindred into which Columba himself had been born. Cumméne and Ségéne also belonged to Cenél Conaill and would probably have counted close kinsmen among the combatants at Mag Roth. It is hardly surprising, then, that they passed a negative comment on the battle. It is less easy to understand why Adomnán chose to omit it from *Vita Columbae*. Perhaps he deemed it irrelevant to the political situation of his own time? As we shall see in a later chapter, the balance of power had certainly changed, in both Ireland and northern Britain, when he embarked on his hagiographical project.

Áedán presumably visited Iona in his role as the monastery's new patron after the death of Conall mac Comgaill. Reciprocal visits by Columba to royal residences in Kintyre are not recorded by Adomnán, at least not directly. One such visit might nonetheless lie behind a story in *Vita Columbae* in which sailors from Gaul arrive in Dál Riata at a place described by Adomnán as *caput regionis*, 'capital of the country'. Here the seamen meet Columba and the monk Luigbe moccu Min who learn from them that a volcano has recently erupted in Italy causing terrible loss of life. What is more interesting in the context of Columba's relationship with Áedán is the saint's presence in the *caput*, the chief centre of power within the *regio*. If, as seems likely, the *regio* is Áedán's kingdom, then the *caput* should be looked for within his core domains on the Argyll mainland. Some historians suggest that the *caput* may have been Dunadd, an imposing hillfort in Knapdale which was certainly a major royal centre in this period. Dunadd has many of the characteristics of a 'capital' including, on the summit, a carved stone footprint that was surely used in royal inauguration ceremonies. The site's Continental links are indicated by numerous shards of Mediterranean pottery, unearthed by archaeological excavation, which provide a plausible context for visits by Gaulish ships. Although not situated directly on the coast, Dunadd has easy access to the sea via the River Add.[10] It was not, however, in Áedán's heartland. In the early eighth century it was a stronghold of the kings of Lorn, rather than those of Kintyre, and this may have been the situation in Áedán's time. If so, it was not the chief place of Áedán's kingdom, the *caput regionis* visited by Columba. Two possible solutions then emerge: the *regio* in question was Lorn or one of its subdivisions, in which case the *caput* might have been Dunadd; or the *regio* lay in Kintyre and the *caput* was Áedán's principal residence on the peninsula. The second possibility makes Dunaverty a strong candidate. It overlooks a beach where ships from Gaul could have berthed with ease. Did Columba and Luigbe speak with Gallic sailors here, while paying a visit to Áedán on the craggy height above?

The Convention of Druim Cett

At some point during his reign, Áedán went to Ireland to discuss important political matters with Áed mac Ainmerech, king of Cenél Conaill and overking of the Northern Uí Néill. The meeting was noted in the annals under the year 575:

> *Magna contio Droma Ceta, in quo erant Colum Cille ocus Aedh mc Ainmerech*[11]
>
> The great convention of Druim Cett, at which were Colum Cille and Áed mac Ainmerech

In *Vita Columbae*, Adomnán refers to this event as a *condictum regum*, a 'conference of kings', and names the royal participants as Áed mac Ainmerech and Áedán mac Gabráin. He undoubtedly drew his information from Cumméne's book which may have given a fuller account. Adomnán gives surprisingly little detail but makes it clear that Columba was among the attendees at the meeting. Twice he refers to the saint's homeward journey from the Convention, apparently on foot. In the first instance we see Columba, 'on his way back to the coast', halting for a brief rest near the Giant's Ring, an ancient fortification outside the village of Drumbo in County Down. In early times this place was called Dun Cethirn and, in 629, it was the scene of a great battle between northern Irish forces. Here, according to Adomnán, Columba paused to drink from a nearby spring. With him was St Comgall, abbot of the monastery at Bangor, to whom Columba relayed a detailed prophecy about the battle that would one day be fought there. Adomnán's second reference to Columba's homeward trek refers to the monastery at Coleraine, not far from the western border of Irish Dál Riata, where hospitality was given by a local bishop. The context of both episodes suggests that Columba was not travelling home with Áedán mac Gabráin, although both were presumably heading back to their respective abodes in Argyll after attending the *condictum regum*.

Historians usually identify *Druim Cett*, 'the Ridge of Cett', as the feature now known as the Mullagh, a low hill overlooking the picturesque Roe Valley in County Derry. Local people in the seventeenth century made an annual pilgrimage to the hill, apparently to commemorate the Convention, and this custom seems to have continued into the 1800s. Although the traditional identification of the venue seems plausible, the royal meeting itself is shrouded in a web of mystery. This is due not only to an accumulation of later folklore but also because Adomnán refers to the event so vaguely. Much of the folklore appears to derive from the preface to *Amra Coluim Chille*, a text discussed in the opening chapter of this book. Although the *Amra* was supposedly composed not long after the saint's death in 597, its preface was added four centuries later, around the year 1000.[12] The preface suggests that three main topics were discussed at Druim Cett: first, the imprisonment by Áed of a certain Scandlán; second, a proposal to expel court-poets and their expensive retinues from Ireland; and, third, 'to make peace between the men of Ireland and Alba with regard to Dál Riata'.[13] According to the preface, a peaceful solution to the dispute over Dál Riata was a pressing need, to prevent an outbreak of hostilities between Áedán and Áed. To this end, Columba attended the meeting as an intermediary, to seek 'a truce for the men of Scotland, so that Áed would not attack them' and to prevent 'the chasing of Dál Riata over the sea'. The preface implies that the dispute between the two kings had indeed brought them to the brink of war, for it states that Columba and Áedán came to ask for truce for the men of Scotland, but it was not given to them. 'Yet there shall be truce for ever,' said Colum Cille, 'without invasion from Ireland eastwards.' The sense of imminent conflict makes Columba's intervention all the more crucial, but the *Amra* tells us that the Convention had a positive outcome. A peace treaty was agreed, by which the men of 'Irish' Dál Riata were to give military service to Áed while rendering taxes and tribute to Áedán.[14]

Although there is nothing outlandish or implausible in the idea of imminent war being averted by high-level debate, the eleventh-century composition of the preface and the twelfth-century date of the surviving manuscripts should arouse our scepticism. We cannot blindly accept any testimony that comes to us so late. Some of it might be reliable, but the rest could be wholly fictitious. Thus, while the avoidance of war might seem a likely topic for discussion at Druim Cett, the *Amra* alone does not prove that it was on the agenda. Looking elsewhere for guidance we find other sources telling us little of value about the *condictum regum*. Our earliest copy of the Old Irish Life, preserved in *Leabhar Breac*, has no mention of it. A detailed account of the Convention appears in two later versions of the Life, but analysis suggests this is an interpolation.[15] It shows Columba being invited to Druim Cett 'to save the poets from banishment', to make peace between the men of Ireland and Alba over the issue of Dál Riata 'which was likely to be a cause of battle' and to release Scandlán 'the king of Ossory's son'. It seems to be drawn from the *Amra* preface, or perhaps from its source. But what was the origin of the belief that the Convention sought to prevent an outbreak of hostilities? If the writer of the preface did not find it in existing lore, did he invent it himself? As his most reliable written source was undoubtedly *Vita Columbae*, he may have known little more about the Convention than we do.

Aside from war and peace, the other matters supposedly debated at Druim Cett are easily relegated to pseudo-history. When the *Amra* preface refers to Scandlán's imprisonment as a key issue it seems to be making an unwarranted inference from Adomnán's text. Only once do we encounter Scandlán in *Vita Columbae*, in a passage describing the saint's prophetic powers. This immediately follows a reference to the Convention and begins thus:

> At the same time and in the same place, the saint desired to visit Scandlán mac Colmáin, who was held in irons by King Áed[16]

Here, Adomnán simply tells us that Áed mac Ainmerech imprisoned Scandlán at Druim Cett, and that Columba visited the captive there. Adomnán does not imply that the visit was connected in any way with the royal discussions. All we can infer from the *Vita* is that the Convention took place at a venue where Áed kept Scandlán in chains. This Scandlán was no common criminal but an Irish prince from Osraige, now Ossory, a kingdom centred on County Kilkenny. At the time of the *condictum regum* he was probably a child, perhaps no older than his early teens. As a hostage at Áed's court, his fate depended on his father's loyalty to the powerful king of Cenél Conaill. Hostage-taking was a normal part of royal diplomacy in the early Middle Ages and often involved a fairly benevolent relationship in which the captive lived with the host's family as a fosterling. In Scandlán's case, the use of chains suggests that Áed wanted to punish or humiliate the royal house of Osraige. The bound prince most likely travelled around Áed's realm as a human trophy among the king's entourage. At Druim Cett, it is even possible that he was placed on public display.[17] We have no reason to doubt that he was visited by Columba, but the incident was merely used by Adomnán as the sideshow to a miraculous prophecy in which Scandlán's future was foretold. This was presented alongside words of comfort spoken by the saint to the unhappy hostage:

> For King Áed by whom you are held in irons will die before you, and though you spend some time in exile, you will afterwards be king over your own people for thirty years.

Here, Adomnán was again in familiar territory. His own childhood and adolescence in Ireland overlapped with Scandlán's reign and he was probably around sixteen years of age when Scandlán died as king of Ossory in 644. Presenting these facts as a retrospective prophecy was therefore easy. He could draw upon his own first-hand knowledge of recent history without needing to consult other sources. If Scandlán's incarceration had been a major item in the discussions at Druim Cett, we can assume that Adomnán was unaware of it, or chose not to mention it, or we might infer from his silence that it was not on the agenda at all. The fate of an Ossory prince may, in any case, have been an unlikely area of interest for Áedán of Dál Riata. Columba, on the other hand, perhaps had genuine anxieties over the captive's welfare. Such sentiments would not be unexpected in a Christian priest who took his vocation seriously. Whether or not any humanitarian concerns were voiced to Áed is unknown, but they surely lay outside the larger issues debated by the two kings. Moreover, it is clear from Adomnán's account of Columba's visit to Scandlán that it changed nothing, for the prince remained a prisoner after the Convention ended.

The *Amra* preface claims that the two kings debated an issue relating to Ireland's poets. This has even less credibility than the claim that they discussed Scandlán's imprisonment, which does at least receive a mention in *Vita Columbae.* Poets or bards were ubiquitous in Celtic society from pre-Christian times to the early modern era and were frequently accorded high social status. Their primary role was to compose praise-poetry for the kings and chieftains whom they served. By extolling the deeds and virtues of a prominent lord, often at the expense of rivals and enemies, a poet provided an effective form of political propaganda. In modern parlance the role was equivalent to that of a 'spin doctor' or public relations expert hired by an ambitious politician. It hardly needs stating that the notion of Áed and Áedán debating whether or not to expel Ireland's poets *en masse* has no historical basis. Nor is it clear why the topic came to be associated with the *condictum regum* in the first place. Later tradition claimed that Columba voiced his support for the poets, thereby preventing their expulsion, and that the *Amra* was composed as an expression of their gratitude. The story is of considerable antiquity, perhaps originating among the legends that began to appear after the saint's death in 597. It surely has no historical connection with Druim Cett.

Returning again to the warfare issue, and to the question of whether it was debated, we find ourselves on somewhat firmer ground. The *Amra* preface refers to a desire by Columba and the kings 'to make peace between the men of Ireland and Scotland with regard to Dál Riata'. As stated above, this appears to be a plausible topic for discussion at a *condictum regum*, where disagreements over territory might be expected to feature. A peaceable solution to some niggling dispute between Áedán and Áed might thus have been a core issue, but the main bone of contention did not necessarily involve 'Irish' Dál Riata. If the Convention took place in 575, as the annalists believed, the items discussed must have reflected one or more pressing political issues of the time. To this end, some historians have suggested that the most important topic on the agenda was the belligerence of a king called Báetán mac Cairill who ruled the Dál Fiatach people of north-east Ireland. Báetán was one of the most powerful figures of his time, and also one of the most ambitious. In 575, he stood at the height of his power and posed a considerable threat to his neighbours. A meeting between two of these – the kings of Cenél Conaill and Dál Riata – would not have been a surprising event. However, a closer examination of sixth-century history reveals that the annalists almost certainly assigned the wrong date to the Convention. Áed mac Ainmerech did not become king of Cenél Conaill until 586, and a further ten years elapsed before he gained the Northern Uí Néill overkingship. Current scholarly opinion now favours a date around 590 for the royal meeting, this being consistent with the chronological context implied in *Vita Columbae*.[18] Adomnán clearly believed that Áed, Áedán, Columba, Comgall and Scandlán were all simultaneously present at the *condictum regum*. Also in attendance, or at some other place nearby, was Áed's son Domnall whom Adomnán describes as 'still a boy' at the time. Domnall became sovereign of the Northern Uí Néill in 628 and secured the overkingship of northern Ireland in the following year as victor at Dun Cethirn. These dates seem broadly consistent with a revised chronology for the Convention. It is unlikely that a prince born before 575 would have been jostling for kingship in 628, when he would have been around sixty years old. By moving the Convention forward by fifteen years or so, we provide a more plausible chronology for Domnall's later career.

Having made a case for redating the *condictum regum* to c.590, we can re-examine its political context more objectively. Báetán mac Cairill, formerly assumed to have been an important figure at the time of the meeting, is no longer in the picture, having died in 581. Neither Áed nor Áedán had much to fear from Báetán's kinsmen, the rulers of Dál Fiatach, whose position of supremacy in north-east Ireland was seized in the wake of his death by the Dál nAraidi or 'Cruithin' of southern Antrim. By 590, the Cruithnian king Fiachna Lurgan, 'Longshanks', is likely to have posed a significant threat to his neighbours.[19] The Cruithnian district of Eilne, bounded by the rivers Bann and Bush, lay sandwiched between 'Irish' Dál Riata and the eastern edge of Uí Néill territory. It is possible that this borderland became a flashpoint for the competing ambitions of Áed, Áedán and Fiachna. If so, two of the trio may have wished to settle their differences at a *condictum regum* rather than on a bloody battlefield, thereby marginalising the third. Fiachna Lurgan's exclusion from the discussions could explain why he receives no direct mention in *Vita Columbae*. On the other hand, the *Vita* does contain a passage that may possibly hint at his indirect participation. Its shows Columba on the homeward trek from Druim Cett breaking his journey at the monastery of Coleraine, where he was welcomed by the local bishop and a large crowd of people.[20] A lodging was prepared for him and the bishop presented an impressive array of food. Adomnán implies that the provender was offered by rich laymen, two of whom he identifies by name. We may note that Coleraine was the principal church of Eilne, the Cruithnian district nestling between the respective domains of Áed and Áedán. As a Cruithnian king, Fiachna may have claimed Eilne as part of his realm and Coleraine as a church under his patronage. Perhaps these claims were disputed and challenged at Druim Cett? The hospitality shown to Columba might then be interpreted as a political gesture by which Eilne's ecclesiastical and secular elites accepted a redistribution of allegiances forged at the Convention. As both Uí Néill prince and Dál Riatan royal abbot, Columba embodied the interests of the meeting's chief participants, one of whom may have been recognised by the other as overlord of Eilne. If Fiachna *in absentia* agreed to relinquish a competing claim, then the Convention perhaps averted an outbreak of hostilities.[21] An alliance between two powerful neighbours would no doubt have provided sufficient incentive for the Cruithnian king to seek a compromise.

Miathi

If the Convention of Druim Cett did succeed in defusing tensions in north-east Ireland, Áedán may henceforth have regarded this area as less draining on his energies and resources. The annals support this scenario by reporting no further involvement by him in Irish affairs for the remainder of his reign. It would seem that he diverted his attention to Britain, especially to lands outside his core territory in Argyll. The sources depict him as a belligerent warrior-king who strove to expand his hegemony far beyond Kintyre. Among the peoples who experienced his aggression were the Britons of the Clyde and Forth valleys, these being his neighbours to east and south. Two major groupings of Britons – the kingdom of Alt Clut and a people called Miathi – appear in *Vita Columbae*. Of these, the former are discussed later in this chapter, while the latter have already been mentioned in the context of a prophecy about royal succession in Dál Riata. Áedán's relationship with the Miathi, and their literary role in Adomnán's narrative, are here examined in greater detail.

The previous chapter referred to the Miathi as a people against whom Áedán fought a battle in which two of his sons were slain. We observed Adomnán's use of this event, which he referred to as *bellum Miathorum*, as a vehicle for one of Columba's prophecies. The prophecy appears quite early in the *Vita*, in the eighth chapter of Book One, and contains the only mention of the Miathi in medieval literature.[22] Armed with nothing but this testimony we would probably disregard this people as one of several whose history eludes us. This does not, however, appear to be the case. A reference to the Miathi occurs elsewhere, in a Classical work pre-dating Adomnán's death by four hundred years. It assigns them a broad geographical setting which gives them a more secure historical context. The work in question is a multi-volume history of Rome written by Cassius Dio, a senator of Greek descent, in the early third century. Dio describes a war waged by the Roman emperor Septimius Severus in northern Britain during the years 208–11. The emperor's main targets were two large groups of hostile natives: the *Calidones* and *Maeatae*. The latter, according to Dio, lived next to one of the great barrier walls erected by Roman troops, while the Calidones dwelt further north. In associating the Maeatae with the inhabitants of 'Caledonia' he indicates that the barrier in question was the Antonine Wall and that both peoples dwelt beyond it in lands outside Roman control. Since the Caledones inhabited Atholl and Strathtay, the Maeatae evidently dwelt south of them, most probably in Stirlingshire and Clackmannanshire.[23] Dio's geographical clues seem to be confirmed by the place-name Dumyat, borne today by a large hill at the western end of the Ochil range above Stirling. The original form of this name was probably *Dun Myat*, 'Fort of the Maeatae', presumably in reference to the ruined stronghold of oval shape, once enclosed by a mighty rampart of stone, which is still visible below the summit. A smaller fort stands on Myot Hill, 2 miles west of Denny in Stirlingshire, and this has also been associated with the Maeatae. If both place-names have been correctly interpreted, they imply that the core territory of the Maeatae included the low-lying lands around modern Stirling. This area is broadly coterminous with Manau, an ancient region bounded by the Ochil Hills in the north, the River Avon in the south and Loch Lomond in the west. Nestling in the shadow of the Ochils we find Clackmannan, formerly the chief town of Scotland's smallest county, with a name derived from Gaelic *Clach Mhanainn*, 'Stone of Manau'. The stone in question is a curiously unremarkable boulder mounted today on a rough pillar next to the Tolbooth in the town centre. Further south, beyond Stirling and Falkirk, the Avon runs along the Lothian boundary past Slamannan, *Sliabh Mhanainn*, 'Moor (or Slope) of Manau'. If the Maeatae have been correctly identified as a people of Stirlingshire and Clackmannanshire, then Manau was surely their heartland.[24] Topography suggests that their leaders would have used Stirling Castle Rock, the region's most imposing natural feature, as a major centre of power. In strategic and economic terms Stirling relates better to its landscape than does Dumyat, the exposed ramparts of which may have been abandoned before the Severan campaign. Historians are in general agreement that the Maeatae whom Severus assailed in 208 and the Miathi who battled Áedán mac Gabráin were the same people.

The precise location of Adomnán's *bellum Miathorum* is unknown. It did not necessarily take place in Miathi territory and could have been a defensive action by Áedán against a predatory raid on his eastern border. However, given the wide scope of his military ventures it is likely that Manau was among the targets of his aggression. If the Miathi were fighting in defence of their territory, the battle probably took place in Stirlingshire, perhaps in the low-lying 'carselands' of the Forth Valley. It may be the event noted by the annalists under the year 584:

> *Bellum Manonn in quo victor erat Áedán mac Gabráin mic Domangairt*[25]
>
> The Battle of Mano in which Áedán, son of Gabrán the son of Domangart, was the victor

Some historians prefer to interpret *Mano*, a Gaelic form of Manau, as the Isle of Man. They suggest that Áedán may have fought there against the Dál Fiatach of Ulster who raided the island in 577–8. The sources, however, offer no support for this idea. Moreover, the annalists who noted the Dál Fiatach expedition referred not to *Mano* but to *Eufania* and *Eumania*, these being variants of *Eubonia*, a medieval Latin name for the Isle of Man. There is no record in the annals, nor in any other source, of a Manx expedition by Áedán. His battle in *Mano* is more likely to have been fought in Stirlingshire, against the Miathi, and was probably Adomnán's *bellum Miathorum*. Another theory associates the defeat of the Miathi with *cath Chirchind*, 'battle of Circhind', an event entered in the *Annals of Tigernach* at 596 or 598. The entry names four sons of Áedán as casualties: Bran, Domangart, Eochaid Find and Artur. Adomnán mentions three of these in his account of Columba's prophecy about royal succession in Kintyre which foretold their deaths in battle. The prophecy came true: Artur and Eochaid Find perished in the *bellum Miathorum*, while Domangart was slain by English foes in 'Saxonia'. Bran receives no mention in *Vita Columbae* but appears in later genealogical tradition as Áedán's son. The battle of Circhind is mentioned only in the *Annals of Tigernach*. A corresponding entry in the *Annals of Ulster* notes the deaths of Bran and Domangart but omits the context, leaving us to infer that this is a truncated reference to the same battle. Artur and Eochaid Find are absent from the the *Annals of Ulster* entry and we know from Adomnán that they did not perish alongside Domangart. We can reasonably deduce that Artur and Eochaid were the only sons of Áedán to fall against the Miathi. Their names seem to have been added retrospectively to the *Annals of Tigernach* entry for *cath Chirchind*. If the latter was not the battle in 'Saxonia' that Adomnán says claimed their lives, Domangart was likewise a late and erroneous addition to the *Annals of Tigernach* casualty list. Circhind is usually identified as the territory known to later chroniclers as *Girgind* or *Gergenn*, the former county of Kincardineshire otherwise called 'The Mearns'. The identification is not certain, and it is possible that Circhind lay elsewhere. In medieval Scottish tradition it was regarded as a Pictish district but this tells us little about sixth-century political geography.[26]

According to Adomnán, the number of casualties sustained by Áedán's army in the *bellum Miathorum* was foretold by Columba, who accurately prophesied a figure of 303. To Adomnán's readers such number-symbolism gave the prophecy sacred value. The number 3 has clear associations in Christian thought with the Holy Trinity and with older biblical concepts. Duplicated as 303 it forms the powerful combination 'three and three hundreds' which would have resonated with literate monks in the late seventh and early eighth centuries. We can, of course, dismiss both the casualty figure and the prophecy as hagiographical inventions. There is no doubt that they originated on Iona many years after the battle. The background story, however, may be based on real interaction between Columba and his royal patron. Perhaps the saint warned Áedán against a showdown with the Miathi, predicting heavy losses even if victory was won? Sure enough, although Áedán emerged victorious, Columba remarked to a fellow monk that the result 'is not a happy one'. Two of Áedán's sons were certainly among the casualties. The total human cost was possibly higher than expected on the Dál Riatan side, even if we ignore the obvious religious symbolism of 'three and three hundreds'.[27]

Some historians identify the Miathi as a Pictish people, even though Adomnán gives no indication of their ethnicity. He refers to them simply as *barbari*, 'barbarians', an imprecise term which might mean no more than that their speech was unintelligible to a Gaelic-speaker. There is no evidence that *barbari* was used here as a synonym for 'pagans' or Picts. In the next chapter we shall take a much closer look at the Picts, but here it may be noted that their lands are usually placed north of the River Forth. The former county of Stirlingshire and ancient Manau are regarded as lying outside Pictland. If the Miathi have been correctly identified as Manau's early inhabitants, then they were not Picts but Britons.[28] Although employed today in the wider sense of all who dwell in Britain, the term 'Britons' conveyed a much narrower meaning in early medieval times. It was borne by a people who considered themselves the island's true natives. Their neighbours, too, regarded them as a distinct group. Today we think of the Britons as Celts, like the Irish and the Scots, but this is a modern notion based on shared cultural traits identified by archaeology and has no real parallel in earlier times. To the inhabitants of Argyll the Britons were simply foreigners whose language was different from Gaelic. This language survives today in the native speech of Wales, Cornwall and Brittany. Historians generally call it Brittonic, Brythonic, or simply 'British'. In Adomnán's time it was still heard in many northern parts of Britain. It was almost certainly spoken by the sixth-century Miathi who fought Áedán mac Gabráin, no doubt in a local dialect. In another variant form it was spoken by the Picts who lived further north. By the early eighth century the main northern bastion of the old British language, as distinct from its northerly cousin 'Pictish-British', lay in what is now south-west Scotland, roughly between the firths of Clyde and Solway. The main political power in this region in Adomnán's time was a kingdom located at the head of the Firth of Clyde. In the late sixth century one of the rulers of this kingdom made contact with St Columba.

The king of Petra Cloithe

Roman writers who chronicled the conquest of Britain in the first century AD referred to the island as *Britannia* and regarded all of its inhabitants as *Britanni*, 'Britons'. By the middle of the fourth century this ethnic label was no longer applied so sweepingly. Late Roman officials distinguished between native communities living within, or immediately adjacent to, the imperial diocese of Britannia and those who dwelt further afield. The 'outsiders' included two groups of Britons whom Roman historians differentiated from the rest by giving them distinct ethnic labels. One group was the *Scotti*, the Scots, whose origins we have already examined. The other was the *Picti*, the Picts, a people at whom we shall look more closely in Chapter 6. Both groups lived north of the imperial land-frontier. This had briefly lain along the Forth–Clyde isthmus in the second century, after the construction of the Antonine Wall, but had withdrawn further south before 300. By c.350, when the Picts and Scots were launching raids on Roman Britain, the northern boundary of the Empire ran along Hadrian's Wall between the River Tyne and the Solway Firth. All natives living south of it were still 'Britons' in the eyes of Rome. So, too, were those dwelling in the region between Hadrian's Wall and the long-abandoned ramparts of the old Antonine frontier. The ethnic labels of the third and fourth centuries survived the collapse of Roman Britain in the early 400s and remained current for the next five hundred years. Thus did Bede use terms such as 'Picts', 'Scots' and 'Britons' in ways similar to the Roman writers who preceded him. Nevertheless, an early medieval chronicler or hagiographer is unlikely to have used such terminology with the precision expected of today's historians. Far from denoting clearly defined ethnic divisions, these terms simply differentiated one loose assemblage of linguistic and cultural affiliations from another. Nor was there likely to have been widespread consistency in how the labelling was applied. One eighth-century writer's Briton, for example, might have been another's Pict. We might wonder, then, whether the Miathi of Manau might on occasion have thought of themselves not only as *Britanni* but also as *Picti*, if indeed they regarded ethnicity as an important factor in their social cohesion. Did they perhaps see themselves, at times, as a southern Pictish people rather than as a northerly group of Britons? We shall never know the answer to this question. The most we can say is that ethnic identities in early medieval times were probably more blurred than Roman historians and later chroniclers suggest.

Notwithstanding these caveats, a large majority of the native population of sixth-century Britain can be identified as 'Britons' in terms of their preferred cultural affiliation. In a very broad sense these people lived below the Forth–Clyde isthmus, in an area encompassing what are now southern Scotland, western England and all of Wales. Their language was sufficiently distinct from the Gaelic of Ireland and Argyll to be unintelligible to the Gaels by c.500. At that time, the lands of the Britons comprised a patchwork of small kingdoms that had arisen in the wake of Rome's departure. Of these, the nearest to Columba's patrons in Dál Riata lay around the headwaters of the Firth of Clyde. Its main centre of power was a fortress on *Alt Clut*, 'Clyde Rock', where the River Leven joins the firth. Today the Rock is the site of Dumbarton Castle, formerly a stronghold of medieval Scottish kings and later an outpost of English authority. In Columba's time it was a seat of mighty kings.

The contours of sea-coast and firthland meant that the realm of Alt Clut shared more than one frontier with the Scots of Dál Riata. Stretches of water connected rather than divided the Clyde Britons from their Gaelic-speaking neighbours and relations between the two were not always hostile. Social and economic interactions were inevitable and most cross-border contact was surely friendly. It would be a mistake to see linguistic and cultural differences making conflict and competition normal rather than exceptional, or that these 'ethnic' factors outweighed a desire for co-operation. There were, nevertheless, periodic outbreaks of hostility. Raid and counter-raid in the frontier zone along the Cowal Peninsula must have been fairly frequent, while seaborne piracy was undoubtedly a feature of life for many coastal communities in the Firth of Clyde. But this kind of endemic, small-scale violence was not necessarily inter-ethnic. Britons are as likely to have raided other Britons if the pickings were easy and worth the effort. Gaelic-speaking pirates would have been similarly indiscriminate in their choice of targets. When full-scale warfare did break out it was not so much inter-ethnic as inter-personal, its primary cause being the predatory ambitions of kings such as Áedán mac Gabráin and his opposite number at Alt Clut.

Áedán's dealings with the Clyde Britons are reported directly in only one source but can be inferred from others. Unfortunately, the sole direct statement appears in a rather less reliable text than Adomnán's *Vita Columbae*. It occurs in a 'triad', a mnemonic device used by bards as a method of retrieving poems from memory. A triad was so-called because it indexed three references from a bardic repertoire under a common attribute or theme. The largest surviving corpus of triads comes from Wales and has been meticulously studied by experts. As an edited collection, with English translation, it has been available to historians for fifty years under the title *Trioedd Ynys Prydein*, 'The Triads of the Island of Britain'. Its contents, commonly referred to as the Welsh triads, refer to people and events from history and legend. Recognisable figures include King Arthur, Queen Guinevere and Merlin, but others are more obscure.[29] Some triads refer to events in northern Britain and mention real people whose historical contexts can be pinpointed. One such example, preserved in a fifteenth-century Welsh text, is the *Three Unrestrained Ravagings of the Island of Britain*, shown here in English translation:

> The first of them, when Medrawd came to Arthur's court at Celliwig in Cornwall; he left neither food nor drink in the court that he did not consume. And he dragged Gwenhwyfar from her royal chair, and then he struck a blow upon her.
>
> The second Unrestrained Ravaging, when Arthur came to Medrawd's court. He left neither food nor drink in the court.
>
> And the third Unrestrained Ravaging, when Aeddan Bradawc came to the court of Rhydderch Hael at Alclud; he left neither food nor drink nor beast alive.[30]

Although the identity of 'Aeddan' is not revealed, the most famous bearer of this name during Rhydderch's lifetime was Áedán mac Gabráin who is clearly the figure intended here. The epithet or nickname *Bradawc* is Brittonic and means 'wily' or 'treacherous', but what Áedán did to earn such a negative image is unknown. The target of his unrestrained action was Rhydderch Hael, 'Rhydderch the Generous', a historical king of Alt Clut who reigned in the late sixth and early seventh centuries. If we take the triad at face value, as an authentic historical reference, it seems to describe a predatory raid on Rhydderch's court. However, although this looks plausible, we cannot be sure that it was the meaning intended by the triad's creator. It is worth noting, for instance, that the other two 'ravagings' appear to be abuses of hospitality rather than military operations.[31] In order to examine the context more closely, we should consider the wider picture of relations between Kintyre and Alt Clut, and also the specific issue of political dealings between Áedán and Rhydderch. As we shall see, this exercise will once again highlight Columba's role as an intermediary between kings.

Áedán undoubtedly fought many battles but only five are entered in the Irish annals. One, the *bellum Manonn* of 584, we have tentatively equated with Adomnán's *bellum Miathorum*, 'battle of the Miathi'. Two others were evidently fought in Pictish territory: *fecht Orc*, 'the Orkney expedition', and *cath Chirchind*, 'battle of Circhind'. A fourth encounter, examined more closely below, was known to the annalists as *bellum Saxonum* ('battle of the English'). The fifth is *bellum Leithreid*, 'battle of Lethreid', fought in 592.[32] The latter has been seen as an attack by Áedán on the Clyde Britons, an event possibly to be associated with the 'unrestrained ravaging' described in the Welsh triads. Lethreid may have lain within the kingdom of Alt Clut, the place-name perhaps surviving today as Leddrie in Strathblane. Alternatively, the battle might not have been fought against the Britons at all, but against other enemies in a district far from the lands of the Clydemen.

A more valuable insight into Áedán's relationship with the Britons is provided by Adomnán in a story about Columba's prophetic powers. This appears in the fifteenth chapter of Book One of *Vita Columbae*, under the heading 'The blessed man's prophecy about Roderc, son of Tothail, king of Petra Cloithe'. Roderc's patronym identifies him as Rhydderch Hael, victim of Áedán's unrestrained ravaging, whose father is shown as Tudwal in a later genealogical text. *Petra Cloithe* is simply a Latin rendering of 'Clyde Rock'. Beneath the chapter heading Adomnán wrote a brief account of Columba's prophecy. It is short enough to be quoted here in full:

> Once, this king – a friend of the saint – sent Luigbe moccu Min to him with a secret mission, for he wanted to learn whether he should be slaughtered by his enemies or not. But the saint questioned Luigbe about the king and the kingdom and his people, and Luigbe answered him as if in pity, saying: 'Why do you put questions about the afflicted man, who cannot know at what hour he may be killed by his enemies?'
>
> Then the saint said: 'He will never be delivered into his enemies' hands but he will die at home on his own pillow.'
>
> The saint's prediction about King Roderc was wholly fulfilled, for he died peacefully in his own home, in accordance with the saint's words.

Rhydderch died in the second decade of the seventh century, probably between 612 and 614. He therefore survived Columba by some fifteen years. The prophecy would, of course, have been meaningless to Adomnán's readers if the saint had not predeceased the king. On one level, then, this is a typical miracle-story, a piece of hagiographical fiction. On another level it may allude to a political relationship between Rhydderch and Áedán, and to Columba's role as intermediary.[33] That this is the real backdrop becomes clear when we note that the main non-hagiographical theme of the story is warfare, with Adomnán portraying Rhydderch as a man tormented by worry about future hostile action by unspecified enemies. The anxious king seeks advice from Columba, described here as his 'friend', and receives a firm assurance that he will not perish by the sword. At that time Columba was the chief priest of Áedán's kin, and of no other royal dynasty, so the only military forces into whose future actions he had any direct insight were those under Áedán's command. Behind the prophecy we may thus be witnessing actual communication between Rhydderch and Columba, with the saint reassuring the king of Petra Cloithe that Áedán would not attack him. Such a promise could not have been made if Columba was not privy to Áedán's military intentions. The implication is surely that Áedán authorised or requested his chief cleric to reveal these plans to the king of the Clyde Britons. In this story, then, we seem to encounter Columba in his dual role as spiritual counsellor and secular mediator. As at Druim Cett, he functions here as a conduit for diplomacy between kings. Moreover, his royal ancestry placed him on equal status with Rhydderch and would have made communication easier. Since Adomnán indicates that the two were already friends before the prophecy, we can envisage an earlier phase of contact between Iona and Alt Clut, presumably on some religious matter. Whether Rhydderch and Columba ever met in person is debatable. Their dealings may have been conducted indirectly, with Luigbe moccu Min and other messengers passing to and fro between them. If the messages were written, then the preferred language of contact was surely Latin. If they were conveyed orally, then we might infer that Rhydderch was illiterate, or that his own priests – whose literacy and Latinity need not be doubted – played no part in the discourse with Iona. If Rhydderch's own preference was for unwritten communication with Columba, and if each party spoke through Luigbe, then either the latter was bilingual or Rhydderch understood Gaelic. We may further note that Columba's presumed role as intermediary should not be seen as proof that he influenced Áedán's decision-making with regard to Alt Clut. Acting as a channel of communication between kings, and relaying their respective policies, was an appropriately passive role for a holy man. It may even have been regarded by some kings as a normal duty of senior abbots alongside various spiritual and ceremonial responsibilities. In that case, Columba was unlikely to have been the only sixth-century churchman who undertook secular as well as spiritual assignments on behalf of royal patrons.

Adomnán believed that Rhydderch's question about his fate was sent as an *occulta legatio*, a 'secret mission'. But from whom was it kept secret? Not from Áedán, surely, because Columba would not have breached the sacred trust between king and priest by divulging matters of military policy to a foreign power without permission. The need for secrecy was more likely to have come from Alt Clut, where Rhydderch's friendship with the abbot of Iona may have caused resentment among local clergy. Or, perhaps, Rhydderch's question to Columba represented one element in a wider process of political peacemaking, perhaps initiated by the anxious Clyde king himself. This might be the context behind Áedán's 'unrestrained ravaging' which, if it was a historical event, could be interpreted as rapacious exploitation of the hospitality of Alt Clut during a visit by Dál Riatan royalty. One implied message in the Welsh triad is that the three hosts who endured the abusive behaviour were unable to prevent it. If Rhydderch invited Áedán as an honoured guest, and if Áedán then used the occasion to behave in an arrogant and boorish manner, we might infer that the political relationship between the two kings was unequal, and that Rhydderch was Áedán's vassal. This, at least, seems to be what the triad implies. It finds support in *Vita Columbae*, which may be telling its readers that Rhydderch feared Áedán and regarded him as a potential nemesis.

Áedán and the English

Columba's prophecy about the violent deaths that awaited Áedán's elder sons was partly fulfilled before his own passing in 597. Eochaid Find and Artur died fighting the Miathi in a battle that may have taken place in Manau in 584. Their brother Domangart perished in *bellum Saxonum*, a battle against the English or 'Anglo-Saxons', his death bequeathing the mantle of heir to the younger Eochaid. Adomnán does not name the place where Domangart fell, nor does he give a precise date for the battle. Turning elsewhere we find this information in Bede's account of Aethelfrith, an ambitious king who ruled the northern English realm of Bernicia. As an Englishman himself, Bede described with grim satisfaction how Aethelfrith ravaged the Britons and conquered large tracts of their territory. Bede noted that the scale of these victories attracted the attention of Aethelfrith's foes:

> For this reason Áedán, king of the Irish living in Britain, aroused by his successes, marched against him with an immensely strong army; but he was defeated and fled with few survivors. Indeed, almost all his army was cut to pieces in a very famous place called Degsastan, that is *Lapis Degsa*, 'The Stone of Degsa'.[34]

This is surely the encounter where Áedán's son Domangart met the fate foretold by Columba. Bede assigned the battle to 603 and we can probably trust him on the date. Unfortunately, he gave no geographical context, despite providing the Latin and English names of the site. Historians in the modern era have suggested various possible locations but none seems particularly convincing. Our best assessment of Degsastan is that it is one of several lost battles of early medieval northern Britain. If it is the place where Domangart died, we can assume, on the testimony of *Vita Columbae*, that it lay in a district perceived by Adomnán as being under English rule. Whether his *Saxonia* meant English-held territory c.700 rather than c.600 is an interesting question. If the former, the battle could have been fought as far north as Edinburgh; if the latter, a location somewhat further south, perhaps in the vicinity of Tweeddale, seems more likely.

Aethelfrith ruled a people whom historians call 'Anglo-Saxons'. These were the ancestors of the English, speakers of a Germanic rather than a Celtic language. In cultural terms they were not indigenous to Britain like the native Britons, Picts and Scots, but claimed descent from settlers who arrived from Continental Europe in the fourth and fifth centuries. The homelands of these immigrants lay in what are now Holland, Denmark and northern Germany in lands inhabited in earlier times by Angles, Saxons, Jutes and Frisians. From the Angles and Saxons we derive the compound label widely used today as a convenient term for all groups involved in the migration. Modern historians, archaeologists and historical geneticists have not yet reached agreement on the numbers of 'Anglo-Saxons' who came to Britain. Migration alone does not, in any case, provide an adequate explanation of the process that eventually turned much of the southern half of Britain into 'England', Adomnán's *Saxonia*. A large amount of assimilation and acculturation must have occurred, this being largely a one-way process in which considerable numbers of Britons adopted the identity of the Germanic newcomers. In some areas, then, ancestral 'Britishness' was apparently rejected in favour of the English language and other cultural traits from the Anglo-Saxon homelands across the North Sea. The areas of Britain most affected during the main migrations in the fifth century lay in the south and east of the island, but, by the middle of the following century, an Anglo-Saxon presence was visible further north in lands east of the Pennines from the Humber Estuary to the River Tweed. By 600, two distinct northern Anglo-Saxon kingdoms had already emerged: Deira, apparently the older, with a focus in Yorkshire; and Bernicia in the north-east coastlands between Hadrian's Wall and the Lammermuir Hills. In 592 or 593, the kingship of Bernicia passed to – or was seized by – the vigorous and ambitious Aethelfrith. His defeat of Áedán mac Gabráin in 603 laid the foundation for swift conquest of nearly all lands south of the Forth–Clyde isthmus and north of the Humber and Mersey estuaries. By the end of the seventh century, when a grandson of Aethelfrith held the Bernician kingship, the English conquest was almost complete. But neither Aethelfrith nor any of his heirs travelled an easy road to supremacy. Their success was won in hard-fought battles that often came at great personal cost to the victor and his kin. Aethelfrith himself died at the hands of English enemies, perishing on a battlefield south of the Humber in 616 or 617. His nemesis was a king of the East Angles, but the principal beneficiary of his demise was Edwin, an exiled prince of Deira, who seized power not only in his own land but in Bernicia too. Aethelfrith's children were then forced to depart in haste, their flight taking them north, beyond the Forth and Clyde, into lands unscathed by their father's ambitions. One son, evidently the eldest and the designated heir, found fosterage with a Pictish king. Some or all of his younger siblings travelled further west, seeking sanctuary with the Scots of Dál Riata. They came to Kintyre, to the royal court of Eochaid Buide, himself a son of their father's erstwhile enemy Áedán mac Gabráin. Eochaid had by then been ruling for nearly ten years, having succeeded Áedán to the kingship of southern Argyll in 608. Setting aside the enmity of the previous generation, he welcomed the young Bernician exiles and gave them a refuge far from the vengeful reach of Edwin. In Eochaid's kingdom the English princes and princesses – born into paganism like their father – were nurtured in a cultural milieu that was not only Gaelic but Christian. Although they never forgot their English heritage, they encountered both the language and the religion of their hosts. They became bilingual and, in time, rejected the religious beliefs of their ancestors. As we shall see in Chapter 7, their embracing of Christianity was to have a significant impact on their homeland and would ultimately open a new sphere of influence for Iona.

Epilogue: Columba and Áedán

How far should we press the notion that Columba served Áedán as a royal abbot and 'high priest'? Does *Vita Columbae* accurately describe their interaction, or does it reflect instead the relationship between their respective successors a hundred years later? These are difficult questions, chiefly because we are so reliant on Adomnán for biographical information on both king and abbot. Nevertheless, even a cautious reading of the *Vita* leaves us with the impression that Áedán saw Columba as a politically useful acquaintance, not least because of the abbot's own royal background. It seems improbable that Áedán would not have regarded having a Cenél Conaill prince as a near-neighbour as anything other than an opportunity to be exploited. For example, Columba's high-level contacts in Ireland made him an ideal intermediary in matters affecting Áedán's Irish territories and this aspect of their relationship may have been evident at Druim Cett. Similarly, it is hard to separate Columba's dealings with Rhydderch from Áedán's policies and ambitions in the Firth of Clyde. What we perhaps need to clarify here is what we mean when we ponder Columba's role as a royal abbot. Thus, although we might choose to accept that he did indeed serve Áedán, and maybe Conall too, in certain political contexts, this is not to say that he exerted real influence over them, or over any other king. His desire or capacity to wield such influence may, in any case, have been smaller than his willingness to assist in particular circumstances where his background and expertise might be deemed useful.[35]

CHAPTER 4
Abbot

Iona

The previous chapter looked at Columba's relationship with Áedán mac Gabráin and highlighted a number of incidents, such as the Convention of Druim Cett, to illustrate the saint's role as 'high priest' of the kingdom. At the end of the chapter we concluded that his dealings with Áedán occasionally drew him into a world of Dál Riatan politics outside his spiritual responsibilities. Nevertheless, his political influence may have been smaller than some modern historians envisage. He was, after all, first and foremost a holy man, and in this chapter we switch the focus back to his ecclesiastical career by looking at his role as abbot and missionary. We begin, quite naturally, on Iona.

Today, the island's eastern shore is dominated by the impressive stone buildings of a major religious settlement. These are the restored remains of St Mary's Abbey, a Benedectine foundation of the twelfth century occupying the site of Columba's monastery. The main phase of restoration at the abbey occurred in the first decade of the twentieth century after an earlier programme of repair and consolidation in the 1870s. Although nothing in the external fabric of the buildings can be traced back to early medieval times, the surrounding landscape preserves crucial hidden evidence. Archaeologists have identified the course of the monastic *vallum* or boundary-ditch mentioned by Adomnán.[1] This runs in a great curve from north to south, enclosing the original settlement within its wide arc. At most points, the vallum lies approximately 100 metres from the abbey. It defines the perimeter of the ancient settlement on all sides except the eastern, where the seashore provides a natural boundary. Interestingly, a radiocarbon date

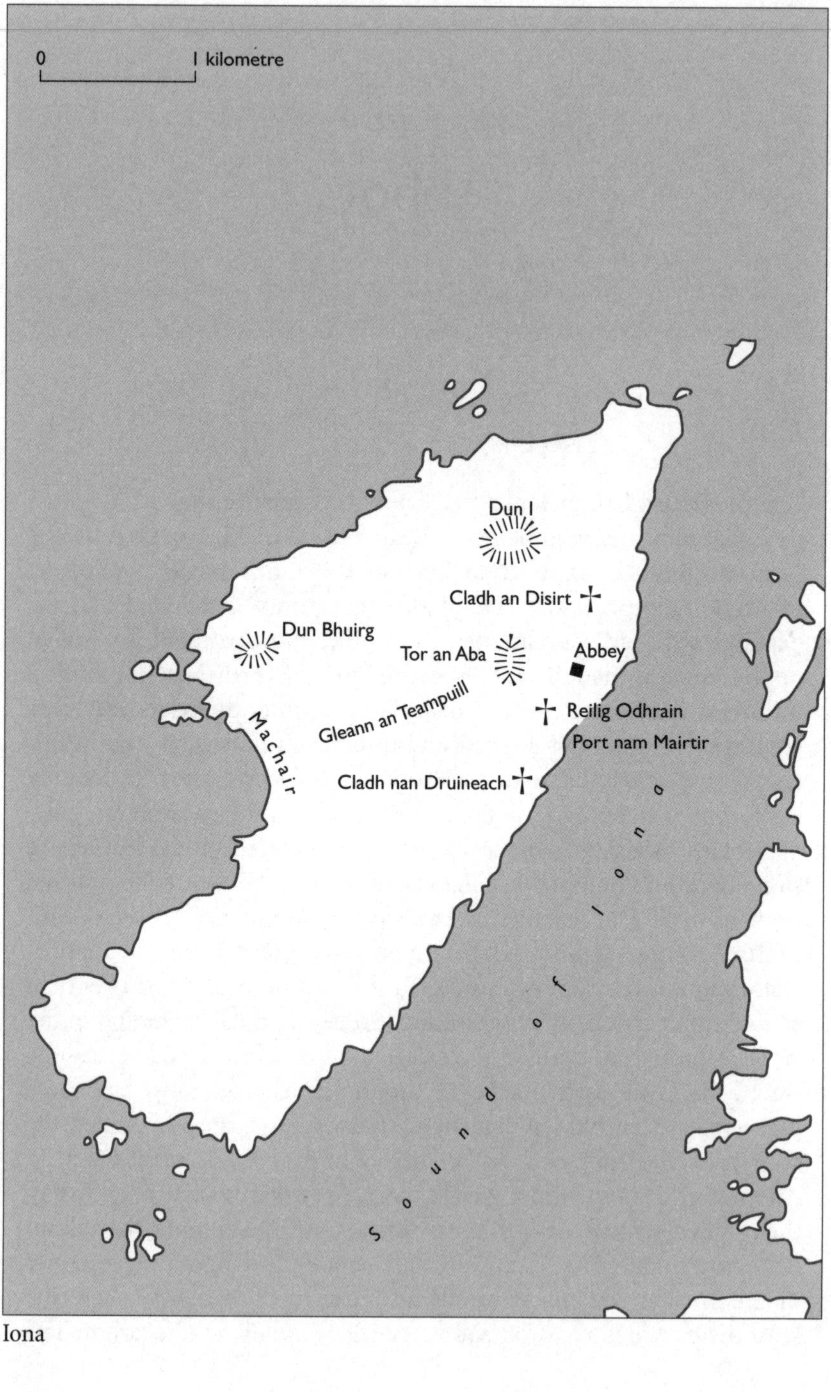
0
1 kilometre
Dun I
Cladh an Disirt
Dun Bhuirg
Tor an Aba
Abbey
Reilig Odhrain
Port nam Mairtir
Gleann an Teampuill
Machair
Cladh nan Druineach
Sound of Iona

Iona

for the earth bank of the vallum in an area north-west of the abbey suggests that the ditch at this point may have been dug as early as the second century AD.[2] The area enclosed by the sixth-century earthworks measures some 8 hectares, part of which was occupied by the monastic buildings. In keeping with the fashion of the time, these were constructed in timber rather than in stone, hence the dearth of surviving traces. This was true of most buildings in Dál Riata so it is unlikely that Columba, or even Adomnán, saw anything other than wooden structures on Iona. Post-holes and trenches associated with timber buildings have been found in various parts of the monastic enclosure, but the evidence is usually meagre. Major edifices, such as the principal church of Columba's time, have not yet been identified. It seems beyond doubt that this and its stone-built successors lie buried beneath the abbey. They cannot be unearthed without causing major disturbance to the Benedictine structure, which is itself of archaeological importance. Only one small portion of the visible fabric seems to preserve a memory of the original layout. This is a tiny stone chapel measuring only 7 metres square, protruding from an angle in the west side of the abbey church. Known today as St Columba's Shrine, its stonework, now restored, pre-dates the arrival of the Benedictines. Rather optimistically, but inaccurately, it has been seen as a sixth-century survivor and even as the founder's mausoleum.[3] Two stone coffins once flanked an altar in the chapel's east wall, but these are no longer extant. They are unlikely to have been contemporary with Columba. Although quite clearly a medieval structure, the 'Shrine' does seem to occupy a position of special importance. It is one of a group of early features that includes three sculptured crosses dating from c.800 and a possibly ancient well. If the chapel is the nucleus of this group, it may mark a place of veneration and ritual reaching back to the beginnings of the religious settlement. Its location might even represent the original core of Columba's monastery.[4]

The domestic buildings where the early monks ate and slept have not yet been located. It is possible that the main living quarters comprised a large dormitory providing accommodation for almost the entire community. Such a building seems to be in Adomnán's mind when he refers to a *magna domus*, a 'great house', at the Irish monastery of Durrow in his own time.[5] He describes this as a round *monasterium* and implies that it housed a great many monks. On Iona, archaeologists have traced the outline of a large circular structure which once stood a little south west of the abbey. If this was not simply a substantial enclosure for livestock, it may be a *monasterium* or dormitory from Columba's time, a *magna domus* serving as the communal abode of his followers.[6] He himself apparently lived alone in a little hut, with a flat stone for a bed, but its precise location cannot be discerned from Adomnán's narrative.

Despite receiving a great deal of archaeological attention, Iona has yet to reveal much evidence from Columba's time, or from Adomnán's. This might surprise modern readers of *Vita Columbae*, especially those who visit in the hope of visualising the scenes of monastic life painted so vividly by its author. The dearth of evidence is not wholly due to the environmental frailty of timber buildings. It has much to do with Adomnán himself, and to his role as hagiographer rather than tour-guide. His references to daily life at the monastery offer little by way of architectural and topographical description and serve poorly as signposts to where particular buildings once stood. His main purpose in giving them was, in any case, hagiographical rather than geographical. In seeking to present an idealised picture of how a religious community should go about its business he not only portrayed Columba as the perfect monk and abbot, but also offered examples of best practice for the monastic community of his own time. His description of sixth-century Iona was therefore the one he considered most suited to this purpose. It cannot be used as a map or guidebook. One problem facing archaeologists looking for traces of the ancient monastery is the possibility that the physical arrangement of later monuments, such as chapels and free-standing crosses, might reflect a similarly idealised view of the past with little correspondence to the original layout. Just as Adomnán's seventh-century narrative tells us little about the plan of the earliest settlement, so an ornate ninth-century cross might be part of an idealised 'ritual landscape' that had little in common with the real monastic landscape of Columba's time.[7] Another factor is the natural evolution of any human settlement which occupies the same site for hundreds of years. Over time, the oldest buildings are refurbished, altered, demolished or replaced. Even within a short period following construction their original functions might be given over to new ones. Any of these changes could muddy the picture for archaeologists, especially where datable material is already scarce and ambiguous. On Iona, where the primary settlement was occupied for a thousand years, successive layers of habitation and labour have put Columba and his monks almost beyond reach.

With scant evidence of the original monastery in the immediate environs of the abbey, our attention moves to the fringe of the vallum and thence to other parts of the island. We find a small number of sites bearing names suggestive of early activity or with traditional links to Columba. Just within the vallum lies a level space, now bare and featureless, known as Cill ma Neachdain, 'My Nechtan's Church'. Although a *cille* place-name need not be as early as Columba's time, the person here commemorated has been tentatively identified as St Nechtan, evidently a Pict, whose death in 679 was noted by the annalists. His *cille* or 'cell' may have been a small chapel used in the seventh century and possibly erected before 600. It lies next to, or is an alternative name for, the equally obscure Cill ma Ghobannain which might commemorate a sixth-century Irish saint called Goban or Gobnenn. Just outside the monastic boundary the medieval chapel of St Oran's nestles in one corner of Reilig Odhrain, an ancient cemetery where, according to tradition, many famous Dál Riatan kings were interred. Reilig Odhrain was still being used for burials in modern times and has therefore not been subject to a major excavation. Limited archaeological work confined to its periphery has not been able to shed much light on how it related to the sixth-century settlement. It is possible that Reilig Odhrain might be the main burial ground of the first monastery, but, again, there is no firm evidence to support or refute this theory.[8] Also outside the vallum stands a feature that might be genuinely and directly associated with Columba: a low rocky ridge called Tor an Aba, 'Abbot's Mount'. Archaeologists in the 1950s found traces of a small hut or 'cell' of considerable antiquity on the top and tentatively identified it as the 'raised wooden hut' mentioned by Adomnán as Columba's private retreat.[9] The archaeological evidence seems broadly consistent with Adomnán's description and, although the identification cannot be proved, the spot was marked in later times by a stone cross suggesting a place of special significance.

South of the vallum the thirteenth-century St Ronan's Church has been shown by excavation to occupy the site of a predecessor which, in turn, was built on a cemetery containing graves from the early medieval period. A precise chronology for the oldest graves proved elusive because the bones had fallen prey to the acidic soil and to the construction of the later church.[10] Further south near the Iona war memorial at Port nam Mairtir, 'Martyr's Port', the place-name Cladh nan Druineach, 'Burial-ground of the Craftsmen', is suggestive of an ancient graveyard, but the surviving traces of what may be a small enclosure are difficult to date. North of the abbey the grass-grown remains of an enclosure containing a small cemetery and chapel lie at Cladh an Disirt, 'Burial-ground of the Hermitage', from where a cobblestone track runs down to the shore at Port an Disirt. These two places suggest the presence of a much older hermitage, perhaps on the site of the chapel itself, which might have been an outlying feature of the original monastic settlement. Iona would certainly have accommodated hermits or 'anchorites' in Columba's time.

Living and working

Vita Columbae gives many glimpses of monastic life. It shows the monks of Iona pursuing their vocation through prayer and scholarship while undertaking a range of non-spiritual tasks necessary for their community's sustenance. We seem to be observing the lives and labours, the comings and goings, of a tight-knit group of holy men in the late sixth century. But the *Vita* was written by a hagiographer, not by a historian. To what extent it painted an accurate picture of life on Iona in Columba's time is therefore hard to ascertain. Much depends on how much of Adomnán's narrative was coloured by his own vision of the monastery's early years: an image of how things might have been, or how they should have been, rather than how they actually were.[11] Nevertheless, the basic routines of monastic life on the island probably changed little in the intervening hundred years. This means that we can probably accept Adomnán's descriptions of day-to-day activities as broadly accurate, as much for the sixth century as for the seventh. We cannot, however, entirely abandon our caution.

Before looking at the details it may be useful to make a couple of broad observations about the population. These are, firstly, that all of Iona's inhabitants in the late sixth century were male and, secondly, that all were members of a single religious community. There were no women and therefore no families. Everyone who lived and worked on the island was in clerical orders, either as monk or layman. Some children were present, as novices in monastic training, but all were boys. The island was therefore an exclusively male preserve, housing a closed community devoted to the religious life. The first members of the community appear to be named in a list of twelve companions who are said to have accompanied Columba on his exile or 'pilgrimage' from Ireland to Britain in 563. The list is appended to an early manuscript of *Vita Columbae* and may have been written simultaneously, in which case it can possibly be assigned to the early eighth century.[12]

Columba's original companions

'These are the names of the twelve men who sailed with St Columba when he first came to Britain from Ireland: two sons of Brendan, Baithéne (also called Conin) who succeeded St Columba, and his brother Cobthach; Ernán, uncle of St Columba; Diarmait his servant; Rus and Fiachna, two sons of Ruadán; Scandal mac Bresail maic Enda maic Néill; Lugaid moccu Temnae; Eochaid; Tochannu moccu Fir Chete; Carnán mac Branduib maic Meilgi; Grillán.'

(from manuscript B of Adomnán's *Vita Columbae*)

Despite its probable early date, the list of companions cannot be taken at face value, at least not in its entirety. Only three of the named individuals are mentioned in *Vita Columbae*: Baithéne who succeeded Columba as abbot; Ernán, Columba's uncle, who served briefly as prior of a daughter-house on the island of Hinba; and Diarmait, Columba's *ministro*, 'attendant'. The historical existence of these three is not in doubt. Of the remaining nine we cannot say as much, for none appears in any other source outside the list. A sceptical opinion might suggest that one or more of the nine are fictional characters created for the sole purpose of inflating the roster to the symbolic figure of twelve, the number of Christ's disciples. Against this we might argue that Iona's own traditions around the year 700 could easily have supplied the names of a dozen sixth-century monks who actually existed. There would have been no need to invent fictional companions for the founder. We should also consider that the Apostolic number, with its powerful symbolism, may have been chosen deliberately by Columba himself when he was assembling his party of pilgrims.[13] One possibility is that the nine 'unknown' companions were simply not famous enough to feature in old tales, or that they were absent from the stories selected by Adomnán. It does, therefore, seem likely that the twelve original pilgrims were real figures of history, and that they accompanied Columba to Britain in 563.

Nothing in Adomnán's narrative suggests that anyone was living on Iona when Columba and his disciples arrived. It appears that King Conall gave them a deserted island. This might seem strange, for the place was hardly barren waste unattractive to human settlement. People had dwelt there in prehistoric times, making good use of the fertile machair and building permanent homes, but their descendants evidently left before the coming of the monks. Whether the abandonment was already a matter of ancient history in 563 is an interesting question. Given the island's agricultural potential, it is hard to imagine a period when nobody chose to live there. Thus, if an evacuation really did precede Columba's arrival, it may have been neither ancient nor voluntary. Perhaps King Conall forcibly removed an existing population of farmers and fisherfolk to make way for his distinguished Irish guests? In considering this question we can disregard the Irish Life's late reference to *drui*, 'druids', who were supposedly living on Iona when Columba arrived.[14]

Guests and visitors

The only laymen on Iona in the sixth century, and presumably in the seventh, were visitors and penitents. The former were mostly persons of high status, such as kings and princes. Some visitors, like Conall mac Comgaill and Áedán mac Gabráin, were royal patrons. Others were exiled princes from lands beyond Dál Riata. Secular guests received the same hospitality as ecclesiastical counterparts and both sorts may have been accommodated in the monastery's *hospitium*, 'guesthouse'. This was no doubt a substantial building, perhaps one of the largest in the entire monastic complex. Its precise location has not been identified, but we know it was built from 'withies' – slender branches interwoven with one another to form wattle panels for walls and roofs. One guest who was not accommodated in the *hospitium* was Taran, an exiled Pictish nobleman, who was billeted instead with a wealthy man on Islay. If Taran is not, as some historians suggest, a figure from Adomnán's own time rather than from Columba's, his placement on Islay might mean that the *hospitium* was full, or that it was not regarded as a suitable abode for him. Another fugitive who came to Iona seeking sanctuary was Óengus Bronbachal, an Irish prince who later became a king. Unlike Taran, Óengus was certainly a real contemporary of Columba and we have no reason to doubt that his visit took place.[15]

Laymen of humbler status cannot be identified among other guests mentioned by Adomnán. It is even possible that such folk were discouraged, or barred, from visiting Iona unless they had a special reason for coming. Those who wished to join the community as penitents, for instance, would first have been granted an audience with the abbot or with another senior member of the brethren. Other laymen came seeking urgent medical help and were given treatment or herbal remedies. Access to the monastery's physician or herbalist is unlikely to have been refused to any sick person, regardless of social position. The monks would have rendered such assistance willingly and without charge, counting it among the normal duties of Christian holy men. Two lay visitors whose social class is not specified were Meldan and Glasderc, who travelled to the island together, each accompanied by a son. Adomnán does not say why they came but depicts each of them asking Columba to foretell the fate of his child. We see the saint prophesying that Meldan's son will die within one week, while Glasderc's will survive to old age. Both, he adds, will be buried on the island.[16] If burial in the monastic cemetery was a special privilege, we can probably assume that Meldan and Glasderc were people of wealth and status. Although perhaps not of royal stock, they may have been prominent members of the landowning class, most probably on nearby Mull. They are unlikely to have been the only laymen permitted to bury dead relatives on Iona.

Adomnán gives the impression of a constant stream of distinguished visitors. The majority were clerics from Irish monasteries. Some appear only in *Vita Columbae* and are therefore obscure, while others are attested in sources outside the *Vita* and have greater historical credibility. A few are well-known saints whose fame, in some cases, is not far short of Columba's. The more obscure figures include Áedán mac Fergnai, described as a disciple of St Brendan the Navigator, and Báetán Ua Nia Taloirc who sought Columba's blessing for a sea-voyage. Of the well-known ecclesiastical guests some were already revered in their own lifetimes. Examples include St Cainnech, founder of a monastery at Aghaboe in Ireland, who arrived on Iona one stormy day.

After being welcomed by Columba and a deputation of monks Cainnech and his companions were taken directly to the guesthouse, where their tired feet were bathed.[17] Others came to Iona when they were not yet well-known, but their subsequent fame, often bestowed posthumously, ensured that their visits were mentioned by Adomnán. One such visitor was Fintan mac Tulchain, a young Irish monk who desired to join Columba. He was preparing to sail to Iona when he learned to his sorrow that the venerable abbot had died a few days earlier. Determined nonetheless to make the journey, he came to the island and was received as a guest. Nobody on Iona knew who he was, or where he came from, or the purpose of his visit. Only when he requested a meeting with Baithéne, newly appointed to the abbacy, did his wish to join the brethren become clear. This was refused, for Baithéne recalled that Columba had once foretold that Fintan's destiny lay back home in Ireland, where he later became a famous abbot in his own right.[18] The tale may or may not be true. It reminds us to tread warily before believing that every visit reported in *Vita Columbae* actually happened, for some famous Irish churchmen whom Adomnán depicts as honoured guests might never have set foot on Iona. The challenge facing the modern reader lies in recognising which visits may be fictional and which might have occurred. A cautious approach is needed, although a rigidly sceptical stance is inappropriate because reciprocal visits between monasteries undoubtedly happened. Moreover, since Adomnán was clever enough to exclude from his narrative any visitor who was not a contemporary of Columba, it is even harder to identify which visits he invented. Thus, although the later renown of Fintan mac Tulchain makes him a prime candidate for any list of fictional visitors, we should allow the possibility that he really did travel to Iona as a young man. It is only when the hagiographical aspect seems obvious, as when four of Ireland's most famous saints arrive together as a group, that we can confidently dismiss the story as an invention.

The visitors mentioned above stayed only briefly before moving on or returning home. Another type of guest stayed rather longer. This was the penitent, a sinner seeking God's forgiveness by undertaking a defined period of penance. Penitents were usually laymen and most returned to their lands of origin after completing their 'pilgrimage' in a monastery. In many respects they were indistinguishable from other monks. They wore clerical robes and lived according to monastic rules.

Adomnán implies that those on Iona constituted a distinct community living under a strict, austere regime. Their daily routine involved work, abstinence, fasting and prayer. Individually they were each allotted a penitential period, the duration of which was defined by the abbot according to the weight of sin. Penance for serious transgressors could be measured in months or, where the sin was especially heinous, in years. Thus did Columba impose a lengthy penance on an Irishman who had murdered his brother after committing incest with their mother. Revolted by the man's crimes, Columba described him as 'wretched' and 'ill-starred'. He assured his monks that this 'son of perdition' would be given a 'truly fearsome' penance. When the sinner arrived on Iona, prostrating himself on the shore, he promised to accept whatever penalty Columba deemed appropriate. The saint's judgement was severe: twelve years as a penitent, these to be served not on Iona, nor indeed in any Gaelic-speaking district, but at a monastery in the land of the Britons. Completion of this penance and atonement for the terrible sins was to be followed by lifelong exile from Ireland. But the 'son of perdition' soon turned his back on his chance of redemption. After only a few days he went back to his home country where, as Columba had already foretold in a prophecy, he was killed.[19]

Others who came to Iona seeking atonement were less daunted by the prospect of penance and accepted it willingly, in spite of the hardship that awaited them. To some the monastic existence began to seem more appealing than the life they had left behind. Adomnán tells the story of Librán, an Irish murderer and fugitive, who completed a seven-year penance at Mag Luinge, a daughter-house of Iona on the isle of Tiree. After a brief homecoming at the end of his penance Librán came to Columba, took the monastic vow, and returned to Mag Luinge as a fully-fledged monk.[20] His story indicates that a penitential period must have been a life-changing experience for those who gladly accepted it. Others attempted to live as penitents but found the challenge too daunting and went home, relapsing into wickedness on their return to the secular world. In *Vita Columbae* we meet one such backslider on Hinba, an island where Iona had a satellite monastery. This fellow, Neman mac Cathir, was an arrogant person whose attitude incurred Columba's wrath. 'But the time will come,' said the saint to Neman, 'when in the company of thieves in the forest you will eat the flesh of a stolen mare.' The prophecy was fulfilled when Neman, after completing his penance and returning to his former life, fell in with a gang of robbers and was seen feasting on horsemeat around a campfire. Adomnán introduced this story by telling his readers that Neman had merely pretended to be a penitent during his time on Hinba. His backsliding into lawlessness was as much a warning for seventh-century waverers as a cautionary tale from the past.[21]

Religious services

Central to the routine of any monastery was communal worship in the primary church. References to religious services on sixth-century Iona occur several times in *Vita Columbae*, usually in the context of a miracle performed by the founder. Sometimes the reference is nothing more than a passing allusion, but in a few cases the picture is more detailed. Thus, we learn that the monks wore white garments for mass.[22] We learn, too, that it was customary for a visiting priest to be asked to celebrate the mass alongside Columba or another senior member of the community. If the visitor was a person of high rank, such as a bishop, he was invited to be the sole celebrant. This custom was, in any case, enshrined in ecclesiastical law across Western Christendom by a decree of the Council of Arles in 314.[23] At other times, the mass was led by an ordinary priest of Iona acting alone. Columba seems to have reserved for himself the role of celebrant on especially solemn occasions, such as when he learned that his friend Bishop Colmán had died. We see him again as lone celebrant during the alleged visit by four renowned Irish saints. This episode, already referred to above, is almost certainly fictional. It describes how the guests were expected to lead mass as a quartet, sharing the responsibilities among one another, but instead they urged Columba to be sole celebrant.[24] Such a diversion from the usual custom would have been extraordinary if it had really happened. As a literary device it informed Adomnán's readers that Columba was held in high esteem by his contemporaries in Ireland, in spite of whatever accusations had been levelled at him by the synod of Tailtiu. The backdrop was a common hagiographical motif: a gathering of famous religious figures at the primary monastery of another, whose importance is thus demonstrated to the reader. Few such meetings occurred in reality, unless a synod was being convened. Most were devised to enhance the reputation of a particular saint by having him or her rub shoulders with others of equal or greater stature. Sometimes the hagiographer paid scant heed to chronology or geography by bringing together saints from different periods or from widely separated regions. Here, at least, the setting is plausible: four of Columba's Irish contemporaries undertake a short voyage to visit him on Iona. We should nevertheless regard it as an invention. If Adomnán did not create it himself, he probably found it in Cumméne's book, or in other traditions circulating among the Columban *familia* at the end of the seventh century.

In addition to attending mass the monks adhered to a regular schedule of services common to all monasteries. This was timetabled around the third, sixth and ninth hours after sunrise, corresponding in modern terms to 9.00am, noon and 3.00pm. At these times a service or 'office' of prayers, hymns and psalms was sung in the monastic church, starting at the third hour with the office of Terce, followed by Sext at midday and Nones in mid-afternoon. The evening service or Vespers was actually regarded as the first of the day. It was followed during the night by several minor services or 'vigils' until the early-morning office of Matins at dawn. Columba and his monks would have prayed in the manner current throughout Western Christendom at that time: standing or kneeling, with arms outspread, or face-down on the floor in a cruciform position. Their prayers included special ones commemorating departed saints whose names, we can assume, were listed in written form. One such prayer is specifically mentioned by Adomnán, who suggests that the list in question began with St Martin of Tours. Alongside the repertoire of prayer a number of hymns and psalms were sung or chanted. Columba himself was said to be particularly adept at amplifying his voice while singing or chanting. On one occasion, in the land of the Picts, he grew annoyed at the disruptive presence of pagan priests while trying to conduct Vespers outdoors. In retaliation he began to chant the forty-fourth psalm and, so Adomnán tells us, 'at that moment his voice was miraculously lifted up in the air like some terrible thunder'.[25] Singing and chanting of psalms in Columba's time probably involved vocal techniques that originated among ancient Christian congregations of the eastern Mediterranean. The sound may have been similar to the Gaelic psalm-singing still heard on the Isle of Lewis. Aside from these theories about singing and chanting we know that the hymns sung on sixth-century Iona were set out in a weekly schedule, for Adomnán refers to 'a book of the week's hymns' falling into a river in Ireland.[26] This precious tome had been written by Columba himself, hence it was miraculously preserved from water damage.

Like many monasteries, Iona observed a tradition of fasting on Wednesdays and Fridays. On these days the monks ate nothing until late afternoon, when the office of Nones ended. Their observance could be suspended if special need arose, such as when food and hospitality had to be given to a distinguished visitor. Thus did Columba set aside the usual Wednesday fast so that the brethren could honour the arrival of a distinguished holy man from Ireland.[27] This relaxation of the normal routine was consistent with contemporary attitudes towards fasting in other Irish monasteries. The ecclesiastical hierarchy not only recommended suspension of the fast when a guest arrived, but also took a dim view of overly rigorous abstinence.

Mass on Iona, as elsewhere, took place on Sundays at noon and on major feast-days such as the anniversaries of saints. The monks were summoned to the church by a bell that was also sounded to gather them together for special announcements.[28] Adomnán describes one instance where the assembled brethren listened to news miraculously relayed to Columba via a clairvoyant vision. They had no doubt come to the church in response to the summoning bell. The bell was sounded again when they gathered to pray for King Áedán's army in his battle against the Miathi. It likewise rang when prayers were offered for the wandering monk Cormac while he was in peril on the open sea. On another occasion monks from St Comgall's monastery at Bangor in northern Ireland were drowned in Belfast Lough. The community of Iona heard the mass-bell and went to the church to pray for the victims. Apart from such exceptional incidents, the daily schedule of church services was marked by bell-ringing at certain times. Thus did Columba hear the bell for the midnight service as he hurried to the church on the night of his death. The sound that reached his ears was not the peal we hear today from lofty spires and towers. A plain handbell similar in design to those fixed around the necks of livestock would have been the norm on sixth-century Iona. Surviving examples in Scotland and Ireland show that the typical church bell was fashioned from a sheet of iron beaten and folded to form a box-like structure, tapering slightly towards a ring or handle at the top. When complete, the bell was given a coating of molten bronze. To produce the required sound the outer surface was struck with some kind of beater, perhaps also of iron.

Books

Those who devoted themselves to monastic life were expected to spend part of their vocation reading and writing. All major monasteries maintained *scriptoria* where books and manuscripts, usually written in Latin, were composed and copied. Reading a religious text was essentially an act of devotion to God. It enabled the reader to gain knowledge of Scripture, theology and ecclesiastical history. Contemplating the words of the Prophets and Apostles, the teachings of the Saviour, the writings of the early Church Fathers and the *vitae* of renowned saints enhanced a cleric's understanding of the Divine. Reading was thus an intensely personal and private pursuit. In *Vita Columbae* it is shown as a solitary activity undertaken in a quiet corner indoors, or in a place of solitude outside. On Iona, each monk probably had his own preferred spot for sitting down with a book. Thus we find Luigbe moccu Min, a young monk who served Columba as messenger and interpreter, 'sitting by the fire in the monastery' and quietly reading. Elsewhere in the *Vita* we see Columba in his private hut, receiving a clairvoyant vision from Ireland, while a monk sits reading alongside him.[29]

Transcription of books was an important task in the daily routine. It was regarded as a sacred duty and had a ritual aspect beyond the simple act of putting ink on a page. The work required patience, skill and concentration. It was intricate and time-consuming. By making a new copy of a revered religious text the scribe was offering to God not only the finished product but also his own energy and devotion. Although great care was taken, an occasional mistake was inevitable, hence each copy was checked line-by-line alongside the original. Thus did Baithéne come to Columba after transcribing a psalter – a book of psalms – with a request for help. 'I need one of the brethren to help me go through the text of the psalter I have copied and correct any mistakes,' said Baithéne.[30] A proof-reader was duly found, but the copy contained only one minor error: a missing 'i' in a single transcribed word. The purpose of this story was to show Columba's miraculous foreknowledge of the mistake and to point out the significance of the missing letter: *I* was the ancient Gaelic name of Iona. Of the volumes transcribed by Columba's own hand none has survived unless, of course, we believe an old tradition that the psalter known as *Cathach*, 'Battler', is one such tome. This famous manuscript, preserved at the

Royal Irish Academy in Dublin, seems to have been written c.600, but its true origin is unknown.[31]

Columba regarded writing as serious business. We see him engaged in copying a manuscript, applying himself so diligently to the task that he did not even look up when a monk interrupted him.[32] On the day of his death, one of his final acts was to continue transcribing a psalter, a task that remained unfinished. He undertook this labour in his private writing-hut which stood close to the monastery. Here he presumably wrote the original literary works credited to him by Adomnán who, unfortunately, gives no further information about them. The author of *Amra Coluim Chille* was somewhat more forthcoming and seems to have believed that Columba composed two songs. These have traditionally been identified as the Latin hymns *Altus Prosator*, 'High Creator', and *Adiutor Laborantium*, 'Helper of Workers', both of which have survived. While modern analysis of *Altus Prosator* supports – but does not confirm – the notion that it should be attributed to Columba, *Adiutor Laborantium* seems more likely to have been composed by Adomnán.[33]

Books in monasteries were treasured and protected. They were regarded as precious items, not only because of the holy texts written on their pages but also because of the immense devotion that went into their making. Most were leather-bound in calfskin or sealskin, but, when extra protection was required on a journey, a wooden case was sometimes used. Such cases were carried around in special satchels and some could hold more than one volume.[34] When not in transit, the books were lovingly stored in the monastic library. How many volumes were present in Iona's collection at any one time is hard to say, but the stock must have grown considerably in the eighty-two years between Columba's death and the start of Adomnán's abbacy. The narrative of *Vita Columbae*, as we have already noted, was influenced by various works with which Adomnán was intimately familiar. Some of these are identifiable and were no doubt consulted by him in the library on Iona. Even if the *Vita* itself had not survived, we would feel justified in assuming that important works such as the Life of St Antony were among the monastery's bookstock. At the beginning of Columba's abbacy the library would have been quite small, its stock consisting of items brought from Ireland on his arrival together with donations from early visitors. In the ensuing years the collection undoubtedly increased as additional copies were transcribed and as new items were acquired from other monasteries. Before the end of the sixth century the monks undoubtedly had access to an impressive store of literature.

Agriculture

Like any island community in the Hebridean seaways, the religious settlement on Iona had to be self-sufficient. A constant supply of food had to be produced and the monastery's 'real estate' – its buildings and the land around them – had to be maintained. This meant that the monks divided their time between religious duties and a range of non-religious ones. One major task was farming and Adomnán makes several references to it in *Vita Columbae*. Much agricultural activity was given over to the growing of crops, especially grain. With the community consuming a substantial amount of bread each day, its grain production would have been undertaken on a fairly large scale. The processes involved were labour-intensive and required not only special skills but also efficient planning and supervision. Fields had to be ploughed and planted; crops had to be tended, harvested and threshed; grain had to be stored, milled and baked. An idea of the scale of these activities within thirty years of the monastery's foundation is shown in an incident on the day of Columba's death. The saint, accompanied by his attendant Diarmait, visited 'the nearest barn' to bless two heaps of grain stored there.[35] Taking Adomnán's narrative at face value, we might infer that these heaps were very large, for he says that Columba considered them sufficient to provide the monks with 'bread enough for a year'. In referring to the barn as the 'nearest', Adomnán implies that there were at least two such buildings and possibly more. There was apparently no mill, despite Adoman's mention of a 'millstone' being used as the base of a memorial cross set up after Columba's death. Buildings specifically set aside for flour-milling were virtually unknown in the British Isles before c.600 and did not begin to appear until the introduction of watermills into Ireland in the late seventh century. The 'millstone' mentioned by Adomnán probably came from a large quern, a hand-operated mill. Alternatively, the commemorative cross supported by the stone might not have been set up until an era when mill buildings appeared. One grain-related structure that does seem to have been present in Columba's time was a kiln where harvested crops were dried and threshed. Adomnán calls this a *canaba*, a Latin term with the simple meaning 'shed'. The same word occurs in two Irish texts where it specifically denotes a kiln for corn-drying.[36] On sixth-century Iona the *canaba* lay between the monastery and the harbour, for Columba's uncle died at its door soon after disembarking from a boat but before the saint could come down to meet him. Corn dried inside the kiln was ground by hand, using quern-stones to produce flour which was then turned into bread at the bakery. A monk called Genereus Saxo, 'the Saxon', one of only two Englishmen named among the brethren during Columba's abbacy, is described as a *pistor*, 'baker', and may have supervised the breadmaking process.[37]

As was usual in northern Britain in this period, the source of grain on Iona was barley rather than wheat.[38] It was grown in fields on the fertile machair and harvested by teams of monks. One area of cultivation lay on the west side of the island, but the exact spot cannot be identified from Adomnán's description. He tells of a group of monks returning to the monastery after a day's toil at harvest time. On reaching a halfway point known as Cúl Eilne each member of this group experienced a strange feeling of joyfulness. It was left to Baithéne, the supervisor of their labour, to identify the sudden sensation as a visit from Columba's spirit.[39] This was no posthumous apparition, but occurred when the founder, although elderly, was still very much alive. As Baithéne explains to his amazed companions, the venerable abbot 'thinks anxiously about us, and is upset when we return home to him so late, for he knows we are hard at work'. Here, as in other miracle-stories, we are given small details of monastic life in what is essentially a hagiographical story. In this particular case we learn that a cultivated area on the west side of the island was connected to the monastery by a well-trodden path. This may have passed along Gleann an Teampuill, a narrow gap in a knot of craggy hills near the centre of Iona.[40] The halfway point, Cúl Eilne, might then be close by Cnoc na Meirghe, a hill at the head of this little glen. At the other end of the gap, where it opens out onto the western shore, traces of old fields of 'rig and furrow' type have been found a little northward of Cuilbhuirg Farm. The fields worked by Columba's monks may have been nearby, or perhaps somewhat lower towards the dunes. Also from the same story we gain an insight into how the harvest teams were managed. They were supervised by a senior member of the community, in this case Columba's cousin Baithéne. Adomnán describes Baithéne as *dispensator operum*, 'allocator of work', a label possibly denoting formal responsibility for allocating tasks not only in the fields but across the monastery as a whole.[41] An older monk among the harvest crew, pausing to speak with Baithéne at Cúl Eilne on the homeward march, bore an unspecified heavy load on his back. If the burden he carried was not agricultural tools and other gear, it was most likely a sheaf of barley or a sack of grain. In addition to working the fields of Iona, Columba's monks also cultivated land around the satellite monasteries on other islands. One of these daughter-houses lay on Tiree, renowned as the most fertile of the Hebrides. On one occasion mentioned by Adomnán, the Tiree monks sent grain to Iona at Columba's request.[42] Such shipments might have been a regular feature of the relationship between the two monasteries, or even the main reason why a satellite was established on Tiree in the first place.

Meat and livestock

As well as tending fields and crops, the monks were engaged in other aspects of farming. Various kinds of livestock were bred and herded, their slaughtered carcases providing meat and hides, their living bodies providing milk and wool. Milk, especially, was a favoured product and *Vita Columbae* gives an insight into its collection and consumption. In one story, Columba sent a trusted monk, Lugaid the Strong, on an errand to Ireland.[43] After being lent the abbot's own boat, Lugaid decided that he wanted milk as refreshment for the voyage, so he searched for a milk-skin. Among various items of equipment stowed on the vessel he eventually found what he sought. Before filling the skin with milk he placed it on the seashore and weighted it with stones to prevent its being washed away by the tide. He did this to saturate it, presumably to soften the dry leather, but Columba correctly prophesied that the sea would carry it away in spite of the weights. One interesting aspect of this story is that a milk-skin, rather than a water-skin, was regarded as a normal item of equipment for sea-travel: Lugaid clearly expected to find one on Columba's boat. Elsewhere in the *Vita* we see a different type of milk container being used, this time on dry land when a young monk 'was returning from milking the cows and carried on his back the wooden pail with the fresh milk in it'.[44] The main point of this story was the young man's request for Columba's customary blessing of the milk pail, which on this occasion concealed a devil whom the saint swiftly despatched. Behind the miraculous aspect we unearth interesting details about dairying on Iona, even as far as learning that the lid of a wooden milk pail was held in place by a peg between two holes. We also learn that monks bringing milk to the monastery paused at Columba's writing-hut so that he could bestow a blessing 'according to his custom'. This appears to have been a normal routine for those assigned to milking duty. The location of the hut in question is unknown, but it seems to have lain on a routeway leading directly to a place where milk cows were kept. Adomnán refers to the milking area as a *bocetum*, 'cattle pen', which indicates that the cows were milked in an open field rather than in a shed.[45] There may have been only one such area designated for this purpose. It was probably enclosed by little more than a wall of unmortared stone piled high enough to keep the animals penned in. This was clearly the wall-building method employed by a party of monks working on the machair when Columba saw them 'engaged in dry-stone work in the little western plain'. They were probably repairing field-boundaries rather than livestock pens, but the *bocetum* was no doubt of similar construction.[46]

Discarded animal bones unearthed by archaeologists show that cattle were slaughtered and eaten on Iona from the time of the first monastery. Religious communities supposedly consumed less flesh than ordinary folk, but, in most places, it would have been rare to find an outright prohibition. A meat-free diet involving no harm to God's creatures was a Christian ideal but hardly a realistic option in early medieval times. The inhabitants of a remote Hebridean island in the sixth century could hardly be expected to adopt a vegetarian lifestyle. The range of foodstuffs was simply not varied enough and, from a nutritional point of view, might have been perilously insufficient in an environment where hard manual labour was the daily norm. The archaeological evidence is unequivocal: beef was on Iona's monastic menu.[47] Whether Columba consumed it we cannot say, but a slight hint of his personal disdain for the killing of animals emerges from a passage in Adomnán's narrative. This reports a conversation between Columba and his trusted attendant Diarmait about a monk called Molua who had brought a tool to be blessed. Columba, deeply immersed in copying a manuscript, made the sign of the Cross over the object without looking up to see what it was. He later inquired of

Diarmait: 'What was the implement I blessed for our brother?' to which the attendant replied: 'A knife for the slaughtering of bulls or cattle.' This so troubled Columba that he added: 'I trust in my Lord that the implement I have blessed will not harm man or beast.' These words turned out to be prophetic, for Molua 'intending to kill a bullock' found that the knife would not even pierce the beast's hide.[48]

In addition to beef, other types of meat were also consumed. Adomnán shows two monks being sent to apprehend Erc moccu Druidi, a thief who had been secretly raiding what Columba described as 'the little island that is the breeding-place of the seals we reckon as our own'.[49] The place in question was evidently a seal colony regarded as exclusive property of the monastery. Although not explicitly stated, the implication is that the creatures living there were periodically slaughtered by the monks. Indeed, the remains of seal calves were found during archaeological excavations within the monastic enclosure. Seals would have been prized not only for their meat but also for useful by-products such as skin and oil. Sealskin is similar to leather and has a naturally waterproof quality while seal oil can be used as fuel or lubricant. In the same story of Erc moccu Druidi we hear of another source of meat when Columba hoped that a gift of sheep carcases might persuade the poacher to give up his thieving ways. This, incidentally, suggests that mutton was another common item on the monastery's menu. The sheep carcases given to Erc presumably came from flocks on Iona, in which case shepherding was as much a part of the economic life of the island in the sixth century as today. Pigs, too, were no doubt among the monastery's livestock. Adomnán refers to a sow being fattened and slaughtered on land owned by a rich man on Islay.[50] He says nothing of pigs on Iona, but it is difficult to imagine their absence. They would have been domesticated and penned, like those on Islay, rather than hunted in the wild. Columba saw a large boar being hunted on Skye by men and hounds, but such a scene could not have occurred on Iona, where a limited area of open countryside denies suitable habitats to any but the smallest wild mammals. No doubt for the same reason there is no mention in *Vita Columbae* of deer being herded, let alone hunted, anywhere on the island. Archaeological evidence nevertheless confirms that the monks ate venison, perhaps in all periods from the sixth century onwards. Deer carcases may have come from Mull, where these beasts were probably present. On one occasion, while visiting Lochaber on the mainland,

Columba sharpened a wooden stake and gave it to a poor man called Nesán. He told Nesán to use it as a hunting tool and said 'as long as you have this stake, your house will never be short of game for the table'.[51] The implement was used successfully in a trap for wild creatures, including a large stag and other deer, but would have been redundant on Iona where such animals had little space to roam.

Fish were obviously an abundant source of food. There are no references in *Vita Columbae* to fishing in the waters around Iona, but it can be assumed that the monks frequently engaged in it. Freshwater fishing in rivers on the mainland is mentioned by Adomnán, but the people involved appear to have been laymen rather than monks. He refers to nets and spear-traps being used and, in one instance, to large salmon being caught.[52] Seals have already been mentioned and were possibly the only marine mammals regularly consumed by Columba's monks. Adomnán refers to a whale swimming in the waters between Iona and Tiree, but there is no evidence for whale-meat being a mainstay of the monastic menu. The animal in question was seen by Columba's cousin, Baithéne, who blessed it as it passed his boat.[53]

Horses were kept on Iona, but, given the island's small size, they were probably few in number. There is no evidence that their meat was eaten by the monks and good reason to believe that it was forbidden. A seventh-century Irish synod issued a prohibition on the consumption of horseflesh by Christians, decreeing a penance of four years on bread and water.[54] Similar disapproval in the previous century is implied by Columba's prophetic warning to the reluctant penitent Neman: 'the time will come when in the company of thieves in the forest you will eat the flesh of a stolen mare'.[55] It seems rather that the main reason for keeping horses on Iona was to use them as working animals. One such beast carried milk pails from the cattle pen to the monastery and, perhaps coincidentally, had a white hide. When we meet this horse in *Vita Columbae*, it is apparently roaming free on a track leading out to the fields, although we may assume that it was stabled at night. In 1906, a horse skeleton was found buried deep under flat stones in a garden at Clachanach, a little to the north of the monastery. The apparent care with which this animal had been interred prompted a suggestion that the bones might be those of the milk-carrying steed described by Adomnán. There is, needless to say, no evidence for the identification. We have no references to other horses on Iona, but one, at least, must have hauled the *curru*, 'chariot', which conveyed the elderly Columba on his travels around the island.

Animals provided the monastery not only with meat but also with a number of useful by-products. Milk from cattle has already been mentioned, but the same beasts had hides that could be worked into leather. Sheep would have been sheared for their wool. Thus, although *Vita Columbae* does not refer directly to leatherworking and garment-making, we can assume that these crafts were undertaken. During excavations on Iona, archaeologists found the remains of leather shoes discarded in early medieval times.[56] These were almost certainly made on the island, presumably from hides provided by the monastery's own cattle. As previously noted, leather with natural waterproofing qualities was obtainable from sealskins.

Wood and metal

One necessary but very specialised craft was metalworking, especially for the manufacture and repair of tools. Monks with this skill would have been in constant demand, not only from companions toiling in the fields but also from others engaged in construction and maintenance around the monastic estate. Ceremonial objects, such as iron bells for the church, would also have been made on the island. Metallic items of a more exotic kind were obtainable via gift or trade. An ornate sword with a hilt of ivory was given by Columba to Librán the penitent so that he could buy his way out of an obligation to a kinsman. This weapon was almost certainly not made by a monastic smith, but must have come to Columba as a gift, its donor being a rich layman or wealthy cleric. The making of simpler bladed implements, not weapons, would surely have been undertaken at the monastery. It would have been hard physical labour. The modern equivalent of a sixth-century metalworker is the blacksmith rather than the foundryman, for the technology of smelting did not appear until much later. In the Middle Ages there was no means of producing enough heat to reduce iron to a molten state. Thus, while softer metals such as bronze could be melted, iron could only be softened and had to be worked with a hammer. Curiously, Adomnán speaks of 'monks who knew the blacksmith's craft' melting down an iron knife to produce a liquid coating that was then smeared on other tools.[57] This could not have happened before the advent of smelting so it must be an anachronism arising from textual error, either by Adomnán or by the source that gave him the story. Perhaps he meant that the iron knife was coated with another metal such as bronze? As both melting and coating were integral to the main point of his narrative a simple error of terminology seems the likeliest explanation.

There were no large woods on Iona. Timber for buildings and other structures had to be imported from elsewhere. When Columba decided to build a guesthouse for visitors he sent monks to fetch the necessary materials from outside the island. They came by boat to *Delcros*, 'Thorn headland', which belonged to a man called Findchán. Columba knew that the place was a good source of 'withies', the long twigs and small branches used for making wattle walls and roofs, but he did not first obtain the landowner's permission. When Findchán became aware that the monks were on his land, loading a boat with withy bundles, he immediately voiced his displeasure. This was conveyed to Columba when the monks returned home with their haul. Keen to avoid giving offence to a neighbour, the abbot sent monks back to Delcros with a gift of barley. The main hagiographical point in this story was the astounding fertility of the grain after Findchán sowed it in his fields. Viewed in a different way, the story tells us how the monastery obtained raw materials for new buildings. If we accept the interaction between Columba and Findchán as historical, the tale is of additional interest in describing relations between Iona's religious community and a secular neighbour. In this case, the latter was a member of the landowning class, a person whose wealth and status meant that his complaint could not be ignored.

Large timbers for constructing new buildings and repairing old ones came from woods on the mainland. Trees such as oak and pine were cut down by work-parties and sent back to Iona by sea. In the late seventh century, during his own abbacy, Adomnán personally supervised the felling of trees near the mouth of the River Shiel at the head of Loch Alsh.[58] The great trunks were towed back to Iona by the monastery's own vessels, some to be used in shipbuilding, others to be shaped as beams for a large house or dormitory. Although this particular instance of tree-felling and log-floating took place c.700, identical scenes were undoubtedly played out in Columba's time.

Travel by land and sea

Most journeys on sixth-century Iona would have been undertaken on foot. Carts and other wheeled vehicles were certainly used, but the island's small size probably meant that only a few were needed. When age and infirmity began to take their toll on Columba, he travelled around in a *curru* or 'chariot'. The typical *curru* in early medieval Ireland, and presumably in contemporary Britain too, was a light, two-wheeled vehicle hauled by a pair of horses. Irish sources associated it with persons of high status, including certain members of the clergy.[59] One episode in *Vita Columbae* refers to a rich cleric called Lugaid whom Columba saw riding in a chariot across the plain of Brega in Ireland. The saint regarded Lugaid's wealth as ostentatious and prophesied a bleak future for him. Clearly, the story's main purpose was to pass comment on clergymen who failed to shun the trappings of wealth.[60] It would be a mistake, however, to believe that Columba's disapproval was aimed at clerical chariot-users in general, or that he viewed such a vehicle as inappropriate for a holy man. Lugaid was nicknamed *Clodus*, 'Lame', and could hardly be expected to walk any great distance. Nevertheless, some clerics evidently felt that a more austere method of travel was appropriate for their image, at least while they were hale in body. Thus did Columba, a man of genuine humility, undertake a number of long journeys on foot. When we see him being conveyed in a chariot on Iona, he is near the end of his life and no longer able to walk the short distance between the monastery and the western shore. His use of a vehicle indicates that at least one route across the island must have been suitable for wheeled transport, at least in fair weather. It was probably no more than a rough bridleway.

Columba's island is separated from Mull by a narrow strait, the Sound of Iona. At its southern end the Sound is 2 miles wide, but further north it narrows to barely a mile. Today a regular ferry service plies between Fionnphort on the Ross of Mull and Iona's main settlement at Baile Mór with a sailing time of only ten minutes each way. The situation has not changed much since Columba's day, when a ferry-boat belonging to the monastery carried travellers back and forth across the Sound. This vessel was moored on the Iona side. Any visitor or homecoming monk on the opposite shore had to shout across the water to summon a ferryman.[61] It may be assumed that a member of the brethren was assigned to this duty each day, perhaps on a rota basis.

At the very least, a traveller on the Mull shore needed to have a reasonable expectation that someone on Iona stood within earshot. There must have been many occasions when the breeze blew so fiercely that not even the loudest shout carried over the strait. In such conditions the traveller presumably had an even longer wait, unless he was able to light a fire to alert the ferryman. Setting a blaze in the heather was a method used by Iona-bound travellers in modern times, apparently even in calm conditions, but this would have been impractical in a stiff wind or in wet weather. The mooring place of the monastery's ferry-boat has not been identified. We need not envisage a permanent fixture like a dock or jetty, nor substantial craft like a modern ferry. The ferry-boat of Columba's time was probably a light, cowhide vessel that could be drawn ashore at need. Part of the shoreline near the site of the ancient monastery is still called Port na Muinntir, 'Harbour of the Community', and might be one of the places where earlier travellers embarked or disembarked.

There were times, of course, when foul weather made even the short trip across the Sound too hazardous. Adomnán tells of one particular day when 'crashing storm and exceptionally high waves' prevented any sea-crossing until a small window of calm, foreseen by Columba, brought a brief respite.[62] Ferocious storms are, of course, a popular hagiographical theme. Foreseeing when and where they are due to strike, and curbing their intensity, form part of the common stock of miracles attributable to saints, but such stories frequently contain useful historical information about boats and sea-voyages. From the miracle-tales in *Vita Columbae* we learn a little of how the waters around north-west Britain and north-east Ireland were perceived by folk who dwelt on their shores in the sixth and seventh centuries. Thus, having already examined a short sea-voyage, the crossing of the Sound, we can now look at some of the longer ones. Adomnán mentions a number of these, most to destinations in Ireland or on mainland Argyll or to Hebridean isles such as Hinba and Tiree. The distances involved were not great in modern seafaring terms: Iona to Antrim is only 74 miles; Iona to Tiree barely 18 miles. Hinba, as we shall see in the next section, has not been located so its distance from Iona is unknown. Some journeys carried members of the Columban community to harbours on the Gaelic-speaking coastlands of Dál Riata, to districts such as Kintyre and Ardnamurchan. Destinations further away included Skye and the Western Isles. Adomnán refers to voyages undertaken by Columba himself, by his cousin Baithéne and by anonymous monks or *nautae*, 'sailors'. The latter were presumably in clerical orders even if their main vocation was not religious. Adomnán gives no precise figures for crew and passengers, but, since the monastery's boats are unlikely to have been large, the typical roster probably ranged from a dozen to twenty. All able-bodied folk on board would have been expected to lend a hand at hoisting sails and hauling oars. Columba once stayed as a house-guest with a *gubernator*, 'helmsman', on Rathlin Island off the Antrim coast. This man was not himself a cleric, but his seafaring skills were undoubtedly shared by specialist *nautae* among the Iona brethren.

The longest sea-voyages described in *Vita Columbae* were undertaken by monks seeking remote places of retreat. These pilgrims hoped to devote themselves wholly to God, living as hermits without the distraction of worldly cares. Finding a suitably isolated site was not a difficult task when the starting-point was Iona. There were many small islands in the Hebridean seaways, some of which were uninhabited but sufficiently hospitable to allow an austere level of subsistence. Those monks who chose this path established small communities where an ascetic lifestyle and periods of solitary contemplation were the norm. One such community, possibly founded in Columba's time by monks from Iona, may have colonised the tiny isle of Eileach an Naoimh in the Firth of Lorn. Here, the remains of a religious settlement comprising individual drystone huts or cells have been found alongside two chapels and a burial-ground. Although the oldest of the visible features dates from no earlier than c.1050, it is clear that the site is of far greater antiquity and could have been founded in the sixth century. It has sometimes been associated with Columba's contemporary Brendan moccu Altae, known today as 'St Brendan the Navigator', the most famous wandering monk of the Gaelic world. Brendan's long search for a place of retreat is thought by some modern scholars to have conveyed him across the Atlantic Ocean to North America.[63] Although no pilgrim from Iona is said to have sailed quite so far, Adomnán mentions one who did roam widely upon the seas in Columba's time. This was Cormac Ua Liatháin, a monk who made at least three attempts to locate a retreat for himself and a few companions. Cormac's first voyage began on the west coast of Ireland, in the district of Erris in County Mayo, and may have been a speculative foray into the Atlantic Ocean. The second embarked from Iona, at that time

Cormac's home monastery, and brought him to Orkney which, for reasons unstated, proved unsuitable. A third attempt, again from Iona, saw him sailing northward with a wind at his back. After fourteen days a horrific event befell his party on the open sea: their boat was attacked by a swarm of what Adomnán calls 'deadly loathsome little creatures' described as being 'about the size of frogs, but exceedingly troublesome because they had spines'.[64] They were probably jellyfish, but Cormac and his friends grew terrified that the vessel's skin-covered hull would be pierced. Only the prayers of the travellers, supported by those of Columba who received from afar a vision of the unfolding crisis, rescued them from deadly peril. We can only guess as to where the event occurred, although a fortnight's sailing may have borne Cormac a long way from British and Irish waters. When he returned to the monastery after this third disappointing trip, he abandoned his quest. Another pilgrim whose efforts similarly came to naught was Báetán, perhaps a native of Argyll, who asked for Columba's blessing on his own expedition, but received instead a disheartening prophecy of failure.[65] Other monks may have set out from Iona, but Adomnán does not tell their stories. Some may have found what they sought, their successful quests being marked by traces of habitation still visible on a number of remote Hebridean islands.

Two types of sea-vessel are mentioned in *Vita Columbae* as being used by the monks of Adomnán's own time: wooden ships built from planks and hide-covered craft known as currachs. The wooden ships were constructed on Iona using timber felled on the Argyll mainland.[66] Adomnán's personal reminiscence of tree-felling at the mouth of the River Shiel tells of oak trunks being towed back to Iona by twelve currachs. We can reasonably infer that these vessels did not comprise the monastery's entire fleet at the end of the seventh century. Twice this number, at the very least, must have been available, given the range of daily tasks involving sea-travel. A fleet of similar size, or perhaps only slightly less in number, can be envisaged for the period of Columba's abbacy. The currach of the Middle Ages little resembled the sleek, narrow craft known today by the same name and still used in some parts of Ireland. The modern version is constructed in the traditional way, its hull being formed by layers of hide stretched over a timber frame, but the currach of earlier times could be a much larger vessel with mast, sail and steering-oar.[67] Its hull length, even accounting for the limitations of hide as shipbuilding material, could be as much as 60 feet. Large currachs of this sort were still plying Irish waters as late as the seventeenth century, but, at some point thereafter, they gave way to wooden ships and only the smaller types of skin-covered craft have survived into modern times. It was probably a small currach that Columba and a few companions used when travelling from Dál Riata to Moray via the Great Glen and Loch Ness. This long and arduous journey incorporated treks between stretches of navigable water, so the boat had to be light enough for overland portage. Adomnán calls it a *navicula*, 'small ship'. It was evidently not needed on the great expanse of Loch Ness which seems to have been plied by fairly substantial sail-powered craft.[68]

Death, burial and funeral rites

The ritual aspects of monastic life included not only communal worship and private prayer but also the more sombre range of ceremonies associated with death. *Vita Columbae* offers a glimpse of what happened to those who died on Iona in the sixth century, but leaves many of our questions unanswered. As with other topics to which he alludes, Adomnán gives a few interesting details without painting the wider picture. Thus, while indicating quite clearly that the early monks who came to Iona in 563 were buried on the island, he does not say precisely where their graves were located. It is possible that Reilig Odhrain marks the site of the first cemetery, especially as simple cross-incised gravestones of very early date have been found there. Some of these could be as old as the seventh century, but it seems doubtful that any belong to Columba's time. Reilig Odhrain appears to have lain outside the monastery's original vallum and might therefore have been used as a burial-ground for laymen – visitors, penitents and local dignitaries – rather than for those who had taken the monastic vow.[69] However, despite its undoubted antiquity, we do not know if it belongs to the earliest period. If it does, and if it served as a cemetery for laymen, the young son of Meldan – previously mentioned – was no doubt buried there. We would then need to look elsewhere for the place where members of the religious community were interred. Cladh an Disirt has been suggested as a possibility, but, as noted above, its age and purpose have not yet been determined.

The original grave of the founder himself cannot now be

identified, although it may have been where St Columba's Shrine now stands. Wherever it lay, it was no ostentatious tomb or richly adorned mausoleum. Even in Adomnán's time, when devotion to the memory of Columba had spread far beyond the Gaelic world, the revered spot was marked only by a simple stone. The funeral rites accorded to the venerable abbot in 597 did, however, acknowledge his special status by mourning him for three days and three nights with prayers and solemn chants. His body, wrapped in a linen shroud, was interred in the ground. There is no mention of a coffin. Although a three-day funeral was clearly exceptional, the simple burial no doubt reflected the community's normal procedure for dealing with its dead. Like their founder, the ordinary monks of Iona would have been mourned and praised in the hours after death before being wrapped in linen shrouds and laid in the earth. Their graves, marked perhaps by simple cross-incised stones of the kind retrieved from Reilig Odhrain, may have been virtually indistinguishable from Columba's.[70]

CHAPTER 5
Iona and her Neighbours

The first satellite monasteries

One daughter-house of Iona features prominently in Adomnán's narrative. It lay on an island called Hinba and appears to have been Columba's most important secondary foundation in Britain.[1] To the frustration of generations of scholars its location has not been pinpointed with any measure of confidence, in spite of the fact that Columba was a frequent visitor. It was on Hinba that he was supposedly persuaded by an angel to anoint Áedán mac Gabráin as king. On other occasions he came to the island in an administrative role, as founding-father of the monastery, although his presence is inevitably linked to a miracle. Once, when four of Ireland's most famous saints supposedly visited him while he was staying on Hinba, he celebrated mass for them.[2] At other times he took an active role in the administration of the daughter-house, appointing his elderly uncle Ernán as prior and relaxing the dietary restrictions for penitents.[3] The latter decision was undertaken jointly with Baithéne who had a supervisory role over the penitential community on Hinba, if not over the entire monastery. Columba was on Hinba when he received 'the grace of the Holy Spirit' in such abundance that it engulfed him for three days. During this time he locked himself in his private dwelling, presumably a hut set apart from the monastic dormitories and reserved for his sole use.[4] By far the most dramatic Hinba-based episode in *Vita Columbae* shows the saint excommunicating a gang of pirates who had been raiding churches. One of these, nicknamed Lam Dess, 'Right Hand', tried to seek a bloody revenge. Tragedy was avoided by the prompt action of a monk who courageously placed himself between Columba and the assailant's spear.[5]

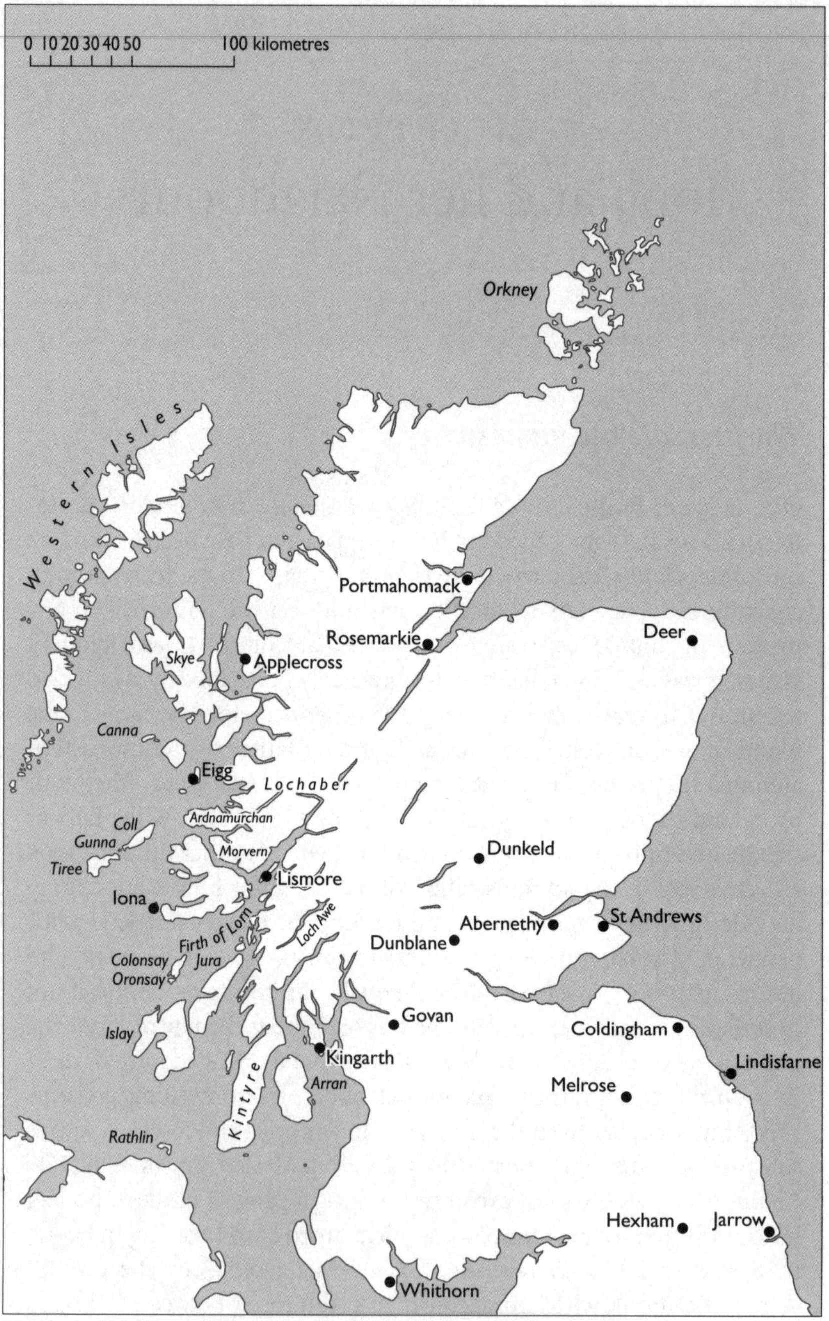

Northern Britain: major ecclesiastical sites, sixth to tenth centuries

In spite of Hinba's obvious importance, we do not know where the island lay. Adomnán gives it a Gaelic name, but this no longer exists, having almost certainly been replaced by a name of Viking origin. Many Hebridean islands still bear names bestowed by Norse settlers in the ninth century and Hinba is no doubt among them. Adomnán nevertheless refers to a number of isles that we are able to identify with relative ease. Thus, his *Malea* and *Scia* are Mull and Skye respectively, his *Colosus* and *Egea* are Coll and Eigg, while *Ilea* and *Ethica Terra* are Islay and Tiree. Other islands are either not mentioned in *Vita Columbae*, or, like Hinba, are given names that have no obvious match on a modern map. Several attempts to identify Hinba were made by scholars in the nineteenth and early twentieth centuries, but no consensus emerged from their deliberations. Among the many locations put forward as possible candidates were Colonsay, Oronsay, Uist, Canna, Jura, Gunna and Eileach an Naoimh.[6] Each theory had to accommodate Adomnán's reference to a place on Hinba called *Muirbolc Mar*, 'Great Sea-Bag', where the monks had a hermitage.[7] This large bay was named because of its shape or for some other characteristic that made it appear 'bag-like'. Any island proposed as a candidate for Hinba should therefore have a feature matching this description. Neither Eileach an Naoimh nor Gunna have anything of this sort in their topography and can therefore be ruled out of the search. Supporters of Jura's candidacy point to Loch Tarbert, the great sea-loch that nearly divides the isle in two, as a possible *muirbolc*, while Canna's natural harbour can likewise be described as bag-shaped. An alternative approach is to define what Adomnán and his contemporaries understood by *muirbolc*. Shape may not have been the only factor, nor the most important, especially if 'sea-bag' is interpreted in a literal sense as a container for seawater. The main characteristic of a *muirbolc* could have been its tendency to empty and fill with the ebb and flow of the tide, like a water-bag being alternately filled and emptied.[8] Such a feature seems to lie between Colonsay and its smaller southern neighbour Oronsay. Perhaps these two islands, joined by the narrow strait of An Traigh that separates them only when the tide is high, together represent the lost Hinba? Colonsay lies only 16 miles south of Iona and would have been a convenient stopping-place for Columba and his monks on their travels to and from the Kintyre heartlands of King Áedán. It is even possible that the Hinba monastery once stood where Oronsay's medieval priory stands today.[9] Although the priory's surviving remains are of fourteenth-century date, its dedication to Columba might preserve a memory of a more ancient past. One old tradition claims that Columba did indeed establish a church on Oronsay, while another derives the island's name from St Oran or Odhran, a semi-legendary figure whose grave was reputedly the first to be placed in the Reilig Odhrain on Iona.

Columba almost certainly founded a monastery on the isle of Tiree at a place called by Adomnán *Campus Lunge*. The name is Latin and seems to mean 'Plain of the Ship' or 'Ship Field'. In Gaelic it would be *Mag Luinge*. Baithéne, Columba's cousin, served as prior there for a time. It may have been the second most important daughter-house after Hinba and, according to Adomnán, both satellites were roughly equidistant from Iona. As on Hinba, the community at Mag Luinge included a number of penitents living under a strict regime of abstinence and prayer. Moreover, although Adomnán does not explicitly state that Mag Luinge was founded by Columba, we may reasonably infer that it was, and that it was not simply a pre-existing monastery brought under his authority after 563. Economic considerations alone would have highlighted Tiree as a logical target for early expansion from Iona. As the most fertile of the Hebrides, with a name meaning 'Land of Corn', its agricultural potential would have attracted Columba's interest. It had the potential to supply Iona with grain and, at only 18 miles distant, could be reached in less than half a day.

Mag Luinge was not the only religious house on Tiree, nor the first. There were at least two others, neither of which was an offshoot from Iona. Adomnán locates one at the unidentified *Artchain*, 'Fair cape' or 'Fair height', and tells a story of its founder, Findchán, who is otherwise unknown outside *Vita Columbae*. Elsewhere on the same island a monastery was reputedly established at *Blednach* by Brendan the Navigator whose own main foundation was Clonfert in County Galway. Blednach has not yet been identified. As it is not mentioned in *Vita Columbae*, nor in any source before the thirteenth century, its historical existence remains unconfirmed. St Brendan, of course, was an older contemporary of Columba and is named by Adomnán as a visitor to Hinba in the company of three other famous saints. Although the visit is most likely a hagiographical invention, it is not improbable that Columba and Brendan had genuine contact at some point between Columba's arrival on Iona and Brendan's death c.580. Adomnán tells of Áedán mac Fergnai, a holy man who for twelve years had been one of Brendan's disciples. Áedán paid a visit to Iona and might have come there from a Clonfert daughter-house in Argyll, perhaps even from the mysterious Blednach on Tiree.[10]

Like Blednach and Artchain, the Columban monastery at Mag Luinge has yet to be located. Archaeologists have identified two sites on Tiree where churches stood in medieval times. These are the old chapels at Kirkapol and Soroby, both of which commemorate Columba in their present-day dedications. It has been proposed that Port na Luinge near Soroby might be 'the harbour of Mag Luinge' mentioned by Adomnán, if the coincidence of names is not merely accidental.[11] There are few other clues, although place-names such as Kilmoluaig, Kilkenneth and Kilbride are suggestive of early churches and any of these might mark the location of a sixth-century monastery. Mag Luinge and Hinba are the Columban daughter-houses in Britain most frequently mentioned by Adomnán. Although he names only two more – respectively on an island and on the mainland – his narrative implies the existence of others. The island in question is *Elena*, a place no more identifiable today than Hinba. An attempt has been made to identify it as Eileach an Naoimh, 'Stony Mound of the Saints', one of the Garvelloch isles in the Firth of Lorn, which has a spring bearing Columba's name. His mother's burial-place is said to be the feature known as 'Eithne's Grave', an arrangement of stones on a hill overlooking the ruins of an early monastery on the island. A small cemetery with simple gravestones of pre-Viking date stands nearby, but none of the visible remains can be associated with the sixth century. It is more likely that they belong to the seventh or eighth, and no more than supposition that the site has any real connection with Columba. We may note also that Brendan the Navigator is said to have built a church on an island called *Ailech* off the coast of Britain. Some historians accept this as a reliable tradition and see *Ailech* as Eileach an Naoimh, drawing support for the identification from two place-names: *Dun Bhrennain*, 'Brendan's Fort', the highest hill on the island, and *Culbrandon*, 'Brendan's Retreat', a smaller isle nearby. Others prefer to identify Eileach an Naoimh as Adomnán's *Elena* or even as the equally mysterious Hinba. The latter theory can surely be ruled out, as it is unlikely that the original Gaelic name behind Latin *Hinba* would have been replaced by another Gaelic one. Wherever Hinba was it presumably bears a name of Scandinavian origin today. The equation of Elena with Eileach an Naoimh seems to be based mainly on an erroneous belief that *eileach*, 'rough or stony mound', must be a corruption of *eilean*, 'island'. There appears to be no evidence that Gaelic-speakers in the Firth of Lorn ever spoke of *Eilean* an Naoimh. In any case, the term *eilean* derives from an Old Norse word and did not enter Gaelic until the Viking era, a hundred years after Adomnán's time. We cannot say much more about Elena. Adomnán seems to think of it as being quite small, perhaps capable of sustaining only one religious settlement, when he refers to *the* monastery on Elena rather than to one of several.[12] In the final analysis we should probably regard both Elena and Hinba as two places that will remain forever lost.

Turning to the mainland, we find ourselves on firmer ground with *Cella Diuni*, another of Iona's early satellites. This lay beside Loch Awe, the longest freshwater loch in Scotland, which runs on a north-east/south-west axis along an ancient boundary between Lorn and Knapdale. *Cella Diuni* is a Latinisation of Gaelic *Cell Diuin*, 'Diun's Church', and appears only once in *Vita Columbae*, in a tale of prophecy.[13] Adomnán tells of Cailtan, prior of this church and brother of the eponymous Diun, and of his return to Iona at Columba's request. Upon arriving on the island, Cailtan was greeted by the saint who told him to expect death within a few days. Peering beneath this story we learn a few things about Diun and Cailtan. It seems likely, for instance, that the former was the founder and first prior of *Cella Diuni*. His brother's readiness to answer a summons from Columba suggests that both had originally been members of the Iona brethren, and that they had been sent to establish a daughter-house on the mainland. Adomnán precedes the tale with the heading 'The saint's prophecy about his monk Cailtan' which confirms that one brother, at least, was a disciple of Columba. Perhaps Diun was already dead before the summons came, with Cailtan taking over the running of their church? Of the place itself we know nothing beyond the name given by Adomnán. The name has not survived into modern times to enable us to pinpoint a specific location beside Loch Awe. The loch itself is very extensive and has a number of old settlements along its shores, several of which could be considered in a search for *Cella Diuni*.

Columba and Dál Riata

In the seventh century, the monks of Iona believed that their founder, St Columba, had served two successive royal patrons. They regarded the earlier of the two, Conall mac Comgaill, as the king who first bestowed the gift of Iona. The other, Áedán mac Gabráin, was seen as having a close bond of friendship with Columba in the final quarter of the sixth century. In Chapter 3 we examined Columba's dealings with Áedán in the light of his dual status as Christian abbot and Uí Néill prince. We looked at his involvement in secular politics as mediator and peacemaker and also at his alleged role as trusted adviser on dynastic matters. One key point emerging from any study of Columba's image as a 'royal chaplain' is the dichotomy between Iona's geographical position off the west coast of Mull and its close links with the rulers of Kintyre and Cowal. It is even possible that the monastery's bond with the descendants of Conall and Áedán was a feature of Adomnán's time rather than of Columba's. In the late sixth century, relations with other secular powers in Dál Riata might have been just as important, if not more so. We may note, for instance, that the early expansion of Iona's influence as presented in *Vita Columbae* could not have been achieved without support and protection from powerful patrons in areas close to the island. This leaves us to wonder how far the respective hegemonies of Conall and Áedán really extended, and whether or not Columba could rely on their protection in places like Skye, Lochaber, Ardnamurchan and Mull. It is possible that he had to gain the favour of other kings as he moved around the Hebridean zone. If so, he may have encountered certain difficulties, for these kings no doubt already had their own 'high priests' serving as abbots of monasteries under their patronage. In this section, then, we examine Columba's relationship with the Dál Riatan religious houses that were not under his authority.

Although much of Dál Riata seems to have discarded paganism before Columba's arrival in 563, the earliest missionaries have left no trace in the documentary record. In a story of conversion carefully crafted on Iona this is hardly surprising: it was important to Adomnán and his contemporaries that Columba had no rivals in his role as evangelist of northern Britain. Thus, although *Vita Columbae* refers to sixth-century monasteries in various parts of Argyll, most are presented as satellites of Iona, founded by Columba himself. The few exceptions include Findchán's community at Artchain on Tiree, mentioned in the preceding section. As we have already noted, Artchain and its Columban neighbour at Mag Luinge were not the only monasteries on the island. The unidentified Blednach, for example, was reputedly established by St Brendan. Other monasteries on Tiree might also have been founded before c.600, their exact locations as elusive today as the names of their founders. They may be invisible in *Vita Columbae* because they owed no allegiance to Iona.

One non-Columban monastery whose existence is not in doubt lay on the small island of Eigg between Skye and Ardnamurchan. It occupied a site where the old parish church of Kildonan stands today. The church, now a roofless ruin, dates from the 1500s but bears the name of St Donnan, the original founder. Donnan was an Irish saint who founded a monastery on Eigg before the end of the sixth century. He may have been there during Columba's final years on Iona, in spite of the fact that Adomnán omits any mention of him or of his monastery. One story in *Vita Columbae* does mention Eigg, but only in the context of a visit by Baithéne who was subsequently trapped on the island by adverse weather.[14] From this lone reference we can infer one of two things: either Adomnán was aware that Donnan's monastery existed at the time of Baithéne's visit, but chose not to mention it; or the visit took place before the monastery's foundation. The first scenario would be consistent with Iona's portrayal in *Vita Columbae* as the premier centre of Hebridean Christianity, to the exclusion of all others. It is therefore possible that Baithéne did indeed travel to Eigg in some formal capacity as an emissary from Iona, conveying messages from Columba to Donnan. Some versions of the *Martyrology of Óengus* report a conversation between the two saints in which Donnan asks for Columba's friendship. The request is refused by Columba who explains that he does not wish for friendship with someone whose life will not end in the peaceful 'white' martyrdom of a non-violent death. He has, of course, foreseen Donnan's murder at the hands of brigands. 'I will not be your soul-friend,' he adds, 'because you and all your community with you will suffer red martyrdom.' This conversation can be regarded as fictional. It was probably derived from an entry in the Irish annals under the year 617: 'the burning of Donnan of Eigg on 17 April, with 150 martyrs'. Despite this catastrophe, the monastery at Kildonan survived and was still in existence in Adomnán's time, its last notice in the historical record being the death of one of its brethren in 752. By then, it may have been a mother-church with its own *paruchia* of satellites, for places called Kildonan are found in various parts of Scotland today.

Another monastery not mentioned in *Vita Columbae* was the one founded by St Moluag (also known as St Lugaid) on the island of Lismore in the Firth of Lorn. This became known as *Cill Moluaig*, 'Moluag's Church', a name subsequently Anglicised to Kilmaluag. In later times, the site was used by the bishops of Argyll who erected a modest cathedral, some portions of which survive in the fabric of the present-day parish church. Like St Comgall of Bangor, Moluag's origins lay in northern Ireland among the Dál nAraidi or Cruithin of Antrim. The hagiography surrounding Moluag portrays him as a disciple of Comgall and locates his early career at Bangor.[15] He reputedly made the sea-crossing to Britain on a floating rock and won the right to settle on Lismore after beating Columba in a swimming race. Behind these hagiographical stories the true origin of Moluag's monastery can be sought in its geographical context. Lismore's proximity to Lorn suggests that Moluag obtained permission for the religious settlement from a local king, perhaps the head of one of the constituent families of what later became the powerful Cenél Loairn kin-group. In exchange for land and guarantees of protection, Moluag's patron would have expected the kind of spiritual services rendered by Columba to the rulers of Cowal and Kintyre. Moluag, like his counterpart on Iona, may have assumed the role of 'high priest' within his patron's kingdom. He died in 592, predeceasing Columba by five years, and was supposedly brought back to Lismore after first being interred in Pictish territory further east. As contemporaries dwelling in the seaways around Mull, these two saints almost certainly communicated with one another. The separate traditions linking them to Comgall of Bangor add weight to the idea that they were in direct contact during their respective abbacies in Britain. It is strange, then, that Adomnán's favourable treatment of Comgall in *Vita Columbae* did not prompt him to mention Moluag. Perhaps Lismore's proximity to Mull made it Iona's major competitor, in which case Moluag's absence from the *Vita* is easier to explain.

In Chapter 2 we noted the likelihood that a system of alternating overkingship operated in southern Argyll in the late sixth and early seventh centuries. Two families descending from a common ancestor Domangart seem to have shared power for several generations until the system eventually broke down. Columba witnessed at first hand the alternating succession in 576 when Áedán mac Gabráin succeeded Conall mac Comgaill. As Áedán's power-base lay in Kintyre we might expect to find his local place of worship at a Christian site on the peninsula. One late medieval tradition claims that he was buried at Kilkerran, near modern Campbeltown.[16] If this has any historical basis, it offers a possible location for the primary royal church of Gabrán's kin. This church, wherever it lay, seems to have been eclipsed by Iona during the seventh century, although the process may have started much earlier, with the original church relinquishing its royal ceremonial functions during Columba's lifetime. Looking back to Conall's reign we might reasonably assume that he, too, worshipped at a religious centre in his home territory, presumably in what would later be the heartland of his sons and grandsons. The territory in question comprised the Cowal peninsula and the Isle of Bute together with other islands and coastlands around the Firth of Clyde. A major early monastery flourished in this region, at Kingarth near the southern tip of Bute, a foundation traditionally assigned to the sixth century. Its reputed founder was a saint called Blane or Blaan whom we can accept as a historical figure. By analogy with Iona we might envisage Blane's monastery being built on land donated by a secular lord, in which case Kingarth's geographical setting suggests a benefactor from the royal family of Cowal, the kindred to which Conall mac Comgaill belonged. This raises the interesting possibility that Kingarth, like Iona, owed its origin to Conall.

The hagiography surrounding St Blane is late and sparse. Our main source is the *Aberdeen Breviary*, a text compiled c.1500 by the bishop of Aberdeen. Among a plethora of information on early Scottish saints the *Breviary* contains a brief account of Blane's life and career. Its reliability is uncertain, but it identifies him as a native of Bute who studied in Ireland under Comgall of Bangor. Returning thence to his birthplace, Blane became a disciple of Cathan, his uncle, whom he succeeded as abbot of Kingarth until his own death in 590. Parts of this story, especially those dealing with Blane's childhood, are based on common hagiographical motifs. In the absence of independent testimony we are left wondering how much of it is true. Fragments of other traditions about Blane have, nevertheless, been preserved. In the ninth-century *Martyrology of Óengus* we find mention of 'triumphant Blaan of the Britons' and of 'Fair Blaan of Cenn Garad'. The context behind the first reference is unknown, but it could relate to lost stories crediting Blane with missionary work among the Britons of the Clyde, perhaps during the kingship of Columba's contemporary Rhydderch Hael. Given its setting, Kingarth

Leac na Cumhaidh, Gartan, Donegal: the cup-marked stone where Eithne is said to have given birth to St Columba, c.521. [© 2007, www.a-wee-bit-of-ireland.com, All rights reserved: http://www.a-wee-bit-of-ireland.com/eire_2007/gartan_06.html]

The Grianán of Ailech, a cashel or ringfort of c.600, was a royal stronghold of the Northern Uí Néill until its destruction in the early twelfth century. [www.pdphoto.org]

Early Christian grave slab at Movilla Abbey, Co. Down, the site of an important monastery founded by St Finnian, c.540. [Reproduced courtesy of the National Library of Ireland]

The towering mass of Ben Bulben, Co. Sligo, overlooking the battlefield of Cúl Drebene where Columba's Cenél Conaill kinsmen defeated the Southern Uí Néill in 561. [www.pdphoto.org]

The Hill of Tara in the valley of the River Boyne, Co. Meath, symbolic seat of the high kings of Ireland in early medieval times. [ianmiddletonphotography.co.uk]

Druim Cett, the 'Ridge of Cett': the Mullagh Hill near Limavady, reputedly the site of the great royal convention attended by King Áedán and St Columba. [Reproduced courtesy of Coleraine Borough Council]

ABOVE. Aerial view of Iona Abbey from the north-east, with the remains of the vallum of the earlier monastery showing clearly above the road in the right of the picture. [© Crown Copyright: RCAHMS. Licensor www.rcahms.gov.uk]

RIGHT. St Martin's Cross, Iona, a finely carved monument of c.800 adorned with religious imagery. It is over 4 metres tall and stands a little to the west of the abbey within the ancient monastic enclosure. [© Royal Commission on the Ancient and Historical Monuments of Scotland. Licensor www.scran.ac.uk]

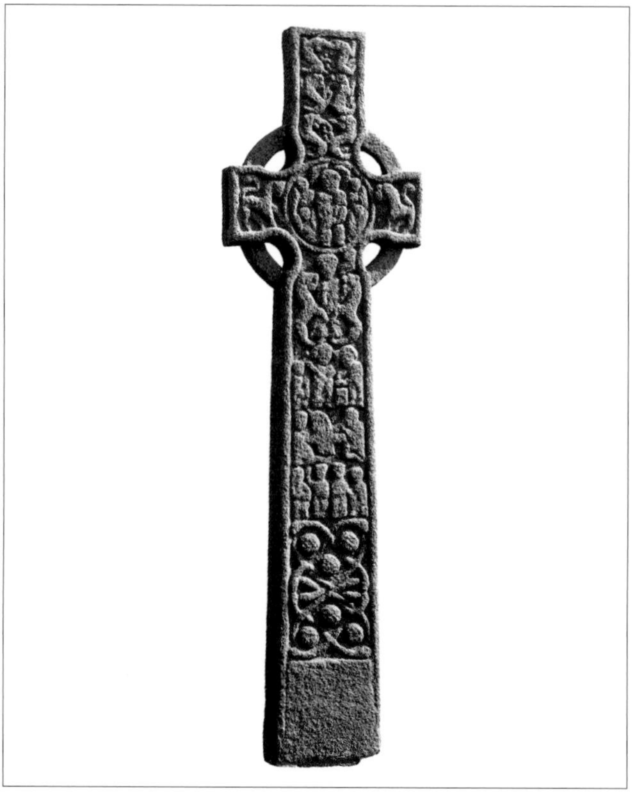

King Áedán's *caput regionis*? The Rock of Dunaverty at the southern tip of Kintyre, an early stronghold of the Scots and the site of a later castle. [Photograph by Barbara Keeling]

The island of Hinba? Looking northwards over Oronsay and Colonsay with Mull in the distance. [© Crown Copyright: RCAHMS. Licensor www.rcahms.gov.uk]

St Augustine's Church, Derry, near the old city walls. The present church, rebuilt in 1872, is believed to stand on the site of a sixth-century monastery founded by St Columba. [iStockphoto/Roger Bradley]

Craig Phadrig: aerial view of the Iron Age hillfort, a possible candidate for the fortress of King Bridei visited by St Columba on one of his journeys in Pictland. [© Crown Copyright: RCAHMS. Licensor www.rcahms.gov.uk]

Clonmacnoise: the ruins of the cathedral built in the tenth century on the site of a monastery founded by St Ciarán in the 540s. [Reproduced courtesy of the National Library of Ireland]

The Book of Kells, a lavishly ornamented Gospel book of c.800, may have been created on Iona before being brought to Ireland. It is now in the library of Trinity College, Dublin. [Reproduced courtesy of the National Library of Ireland]

The great cathedral at Dunkeld on the north bank of the River Tay reputedly possessed relics of St Columba throughout the medieval period. [© Courtesy of RCAHMS. Licensor www.rcahms.gov.uk]

The Monymusk Reliquary, a house-shaped shrine of the eighth century, is believed by some to be the Breccbennach of St Columba, a battle-talisman borne by the victorious Scottish army at Bannockburn in 1314. [© National Museums of Scotland. Licensor www.scran.ac.uk]

might even have served as a link between the respective secular powers of Cowal and Alt Clut. If so, Columba's communications with Rhydderch were perhaps intended to extend Iona's influence into a region where the abbots of Kingarth had traditionally wielded spiritual authority. An additional point of interest in any discussion of Blane is the location of his primary cult-centre in later medieval times. From the mid-ninth century, if not before, this lay not at Kingarth but at Dunblane in Perthshire. A plausible explanation for the shift might be the transfer of the founder's relics to a safer location at a time when Viking marauders were active in the Firth of Clyde.[17]

Although *Vita Columbae* makes no mention of Kingarth, it was almost certainly a major Dál Riatan monastery in the late sixth century. It may have been the preferred church of Cowal kings during the reigns of Conall mac Comgaill and his immediate successors. Perhaps its abbots established daughter-houses elsewhere in southern Argyll? Our attention inevitably falls on ancient churches bearing dedications to Blane, and also to Cathan, or to places where these two saints are otherwise commemorated. The Gaelic place-name *Cill Blathain*, 'Blane's Church', occurs in Anglicised form as Kilblain near Kingarth, Kilblane in Kintyre and Kilblaan at the head of Loch Fyne. Cathan's name is similarly preserved in *Cill Chatain*, Anglicised as Kilchattan, a toponym found not only on Bute but on other islands such as Gigha, Islay and Colonsay as well as in Kintyre. Not all of these names are likely to mark genuine satellites of Kingarth, but some probably do and one or more might be quite early, perhaps dating from the sixth or seventh centuries. A prime candidate is the monastery recently excavated on Inchmarnock, a tiny island off Bute's western coast. Here, the place-name commemorates a saint called Marnock, Gaelic *Mo-Ernoc*, 'My Little Ernán', a namesake of Columba's uncle Ernán but apparently a different individual. Archaeological evidence indicates monastic activity in the eighth and ninth centuries, but an earlier foundation, perhaps an offshoot from Kingarth, cannot be ruled out.[18]

The foregoing discussion gives some insight into the distribution of major monasteries in sixth-century Argyll. We can be fairly sure that the picture is incomplete. The Iona-centred narrative of *Vita Columbae* has undoubtedly omitted crucial information about what was happening elsewhere, leaving us with many unanswered questions. We should like to know, for instance, if Eigg, Lismore and Kingarth were the most important non-Columban foundations in Dál Riata. The combined testimonies of hagiography, annals and archaeology imply that these three, together with Iona, were the principal centres of Hebridean Christianity between 550 and 600. Matching them to their respective secular patrons is a difficult exercise. Seventh-century Iona had strong ties with the kings of Cowal and Kintyre and plainly believed that these connections originated in the 560s. This is a consistent thread running through Adomnán's narrative and can be accepted, to some extent at least, as a true reflection of Columba's political relationships. What is missing from the *Vita* is a glimpse of the saint's interaction with other secular powers, especially those closer to Iona in places like Mull and Lorn. Some historians wonder if his unrecorded contact with the ancestors of Cenél Loairn might have been more important to him than his well-attested dealings with Conall and Áedán. Such musings are based on what appears at first sight to be a logical deduction from Hebridean geography, namely Lorn's proximity to Mull, and Mull's proximity to Iona. This might be assuming too much, for we know too little about the distribution of power in early medieval Argyll. For all we know, the western half of Mull – and Iona too – may have lain under the authority of Kintyre-based kings in the late sixth century. If so, Columba may have had few dealings with the rulers of Lorn, since most of his Dál Riatan monasteries would have been founded in districts where Conall or Áedán held sway. In any case, the only Columban daughter-house certainly identifiable in Lorn was *Cella Diuni* beside Loch Awe. The rest lay in territories that might not have traditionally leaned towards Lorn-based rulers. An example is Tiree, an island only marginally closer to Lorn than to Kintyre. All of its monasteries, including the Columban daughter-house at Mag Luinge, might have expected patronage not from Lorn but from Kintyre and Cowal. Tiree's own indigenous elite – her chieftains and landowners – may have naturally gravitated to Domangart's heirs rather than to kings in Lorn, Islay or elsewhere.[19]

Columba's dealings with secular authority in Dál Riata were not restricted to high-level communication with kings. His own travels, and those of his disciples, inevitably brought him into contact with other powerful individuals, some of whom claimed royal blood. Not all of these folk treated him with the benevolence and respect shown by his patrons. Some were openly hostile. In one startling episode reported by Adomnán a direct attempt was made on Columba's life. This happened in an atmosphere of simmering tension between the saint and a gang of violent marauders led by one Ioan mac Conaill mac Domnaill. Ioan is described as belonging to 'the royal lineage of Gabrán' and is usually seen as a kinsman of Áedán, perhaps a cousin. He had, however, fallen into evil ways, leading a band of ruthless pirates who roamed the seaways. These men began targeting a farmer called Colmán who lived on the coast of Ardnamurchan. Adomnán says of Colmán that he was rescued from poverty by Columba, whose blessing increased his tiny herd of five cattle by a hundred. In return, Columba availed himself of Colmán's hospitality and appears to have been a frequent house-guest. He was not there, however, when Ioan mac Conaill and his band sailed into the nearby bay. The pirates came ashore to pillage Colmán's house before making off with a boatload of plunder. So easy were the pickings that they came back twice, their third raid coinciding with one of Columba's visits to Ardnamurchan. On this occasion the saint seems not to have been staying with Colmán, for the marauders were unaware of his presence in the district until he unexpectedly appeared as they prepared to sail away.[20] He confronted them on the seashore, trying to persuade them to give up their loot and reproaching them for their crimes, but his words were greeted with scorn. Ioan mocked him openly and ordered the vessel to put out to sea. At that moment Columba waded knee-deep into the water and lifted his hands in prayer. There he remained until the pirates were out of sight, before returning to his companions who stood waiting on the shore. He then went up onto higher ground, seeking a place with wide views across the sea. There he prophesied that Ioan, 'this wretched fellow who has despised Christ in his servants', would drown in a coming storm. To the amazement of the monks, the weather in the distance worsened dramatically and a fierce storm arose. It caught the pirates in open water as they headed south-west from Ardnamurchan towards the wide channel between Mull and Coll. Their boat capsized and none survived. This did not, however, entirely remove the menace, for not all of Ioan's men were with him on his final raid. Others continued in their evil ways, rallying around his brothers. Thus we meet the same gang again, in yet another confrontation with Columba. In introducing this new tale of 'the sons of Conall mac Domnaill', Adomnán reminds his readers that 'we have already told the story of one of them'[21]. If the ordering of his narrative reflects a chronological sequence, the encounter in question took place after Ioan's death. This time, Columba found himself in an even more perilous position. The setting was Hinba, the island where he had a satellite monastery. Having learned of attacks on churches by Ioan's brothers he decided to excommunicate them, this being the strongest sanction available to him. At that time the pirates were either dwelling on Hinba or lurking around its shores. Among them was one called 'Right Hand', a nickname given by Adomnán in its Latin form *Manus Dextera*. In modern Gaelic it would be *Lam Dess*, this no doubt being similar to how the name sounded to sixth-century ears. How such a nickname was acquired is unknown, as is the real name it masks, but it is tempting to suggest that its bearer may have been a favoured deputy or 'right-hand man' of the pirate chief Ioan. Seized by a murderous rage, Lam Dess attacked Columba with a spear, plainly intending to kill him. In a selfless act of courage and loyalty a monk called Findlugán, who happened to be wearing Columba's cowl, stepped in front of the saint to shield him. The spear failed to pierce the cowl, leaving both Columba and the brave Findlugán unharmed, but Lam Dess believed that the thrust had struck deep. Fooled perhaps by the swapping of garments, he mistook Findlugán for Columba and assumed that the saint himself was mortally wounded. The confrontation ended, but justice was served one year later when Lam Dess was killed in a skirmish on the island of *Longa*. The island might be Luing at the southern end of the Firth of Lorn if it is not the 'Long Island' formed by Lewis, Harris and the Uists.[22]

Outside *Vita Columbae* we learn nothing more of Lam Dess and he remains an enigmatic character. He was evidently not one of Ioan's brothers, a son of Conall mac Domnaill, for Adomnán describes him as 'a man from the band of these men of evil' rather than as a kinsman. A more puzzling aspect of Columba's enmity towards these scions of 'the royal lineage of Gabrán' is Adomnán's reason for mentioning it at all. Elsewhere, his treatment of Gabrán's family is generally favourable, especially with regard to Áedán, yet here we apparently see members of the same kin-group portrayed as merciless thugs. They harass defenceless farmers, attack churches and even attempt to slay a senior abbot. They seem, in fact, to be a rather unsavoury group of characters. Reconciling this negative image with Adomnán's customary eulogising of Gabrán's kin is difficult, but the solution may lie in looking at the data in a different way. We could, for instance, envisage not one Gabrán but two, one of them Áedán's father. Ioan and his brothers might then be the descendants of an otherwise unknown King Gabrán who lived a generation or more before his namesake. Both Gabráns could have been related in some way, but even this is not a necessary deduction from *Vita Columbae*, for the ancestor of the pirates may have ruled a domain far from Kintyre. If so, where was it? Ioan was drowned in the waters between north-west Mull and Coll while sailing away from Ardnamurchan. Lam Dess was slain on the unidentified island of *Longa* which might be Luing or the elongated arc of the Western Isles. Neither location suggests a particular place of origin or principal residence for the pirates. A clue may nonetheless be given by Adomnán when he says of Columba that he was residing on Hinba when 'he set about excommunicating those men who persecuted churches, in particular the sons of Conall mac Domnaill'. Might we infer from this that Columba excommunicated Conall's sons on Hinba because they lived on that island? It might even have been their ancestral home, a place their forefather Gabrán had once ruled. Colonsay, previously noted as a possible candidate for Hinba, would neatly fit the geographical context suggested not only by Ioan's demise in the sea off north-west Mull but also by his henchman's possible slaying on Luing. We may suggest, by way of an endnote, that if the leaders of the pirate band really belonged to the royal dynasty of Kintyre, their relationship with Áedán mac Gabráin was surely hostile. Twice we see them in verbal or physical confrontation with the most senior abbot of Áedán's realm. In any event, the enmity they showed to Columba might reflect a similar attitude towards Áedán himself, whether or not they considered him a relative.

The sons of Conall mac Domnaill, although not described as kings, claimed royal ancestry. In terms of social rank they were noblemen, occupying an upper tier of the landowning aristocracy. Their activities as sea-rovers should not blind us to the likelihood that their home base was a substantial estate capable of supporting them through the winter months. They were members of a prosperous social class represented elsewhere in *Vita Columbae* by men such as Feradach of Islay whose rich lifestyle was described by Adomnán.[23] To the same class also belonged the disgruntled Findchán who complained about monks of Iona taking withy sticks from his land. Findchán probably owned a large estate on the Ross of Mull.

Being himself of high social status Columba would have moved easily among the elites of Dál Riata. Even wealthy landowners such as Feradach and minor royals like the pirate chief Ioan were less than his social peers, for he came from the topmost stratum of Gaelic society. As the highest-ranking Irish exile in Britain, only the upper echelons of Dál Riatan royalty were his true equals. However, his exalted status proved no obstacle to his religious vocation. As a dutiful Christian priest he saw humility as a virtue when dealing with people at the lower levels of society. This, of course, is how his hagiographer painted his portrait, but we have no real cause to reject it. Columba's displays of humility were surely heartfelt and genuine and we would not be naïve in accepting them. On the contrary, we should keep in mind that the saint depicted in *Vita Columbae* was not merely a hagiographical creation but also, and perhaps more so, a devout and committed holy man. He was not averse to staying as a house-guest with folk of low economic standing. In Lochaber on the Argyll mainland he accepted the hospitality of Nesán, 'a very poor man', who offered accommodation for one night 'as far as his means would stretch'.[24] In gratitude the saint prophesied that Nesán's tiny herd of five cows would swell by a hundred before telling him that 'your seed will be blessed in your sons and grandsons'. A similar rise in economic fortunes had come to Colmán, the Ardnamurchan farmer victimised by the pirate chief Ioan mac Conaill. Both Colmán and Nesán were poor people for whom Columba prophesied prosperity after they gave him friendship and hospitality. Their stories are probably based on real events remembered by their families and preserved in succeeding generations. In Nesán's case, his grandsons may have made no secret of their family's miraculous escape from poverty. Perhaps they reported the story of their grandfather's encounter with Columba to Abbot Ségéne in the second quarter of the seventh century? Like Nesán, Colmán of Ardnamurchan was rewarded with an increase in cattle from a paltry five to one hundred and five, as well as with a blessing on sons and grandsons. Although these two tales follow a hagiographical template with names and circumstances altered, we have no reason to disregard their core elements as unhistorical. The essential facts of both may have been reported to Ségéne by the grandchildren of Colmán and Nesán before being woven by Cumméne into his book of miracles. Behind the hagiography of each story we see Columba the advisor of kings moving comfortably among folk on the margins of society.

While staying as a guest at a place called *Coire Salcháin*, 'Willow Corrie', Columba was visited by a *plebeus*, 'layman', who was being terrorised by thieves. On learning that the victim lived in a district beside *Stagnum Crog Reth*, 'Crog Reth Lake', Columba informed him that brigands were at that moment looting his house and stealing his small herd of cattle, having forced his wife and children to flee.[25] Here, Adomnán draws on a common stock of motifs that appear later in the story of Colmán of Ardnamurchan: a poor family targeted by robbers; a humble abode looted; a small herd stolen. The main differences here are the anonymity of the *plebeus*, the fact that he is not Columba's host, and the lack of a happy ending via an upturn in the family's fortunes. As with Colmán's tale, the geographical setting appears to be mainland Argyll, but *Coire Salcháin* has so far defied identification. Several possible locations have been proposed, but the likeliest may be in the vicinity of the now-deserted hamlet of Salachan in Morvern.[26] A corrie, from a Gaelic word meaning 'cauldron', is a common feature in the Scottish landscape, usually taking the form of a round hollow on a hillside. On modern maps a corrie slightly west of Salachan bears the name Corrie an Lagain (perhaps 'Corrie of the Dell'). This lies below the knoll of Dun Shalachain which looks out over the Sound of Mull to the narrow isthmus dividing the northern and southern parts of the island. Being within easy reach of travellers from Iona this seems a plausible location for the place where Columba stayed as a guest, although the whereabouts of his host's residence remain elusive. If this district is the approximate setting of the tale, we should expect the layman's house at *Crog Reth* to be situated in the same district, and a possible candidate exists. One mile east of Salachan, the present-day village of Ardtornish stands on the Rannoch River which flows into the Sound of Mull via the tiny Loch Aline. The river runs down from a small upland loch, called Loch Tearnait, 'Loch of the Sanctuary', which contains a crannog or artificial island. Part of the loch's northern shore is marked on modern maps as Leacraithnaich, a name preserving the Gaelic form of *rannoch*, the root of which is *raith*, 'fern'. Leacraithnaich might here mean 'Fern slope' or 'Fern stone'. The same second element seems to occur in Adomnán's *Crog Reth* which may represent an archaic form, perhaps ultimately of Brittonic origin, of modern Gaelic *Cruach Rannoch*, 'Fern Hill'.[27] The medieval 'sanctuary' from which Loch Tearnait is named lay on the crannog which, according to local tradition, was used as a hideout for fugitives. The name must have arisen long after *Vita Columbae* was written. If so, it may have replaced an earlier name that once described a surrounding landscape of fern-covered slopes, this aspect being suggested by today's Leacraithnaich. It

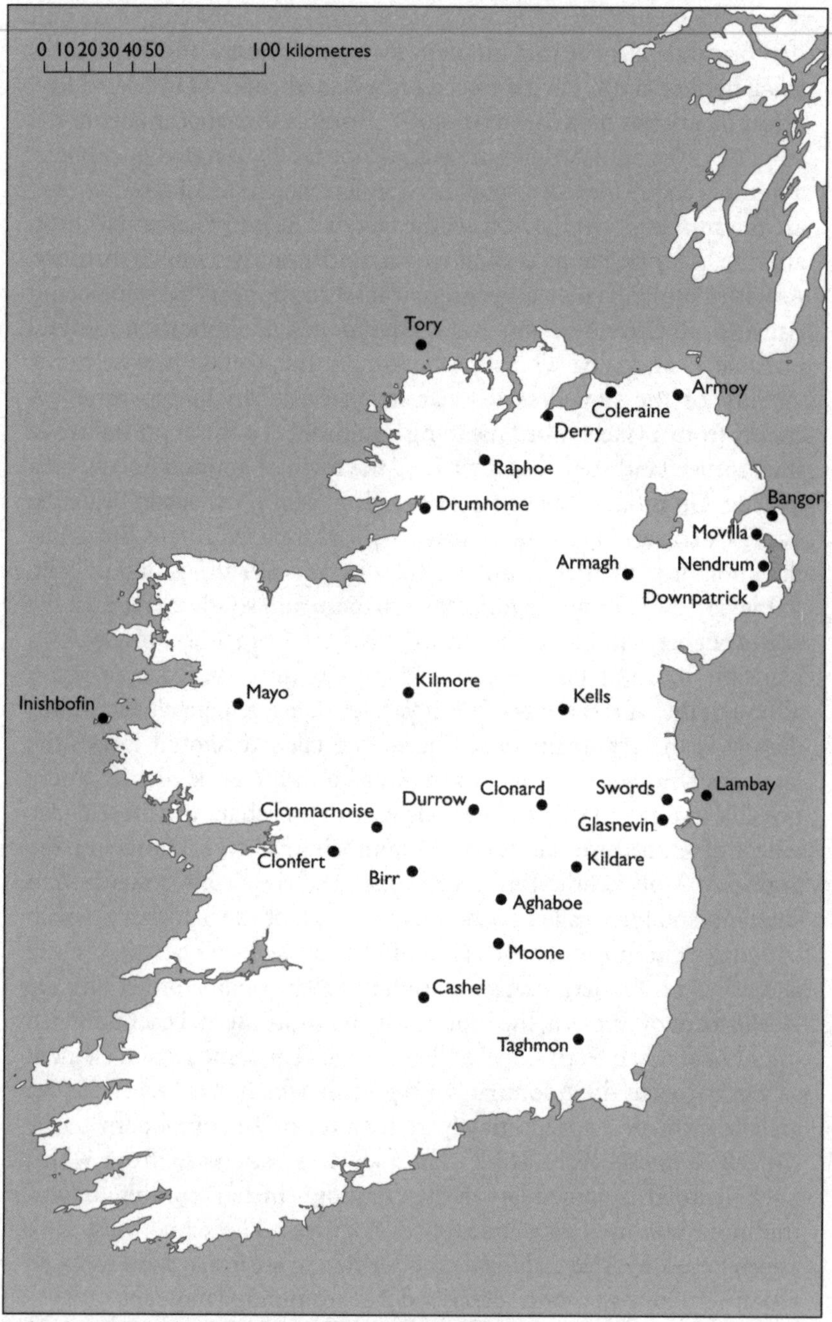

Ireland: major ecclesiastical sites, sixth to tenth centuries

is therefore possible that Loch Tearnait was originally called *Loch Cruach Rannoch*, 'Fern Hill Loch', a name rendered into Adomnán's Latin as *Stagnum Crog Reth*, and that Columba's host at Coire Salcháin did indeed reside near Salachan in Morvern.

The episodes noted above show Columba travelling freely around Dál Riata, typically with a small group of companions. Although clearly revered and respected by most of the lay population, his safety was by no means guaranteed. In the dramatic encounter with Lam Dess he found himself in extreme danger and narrowly escaped being killed. At no point is he shown accompanied by armed bodyguards, even when he ventures to places where the authority of his patrons in Cowal and Kintyre must surely have had no remit. Although the secular powers in districts such as Morvern, Lochaber and Ardnamurchan cannot be identified with certainty, the geographical context points to the ancestral kindreds of Cenél Loairn.[28] It is likely, then, that Columba had close dealings with this group of families and maintained amicable relations with them. How far such interaction impacted on his friendships with Conall mac Comgaill and Áedán mac Gabráin is unknown.

Columba's foundations in Ireland

Columba's 'pilgrimage' in Britain began when he left Ireland in 563. The circumstances of his departure appear to be connected in some way with his excommunication by a synod of Irish clergy. It is possible, then, to view Iona as his place of exile, not merely as a home for pilgrims and missionaries. From Adomnán we learn that neither the period of exile nor the excommunication were permanent. We see Columba returning to Ireland to attend the Convention of Druim Cett, an event that can be dated to c.590, but this was not his only homecoming visit. At some point after 585, perhaps even before he attended the Convention, he founded a monastery at *Daru*, 'The Plain of Oaks', now Durrow in County Offaly.[29]

Durrow lay in the kingdom of the Uí Failge, an ancient royal kindred from whom the name *Offaly* derives. The Uí Failge seem to have fallen under the sway of the Southern Uí Néill around the middle of the sixth century, their rulers acknowledging Diarmait mac Cerbaill and his son Colmán Bec as overlords. When Colmán was defeated by

Columba's cousin Áed mac Ainmerech in 586 the Uí Failge and other midland groups presumably fell under Northern Uí Néill overlordship, at least until Áed's death eleven years later. The monastery at Durrow was perhaps founded during this period, on land granted by Áed to Columba. Such a chronology fits Adomnán's belief that the founding of Durrow coincided with a visit by Columba to the monks of Clonmacnoise. Adomnán identified the abbot of Clonmacnoise at that time as Alither whose tenure ran from 585 to 599, a period contemporary with Áed's dominance of the Southern Uí Néill. The likelihood of Áed being the patron of his kinsman's new monastery is high, for the foundation would have installed what was essentially a Cenél Conaill religious house in the territory of Áed's southern rivals. The main benefit for Columba was a useful foothold for Iona in the midland region of his homeland. Later Irish tradition identified a different king, also called Áed , as Durrow's first patron. This namesake of Ainmere's son was Áed mac Brenainn, ruler of Tethba on the northern border of the Uí Failge. He enjoyed a brief hegemony in the Irish midlands after defeating Diarmait mac Cerbaill, king of the Southern Uí Néill, in 562. Nevertheless, his alleged patronage of Durrow appears to be a fictional link created by later kings of Tethba to legitimise their connection with the Columban monastery.

We cannot establish a precise date for Durrow's beginnings, nor do we know if the foundation occurred before or after the Convention of Druim Cett. Bede thought Durrow preceded Iona, but this was just a guess based on a mistaken assumption that Columba's Irish monasteries must have been founded before he came to Britain. Of the original monastery on the 'Plain of Oaks' little has survived. The monastic enclosure is still visible, as is a medieval church on the site of the twelfth-century abbey which, presumably, succeeded the original settlement. Durrow's most famous monument is the finely carved High Cross of c.850 which formerly stood within the enclosure before being moved into the church in recent times. Equally well-known is the Book of Durrow, an illuminated manuscript containing the Gospels, which might date from c.700. Although it was noted as being at Durrow in 916, the book apparently came from elsewhere, possibly from Iona or from the Northumbrian monastery on Lindisfarne.

After receiving a grant of land on which to build a religious settlement, Columba probably remained at Durrow to supervise the early stages of construction. At some point thereafter he returned to Iona, leaving his kinsman Laisrán mac Feradaig in charge as Durrow's first prior. Laisrán, a son of Columba's cousin Feradach, had hitherto been a monk of Iona. We first encounter him as a companion of the saint on a visit to Ardnamurchan in 572. He was no doubt a young man at the time of the visit, but his presence alongside Columba and Diarmait on their travels suggests that he already held a position of trust and seniority. As a member of the royal house of Cenél Conaill he was a suitable choice for the priorship of Durrow. Moreover, the appointment may have been suggested or approved by Áed mac Ainmerech as a means of further strengthening his family's position in the region. One of Laisrán's first tasks would have been to oversee the building of the monastery, a project that seems to have been well underway in a story in *Vita Columbae*. The setting is Iona in winter, on a bitterly cold day. We see Columba stricken by sadness after miraculously receiving a vision from Durrow.[30] When questioned by Diarmait, the saint reveals that his unhappiness has been caused by none other than the prior of the new monastery. 'For I see my monks worn out with heavy labour,' he explains, 'yet still Laisrán puts pressure on them in building a great house.' At that very moment, far away in Ireland, Laisrán orders the back-breaking toil to cease and sends the exhausted workers to their rest. He also decrees that, in future, all such work shall be suspended in harsh weather. Upon learning of this sudden change of heart, via a second miraculous vision, Columba's sorrow vanishes and he joyfully declares his kinsman to be the 'comforter' of the monks. As well as highlighting Columba's special powers of farsightedness, the tale may have served a secondary purpose in its portrait of Laisrán as both hard taskmaster and benevolent prior. He emerges from it as a rather stern individual who was nevertheless capable of showing kindness to his monks. The key narrative elements – grim winter weather and the construction of a large residence or dormitory – surely originated at Durrow and are probably factual, but Laisrán's sympathetic gesture may have been a later addition to the story, perhaps originating among those who venerated him after his death. He died on Iona in 605, having succeeded Baithéne as abbot five years earlier.

How often Columba visited Durrow is hard to say. One visit seems to be mentioned by Adomnán in a miracle-story about a tree growing near the monastery, but the source may be local folklore circulating in his own time. In this story the tree's bitter fruit prompts Columba to bestow a blessing upon it, thereby turning the bitterness into a wonderfully sweet flavour.[31] Perhaps such a tree really did grow at Durrow, its sweet-tasting fruit being attributed in local tradition to a blessing bestowed by Columba, but the story is almost certainly fictional. No other visits to Durrow are reported in *Vita Columbae*. This does not necessarily mean that none took place, but rather suggests that Adomnán chose not to include them.

Durrow appears to have been the most important of Columba's Irish foundations, a position it held until its eclipse by Derry in the eleventh century. Present-day Derry, also known as Londonderry, straddles both banks of the River Foyle in northern Ireland. The city stands near the border between the counties of Londonderry and Donegal. Its modern name, an Anglicised form of Gaelic *doire*, 'oak grove', is a shortened form of *Daire Coluim Chille* which itself was preceded by the even older *Daire Calgaich*, 'Calgach's Oak Grove'. The latter name was current in the seventh century when we encounter it in both *Vita Columbae* and the Irish annals. In the annals it appears in the death-notice of King Fiachra mac Ciaráin who is described as 'the second founder of Daire Chalgaigh' at his death in 620.[32] Fiachra, a grandson of King Ainmere of Cenél Conaill and thus Columba's kinsman, is otherwise an obscure figure. It is usually assumed that the other founder alluded to in this entry was Columba, in spite of Adomnán's vagueness about the place he calls *Daire Calcig*. Adomnán describes Derry as a point of embarkation for monks travelling from Ireland to Iona, but makes no direct reference to a monastery being founded there in the late sixth century. He does, however, imply the existence of one in the early seventh. Thus, he tells of Báetán Ua Niath Taloirc – a monk of Iona during Columba's abbacy – who was buried at Derry sometime after 597 in what was surely a monastic cemetery. The same story mentions a nearby church in which local people took refuge during an attack by brigands.[33] Later Irish tradition firmly believed that Columba himself established the first monastery at Derry and, although the sources are rather late, the belief is not at odds with Adomnán's narrative. We might infer from *Vita Columbae* that the reason why Daire Calgaich was regarded as an appropriate place of departure for Iona-bound travellers during Columba's lifetime was because a settlement of his disciples already existed there. Such an inference is supported by the Irish Life which, although controversial, may preserve authentic history about Derry's origins in the following passage:

> Then Colum Cille went to Daire, the royal fortress of Áed mac Ainmerech. The latter was king of Ireland at that time. The king offered the fortress to Colum Cille, who refused on account of Mobhi's precept . . . Afterwards, Colum Cille settled in Áed's fortress and founded a church there, in which were performed numerous miracles.[34]

St Mobhi, founder of the monastery at Glasnevin near Dublin, died in 545 when Columba was in his twenties. He appears elsewhere in the Irish Life as a teacher of the young Columba and it is possible that the two did have some contact. The annals give 546 for the foundation of 'Daire Coluim Chille', but the use of this place-name, unknown before c.900, indicates a late and spurious entry. The rest of the tale in the Irish Life looks fairly plausible. If Áed and Columba had already co-operated in the founding of Durrow, and if Derry lay on the edge of Cenél Conaill lands in the late sixth century, it is possible that an early satellite of Iona was founded there. The political context might then be Áed's defeat of Cenél nEógain, the rulers of Tyrone, at the Battle of Druim Meic Ercae in 578, especially if this unidentified site lay near Derry. If we accept what the Irish Life tells us, Áed's 'fortress' at *Daire* was perhaps a much older structure, formerly associated with the mysterious 'Calgach', that came into Áed's possession after the battle. Inevitably, the modern city has obliterated medieval Derry and whatever ancient settlements preceded it so we can only guess where they might have stood. The site of the early monastery is believed to be marked by the present-day St Augustine's Church, formerly an abbey of the Augustinian Order, near the old city walls on the west side of the River Foyle. In the absence of other data we can cautiously envisage our presumed Columban daughter-house standing on this spot. An alternative view of Derry's origins sees the monastery being founded not by Fiachra and Columba but by Fiachra and Áed, the latter here being identified as the unnamed co-founder whose existence we infer from the annalists.[35]

Adomnán's description of Columba as *multarum columna ecclesiarum*, 'pillar of many churches', could imply that he personally founded a number of daughter-houses. Alternatively, it might be a metaphorical reference to places established by his disciples in the seventh century. The first interpretation would be consistent with the Irish Life which gives the names of Irish churches and monasteries allegedly founded by Columba. Adomnán, by contrast, produces no similar list and is largely silent on the issue. Thus, although the Irish Life shows Columba founding settlements all over Leinster and Connacht, this scenario finds little support in Adomnán's narrative. Given the late date of the Irish Life, we need not feel unduly surprised by this. Generally speaking, the Life is not a reliable guide to sixth-century history. It drew its information on Columba's alleged foundations from origin-legends devised long after his death. We must, in fact, adopt a minimalist view of the daughter-houses he founded in Ireland. Setting aside the Irish Life, we turn back to Adomnán who seems to offer only Durrow, Derry and three other sites. Of these five, Durrow and Derry can be accepted because Adomnán implies their membership of Iona's *paruchia* in Columba's lifetime. None of the other three appears in the Irish Life, but, based on hints given by Adomnán, this trio might also have sixth-century beginnings. The first lay on the southern edge of Cenél Conaill territory at Drumhome, two miles west of Ballintra in County Donegal, on a site occupied today by a ruined parish church. Adomnán calls it *Dorsum Tomme*, 'Ridge of Toimm', and gives a strong hint that it housed a community of Columban monks before c.650.[36] He recalls meeting in his youth an old monk called Ernéne moccu Fir Roide who had formerly served at Derry. On the night of Columba's death, while fishing in the River Foyle alongside other Derry monks, Ernéne saw a huge column of fire ascend to the sky. Many years later, perhaps in the late 640s, Ernéne recounted the story of this vision to a young Adomnán who subsequently incorporated it into *Vita Columbae*. Adomnán adds that Ernéne 'is buried in the burial-ground of the monks of St Columba at the Ridge of Toimm'. If, as the tale seems to imply, the monastery at Drumhome was already in existence in the first half of the seventh century, a foundation-date in the final decades of the sixth seems possible. The same might be said of *Lathreg inden*, another place mentioned by Adomnán but absent from the Irish Life. In *Vita Columbae* it is described as a small church overseen by Báetán Ua Niath Taloirc, formerly a monk of Iona. Because Báetán was buried at Derry it seems likely that *Lathreg inden* lay at no great distance away, even if its precise location cannot now be identified. It has been suggested that it lay in the township of Larraghirril on the Inishowen Peninsula, some 20 miles north of Derry. Its Gaelic name was probably *Laithreach Finden*, 'Finden's Place'. And so we come to the third in our trio of possible sixth-century satellites, the one with the weakest case. Adomnán Latinises its name as *Cella Magna Deathrib*, which in Gaelic would be *Cell Mór Dithruib*, 'Big Church of the Desert'. He describes it as a place where local people offered gifts to Columba. It has been convincingly identified as Kilmore on the River Shannon in County Roscommon, south-east of Jamestown, but Columba is depicted merely as a visitor to this monastery, not as its founder. Our only reason for considering it as a possible early daughter-house of Iona is its appearance in an eighth-century *vita* of St Fintan of Taghmon who, according to Adomnán, visited Iona not long after Columba's death. Fintan's *vita* has him studying Scripture under Columba's supervision in the monastic school of Cell Mór Dithruib at a time when Baithéne was also there. Although the relatively early date of the source seems to add weight to the story, we should note Adomnán's clear assertion that Fintan and Columba never met in life. Nor does Columba appear in *Vita Columbae* as a holder of rank at Cell Mór Dithruib. It seems more likely that he went there as an honoured guest whom local laymen welcomed with gifts. There is no hint that the gifts were demanded by the monks of Cell Mór Dithruib as tribute-payments for the head of a federation to which their monastery belonged. That gift-giving rather than tribute-levying is indeed what Adomnán intended is implied by the story's wider context. He appends the episode at Cell Mór Dithruib to a story about gift-giving at Coleraine, a church over which Columba certainly had no authority. At both places the context seems to be a visit by an ecclesiastical dignitary who arrived as a guest. If, then, Columba had no direct authority at Cell Mór Dithruib, we should dismiss the story in Fintan's *vita* as fictional. The place was probably not a sixth-century satellite of Iona. Its true origins are unknown, although the Gaelic *dithrub*, 'desert' or 'wilderness', suggests that it may have begun as a retreat for hermits.[37]

CHAPTER 6
The Picts

Bede and Pictish Christianity

The conventional story of the arrival of Christianity in the far north of Scotland is well-known. It is largely based on the testimony of Bede, who left his readers in no doubt as to who was responsible.

> A priest and abbot named Columba, distinguished by his monastic habit and life, came from Ireland to Britain to preach the Word of God in the provinces of the northern Picts, which are separated from those of the southern Picts by a range of steep and desolate mountains.[1]

Bede wrote these words in the early eighth century, at the Northumbrian monastery of Jarrow. He was separated from Columba by four or five generations and from Iona by more than 200 miles. Where, then, did he acquire his information on the conversion of the Picts? He certainly did not borrow it from *Vita Columbae* for Adomnán's account of Columba's activities in Pictland is rather vague. In the *Vita* we are not presented with a large-scale programme of evangelisation but with a series of episodes in which individual Picts choose to reject paganism. There can be little doubt that this was how the Iona brethren of Adomnán's time viewed their founder's dealings with the Picts. Bede's version was different and plainly did not come from Iona, nor from the Columban churches in Ireland. Its origin lay elsewhere, and the trail of clues leads back to the Picts themselves.

Relations between the English of Northumbria and their Pictish neighbours across the Firth of Forth underwent a transition in the early eighth century. In 685, when Bede was around twelve years old and already a monastic pupil at Jarrow, the Northumbrian king Ecgfrith and his army were slaughtered by Pictish foes in a great battle. The Picts were led to war by King Bridei (Gaelic: *Brude*) who seems to have ruled from a power-base in Fortriu, an ancient kingdom centred on what later became the medieval earldom of Moray. The battle was probably fought further south, near Dunnichen in Angus, and its outcome is often thought to be commemorated on a magnificent carved stone at nearby Aberlemno. Northumbrian and Pictish forces clashed again, in 698, the conflict spilling over into the next century with another battle in 711, this time in Manau. At some point thereafter a *foedus pacis*, a peace treaty, was forged between the two peoples. The ensuing suspension of hostilities lasted for some thirty years, outliving even Bede himself. In 731, the year when he published the *Ecclesiastical History of the English People*, his overview of the contemporary political situation referred to continuing friendship between Northumbria and Pictland.

The *foedus pacis* represented a significant thawing of relations across the Forth. It may have been forged within a year or two of the Battle of Manau, during the reign of Naiton (Gaelic: *Nechtan*) a powerful Pictish king. Naiton was a son of Derile or Der-Ilei who was possibly his mother rather than his father. He and his brother, whom he succeeded in 707, ruled as overkings of a large realm that may have stretched from southern Perthshire to the Moray Firth. Naiton occupies a special place in the *Ecclesiastical History* as the architect of a major programme of religious reform throughout his kingdom. The reform coincided with major changes on Iona that we shall examine in a later chapter. Here, we may note that Naiton sought advice and assistance from Ceolfrith, abbot of Jarrow, who sent helpful letters in response. Ceolfrith's replies were perhaps written by Bede, and it may have been during these exchanges that the latter encountered a story about Columba's mission to Pictland.

Who were the Picts?

The *Picti* or Picts enter the historical record in AD 297 when a Roman writer described them as barbarian inhabitants of the far northern parts of Britain. Later, in the fourth and fifth centuries, they appear alongside various Gaelic and Germanic groups as ruthless pirates. Although the Romans drew a distinction between the Picts and their Romanised neighbours further south, it is clear that they regarded both groups as indigenous Britons. Today the distinction is hard to define and might not, in any case, have been applied consistently by the Romans themselves. Modern historians often attempt to clarify the situation by drawing a line along the River Forth and assigning the Picts to the region north of it. The natives south of the line are likewise labelled as Britons. This convenient demarcation has long held sway but is increasingly being viewed as an over-simplification. It seems at odds with a growing awareness that the Picts were not, in fact, one people but many peoples. Some, it seems, were more 'Pictish' than others. Moreover, not all communities dwelling south of the River Forth and north of Hadrian's Wall can be cleanly separated from the Picts and given the label 'Britons'. We simply do not know enough about the cultural affiliations of these frontier people to say that they were definitely not Pictish, or that they never embraced certain traits of Pictishness. Looking further north, we can deduce from the works of Adomnán and Bede that the people of the central and eastern Highlands in the sixth, seventh and eighth centuries were regarded as Picts, but we are on less firm ground when we try to say the same of the inhabitants of Orkney, Shetland, or the Western Isles. Items associated with Pictish culture, such as symbol stones, are found in these areas but do not necessarily identify their makers as Picts. The belief that the symbols were used only by Picts is, in any case, a modern inference based on long-standing notions about the extent of 'Pictland'. Nonetheless, for the purposes of this book, a fairly conventional view of Pictish geography is adopted. The Picts are here portrayed as an indigenous people of Britain who lived north of the River Forth and east of Argyll in early medieval times.

The tale of the 'Pictish mission' was not the only story of Columba acquired by Bede. We have previously encountered a tradition, reported in the annals, that Columba received Iona as a gift from King Conall mac Comgaill. This was clearly Iona's own story of its beginnings and therefore, in all likelihood, a broadly accurate foundation-tale. An alternative vision was related by Bede, who credited the grant of Iona to Bridei, son of Maelchon, a Pictish king who was Conall's contemporary. Adomnán's silence on Iona's origins should not tempt us to accept Bede's testimony over that of the monastery's own annalists. The tale reported in the *Ecclesiastical History* puts a Pictish king, not a Dál Riatan one, in the central role and should probably be seen as propaganda invented by the Picts themselves. It may have been devised c.700 to support a fictional claim that Iona was not a Dál Riatan monastery but a Pictish one.

Bede's reference to Columba's mission among the northern Picts mentions their southern compatriots, whom he locates south of a mountain range that can only be the Grampians. These southerners, he adds, were not converted by Columba, but instead 'received the true faith through the preaching of the Word by that reverend and holy man Bishop Nynia, a Briton who had received orthodox instruction at Rome in the faith and the mysteries of the truth'.[2] Nynia, or Ninian as he is more widely known, is a controversial figure whose true identity has long been a matter of debate. Bede associates him with Whithorn in Galloway, but later traditions link him to other sites in southern Scotland and further afield. As we saw in Chapter 2, it is possible that the names 'Ninian' and 'Nynia' arose from a misreading of 'Uinniau' and that the person credited by Bede with bringing Christianity to the southern Picts was the figure we have previously referred to as Uinniau or Finnio. Some corroboration of Bede's account appears in the archaeology of southern Pictish areas such as Fife where early Christian cemeteries appear to have been established during the sixth century. Whether these sites had anything to do with missionary activity attributed to Nynia is unknown, but they do seem connected in some way to contemporary religious developments south of the Forth–Clyde isthmus in the lands of the Britons. Perhaps Nynia, or one of his countrymen, brought Christianity to Fife and founded a small number of churches? If this is what actually happened, there is little evidence that other parts of 'southern Pictland' witnessed similar evangelising activity. On the northern side of the Firth of Tay we find what may be slight traces of early Christian burial, but the evidence does not amount to much and there is no reason to connect it with the data from Fife. A lone literary hint suggests rather that the lands between the Firth of Tay and the Grampian Mountains received a mission from Iona, despite the people of these lands being southern Picts like those supposedly converted by Nynia. The hint comes from *Amra Coluim Chille* which calls Columba 'the teacher who would teach the peoples of the Tay', an apparent contradiction of Bede's claim that the Columban mission operated further north. In truth, we cannot hope to make sense of these enigmatic scraps of information.

Returning, then, to Bede's description of Columba as missionary to the northern Picts, we are faced with an issue of reliability. There has long been a tendency to accept Bede at face value by seeing Columba as the 'Apostle of the Picts' who guided them away from paganism. The flaw in this notion is that it ignores Adomnán's silence on the topic. While it is certainly true that Adomnán refers to Columba's dealings with various Picts, he mentions no northern equivalent of the alleged Ninianic mission to southern Pictland. Any belief that the testimony of the *Ecclesiastical History* should always be preferred to that of *Vita Columbae* is, in any case, mistaken. Both Bede and Adomnán were skilled hagiographers, the former demonstrating his mastery of the craft in his writings on St Cuthbert. Bede's reliability as a historian should not, therefore, be overestimated. On the matter of Columba's Pictish mission we have no reason to accept his words over those of Adomnán, who does not seem to regard it as a large-scale undertaking.

Pagan Picts in Vita Columbae

Adomnán undoubtedly had access to more information about Columba than Bede could ever have learned from either the monastic library at Jarrow or from Abbot Ceolfrith's Pictish contacts. We know, for instance, that *Vita Columbae* incorporates material from an earlier work written by Cumméne in the 640s. It is very unlikely that Cumméne would have been unaware of significant activity by Iona missionaries in Pictland during the founder's lifetime. If a large-scale mission had taken place, Cumméne would surely have mentioned it and it would have appeared in Adomnán's work two generations later. Instead, we find in *Vita Columbae* a number of more or less unconnected episodes in Pictish territory. These give useful insights into how the Columban community in Adomnán's time viewed its founder's relationship with the Picts. Taken together, they provide our best evidence for Columba's Pictish 'mission'. To compare them with Bede's statement about the conversion of the northern Picts we must examine each episode individually.

Adomnán first introduces the Picts in his opening chapter which gives a summary of Columba's 'miracles of power'. Listed among these is an incident that occurred *in regione Pictorum*, 'in the region of the Picts' where Columba miraculously hoisted a sail against a head wind. Two other miracles took place 'in the same province', one of which involved resurrection while the other – a somewhat less awe-inspiring deed – happened 'in the sight of King Bridei and his household'. Adomnán's first detailed story about a person of Pictish stock appears in the thirty-third chapter of Book One. Here he tells of an elderly man called Artbranan who came to Columba while the latter was visiting Skye. One hour before Artbranan's arrival, Columba had prophesied that this old pagan, the *primarius* or 'chief commander' of a group called *Geonae cohortis*, 'the warband of Geona' would arrive on the seashore seeking baptism. The prophecy was duly fulfilled, as was another in which Artbranan's death immediately after baptism was foretold. The old man was buried nearby, his grave being marked by a cairn. Adomnán added that local people in his own time called an adjacent stream *Dobur Artbranain*, 'Artbranan's Water'.[3] The stream is unidentifiable today.

During the baptismal ceremony an interpreter had to communicate Columba's words to Artbranan, who was clearly not a Gaelic-speaker. We can assume that the 'warband of Geona' was a Brittonic-speaking group and, given the geographical setting of the story, its members presumably spoke a Pictish dialect. However, although the incident took place on Skye, we cannot be certain that Artbranan lived there. He arrived by boat and could have sailed over from another island, or from the mainland. Unfortunately, neither Adomnán nor any other source gives any clue as to where the *cohort* was based. Its elderly *primarius*, who had to be carried from his boat by two younger men, was clearly infirm. Age and ill health would surely have precluded a long or arduous journey so we may assume that he lived not far from his place of baptism.

If the *Geonae cohortis* were Picts, as seems likely, this would be sufficient to explain the presence of an interpreter. It need not imply that Skye itself was predominantly Pictish in the late sixth century. The survival of three carved stones bearing Pictish symbols merely suggests that one or more communities on the island displayed a Pictish cultural affiliation. This does not necessarily mean that their preferred language was also Pictish for the term *dobur* is Gaelic and was clearly used by people living near Artbranan's Water in Adomnán's time. Moreover, a sequence of annal entries relating to events on Skye around the middle of the seventh century indicates that at least one family on the island was Gaelic-speaking.[4] Perhaps Gaelic was already the main language of Skye when Columba came there? This leaves us wondering where the non-Gaelic-speaking Artbranan originated. One theory sees the nominative of *Geona* as *Geonus*, which in turn might be a Latinisation of Ce, a Pictish region roughly corresponding to the modern counties of Aberdeenshire and Banffshire.[5] Although this works linguistically, it requires us to imagine the ailing Artbranan undertaking a wearisome 120-mile journey from his home east of the Grampian Mountains to the Hebridean coastlands. An alternative is to see him and his people inhabiting a western coastal district where Pictish was spoken and where pagan beliefs still persisted in the late sixth century. So, although Artbranan might not have been the first of Columba's Pictish converts, he does seem to be the first mentioned by Adomnán.

Several journeys made by Columba across *Britanniae Dorsum*, 'Spine of Britain', are reported by Adomnán who describes this feature as a range of mountains separating Scots and Picts.[6] It is unlikely that he saw it as a rigid cultural or ethnic frontier, but it nevertheless served a useful literary purpose as a spiritual divide between Gaelic Christianity and Pictish paganism. In reality, the boundary between Dál Riata and Pictland was not so easily defined. Adomnán certainly knew this, but the notion of a simple east–west split between Picts and Scots suited his narrative better. The same simple demarcation still exerts a powerful influence today. Recognising it as an erroneous perception allows us to step back for a more objective look at the different cultural groups who inhabited early medieval northern Britain. We soon observe that the interfaces between them are far more blurred than the author of *Vita Columbae* suggests.

When referring to the 'Spine of Britain', Adomnán uses the Latin *dorsum* in its topographical sense, as the equivalent of the Gaelic *druim*, 'ridge'. The 'Spine' in question appears in later Gaelic texts as *Druim Alban*, 'Ridge of Alba', where *Alba* is a term in common use today as the preferred Gaelic name for Scotland. Much uncertainty surrounds the origin of *Alba*, a term largely absent from the historical record before c.900. In the tenth and eleventh centuries it defined a kingdom ruled by a Gaelic-speaking dynasty whose main centres of power lay in the former Pictish territories of eastern Scotland. By then, the Picts themselves had lost or relinquished their separate identity. In other words, they had become 'Scots' in terms of linguistic and cultural affiliation. How and why this happened are complex questions beyond the scope of this book. In any case, the changes took place a hundred years after Adomnán's death and have little bearing on relations between Picts and Scots in the sixth and seventh centuries.

Adomnán's *Britanniae Dorsum*, the later *Druim Alban*, is the mountainous mass separating Argyll from Perthshire and other eastern regions. Today, as in Columba's time, a number of routes traverse this imposing barrier via a network of passes and glens. Of these, the one preferred by Columba on his journeys to Pictland went north-east from Dál Riata along the Great Glen and thence towards the Moray Firth. It is clear from Adomnán's narrative that Columba travelled much of this route by boat, a far easier option than an overland trek through rugged, tree-clad glens. A line of lochs runs from the Firth of Lorn to the River Ness, all of them navigable by small vessels, with only two short stretches of dry land where boats need to be carried from one loch to another.[7]

Columba's journeys to the eastern side of Druim Alban brought him into Pictish territory. Adomnán does not indicate where this began but the boundary between Gaelic-speaking 'Scots' and Brittonic-speaking 'Picts' may have been crossed as soon as the travellers reached Loch Ness, perhaps near where Fort Augustus stands today. Men bearing what seem to be Pictish names were encountered by Columba near the northern end of the loch in the vicinity of Glen Urquhart. Here the saint baptised an old pagan called Emchath whose imminent death he foresaw in a prophetic vision. Emchath's son Virolec also received baptism, as did their entire household.[8] In this episode we appear to be witnessing the Christian conversion of prosperous Picts and their servants. Adomnán wrapped it in a tale of prophecy, but the true context may have been an invitation to Columba from a dying man who wished to renounce paganism. The baptismal ceremony took place at 'the fields of Airchartdan', presumably an agricultural estate that supported Emchath and his family. *Airchartdan* is clearly an older form of *Urchardan*, the modern Gaelic name of Urquhart, but its ultimate origin is Brittonic. The first element is the prefix *air*, meaning 'near' or 'next to', while the second is an early form of Welsh *cardden*, 'copse', thus giving a compound name meaning 'next to the copse'. An approximate translation into modern English is 'Woodside'.[9] Both the geographical context, the Brittonic place-name and the names born by Emchath and his son suggest that the family was Pictish.

Adomnán refers to another land-owning kindred being similarly baptised as a group 'during the time when Columba spent a number of days in the province of the Picts'.[10] The head of this family had heard the Christian message being preached by Columba *per interpretatorem*, 'through an interpreter'. He thereupon requested baptism for himself, his wife, their children and servants. Like Emchath and Virolec, this unnamed Pict included his whole household in the baptismal ceremony. In both instances the servants evidently had little choice but to follow their masters in switching to Christianity. In the second case, the baptism was followed a few days later by the death of the householder's son, a boy whom Columba subsequently restored to life. To this story of miraculous resurrection Adomnán added a group of pagan Pictish priests whom he calls *magi*, 'wizards'. They taunted the bereaved parents for abandoning the old gods in favour of one who was too feeble to prevent their son's death. For Adomnán and his contemporaries the key point was that Columba's resurrection of the child turned the tables on the sneering wizards. For us, the story offers a brief but fascinating glimpse into the life of a Pictish community. We see Columba returning to the house to ask the whereabouts of the dead boy. He enters an adjoining room or building while an anxious crowd waits outside. Adomnán seems to be describing a lordly hall, or a complex of several dwellings, to which a large number of local people has congregated. The setting is clearly a substantial residence inhabited by a prominent family whose dealings with Columba are of interest to the wider community. Given the high status of the dead boy's parents, it is likely that the heathen priests showed them rather more deference than Adomnán would have us believe. We may note, too, that there is no hint of a mass-conversion of the local populace after the boy's miraculous return to life. Although we hear that 'a great shout went up from the crowd', we cannot interpret this as a prelude to communal rejection of paganism. Adomnán adds that 'mourning gave way to celebration and the God of the Christians was glorified', but this might indicate no more than joy at the unexpected recovery of a perilously sick child. As at Airchartdan, Columba baptised a few individuals among the landowning class but made no major inroad against local pagan beliefs. This is not to suggest that his 'mission' failed in these two cases. For all we know, he may have accomplished precisely what he set out to do.

Another encounter with Pictish *magi* occurred when Columba learned of a well supposedly endowed with demonic powers. The local populace personified the well as an evil god and believed that disease afflicted anyone who bathed in it or who dared to drink its accursed waters.[11] Columba resolved to confront these superstitions by visiting the site, much to the delight of the heathen priests who expected him to come to harm. After blessing the water he washed his hands and feet before taking a drink and encouraging his monks to do likewise. No adverse effects were seen and the evil aura was judged to have been vanquished, the well being used thereafter as a place of healing. No baptism or preaching is mentioned in this story, which appears to be a conventional explanation of how a place associated with pagan beliefs became a Christian holy well. The tale presumably arose in the folklore of a particular district where a sacred well, revered since time immemorial, had recently been stripped of pagan connotations. Adomnán may have heard the story during one of his own journeys in Pictland, unless it came to Iona via a visiting Pictish cleric. Any real connection with Columba may be doubted, but the tale's inclusion in *Vita Columbae* suggests that it was popular in Adomnán's time, as much on Iona as in its place of origin. Today the location of the well is unknown, but it was no doubt identifiable in the late seventh century, especially among local Pictish clerics who claimed Columba as their patron saint.

The most famous episode in *Vita Columbae* concerns a savage beast that lived in the River Ness.[12] Adomnán locates this incident in Pictish territory in the presence of 'heathen natives', at a place where Columba and his companions were seeking to cross the river. A man who had been mauled to death by the beast was being buried at the waterside when the saint's party arrived. Columba ordered one of his monks, Luigne moccu Min, to swim across and retrieve a small boat from the opposite bank[13]. The beast duly rose from the depths to pursue the swimmer and was within a few feet of catching him when Columba commanded it to desist. 'Go no further!' he cried, making the sign of the Cross, and the creature turned away in fear. Adomnán wrote that the Pictish onlookers were 'so moved by the greatness of the miracle they had witnessed that they too magnified the God of the Christians'. There is no hint that these pagans subsequently asked for baptism. Although clearly impressed by Columba's powers, they seem to have had no immediate desire to adopt his religious beliefs. The story in fact conforms to a common type where a fabled hero confronts and vanquishes a savage water-creature. Adomnán was not the only hagiographer to exploit this theme, but the geographical context of his tale has made it the best-known example.[14] Inevitably, it has been interpreted as the oldest recorded sighting of the fabled monster of Loch Ness. Alternative explanations, including a theory that Columba may have encountered a large marine mammal such as a walrus, have failed to dampen the enthusiasm of those who believe in the existence of 'Nessie'. For our present purposes we can probably accept the basic elements of the story as authentic. It may describe a real event, perhaps the slaying of a local man by a ferocious sea-creature that lurked in the river. Columba and his companions might have learned of the tragedy as they passed through the district. Later, on Iona, the bare facts were no doubt embellished with the addition of a saintly miracle. As with other stories of Columba's travels in Pictland we glean no sense of a formal Christianising 'mission', still less the great achievements envisaged by Bede. Columba's gains at the expense of Pictish paganism seem to have been token successes involving a few high-status converts. The wider populace apparently remained unbaptised.

King Bridei

In the final chapter of the *Ecclesiastical History* Bede gives a useful chronology of dated events. He assigns Columba's arrival in Britain to the year 565, two years later than the date given by the Iona annalists, and places the foundation of Iona in the same year. In an earlier chapter he provides a political context for both events:

> Columba came to Britain when Bridei, the son of Maelchon, a very powerful king, had been ruling over the Picts for over eight years.[15]

Bridei's reign can be dated fairly precisely. The Pictish king-lists assign him a reign of thirty years, while the annalists place his death at 584. Drawing these traditions together we can say, with some confidence, that he became king in 554 or 555. The location and extent of his kingdom are less easy to define. Adomnán believed that one of Bridei's main royal residences was a fortress near the River Ness.[16] This suggests that the tradition on Iona in the late seventh century was that Bridei had ruled the northern Picts. Here, then, we appear to have a close correlation between Adomnán and Bede on the geography of Columba's Pictish ventures. But where was Bridei's centre of power and what was the extent of his realm?

The first part of the question remains unanswered. Three sites near the River Ness have been offered as possible candidates for Bridei's stronghold. Of these, the front-runner is the Iron Age hillfort on Craig Phadrig, a mile and a half west of Inverness. Excavations have revealed that a double circuit of ramparts enclosing the hill's oval summit was built in the fourth century BC. Both the inner and outer defensive rings were of drystone construction laced with timber. Access to the summit appears to have been via a steep path leading to an entrance in an additional 'third wall' flanking the eastern side of the outer rampart. Curiously, the defences seem to have been destroyed soon after they were built, but occupation continued thereafter to the middle of the first millennium AD. A metalworking mould, probably of fifth-century date, suggests that the occupants of the fort in its final phase were people of wealth and status. Their presence provides a context for King Bridei's possible use of the site.

Much closer to the River Ness is the second of the three candidates, an imposing hilltop site now occupied by Inverness Castle. The current structure, built in Victorian times, is the latest in a sequence of castles dating back to the eleventh century. It is possible that the first of these replaced a much older stronghold, perhaps a stone-walled fortress like Craig Phadrig, formerly used as a royal residence in the sixth century. The location certainly fits the vague clues given in Adomnán's narrative: the impressive eminence of Castle Hill looms directly above the south bank of the river. However, in the absence of a thorough archaeological excavation, the antiquity of the site is unknown. Somewhat less imposing is Torvean Hill, the last of the trio. Like Craig Phadrig it lies roughly one and a half miles from Inverness and is closer to the river, but its single rampart and ditch convey little sense of importance. We cannot, as yet, rule it out of the search, but its unimpressive character makes it the weakest of the three.[17]

Wherever Bridei's stronghold lay it was clearly a hilltop settlement. It was accessible only by a steep path, as Columba and his fellow travellers discovered on their first visit to the king.[18] The wearisome ascent brought them to the entrance where they found the gates barred against them. This frosty welcome was Bridei's doing, or so Adomnán tells us. The king, 'puffed up with royal pride', refused to let them in, but his aloofness was swept away by a saintly miracle which unbarred the gates. Columba then strode into the fortress, much to the consternation of Bridei and his *senatus*. The latter term's Roman connotations should not tempt us to imagine a formal institution of Pictish government but rather a group of noblemen who supported and protected the king. After witnessing the miraculous opening of the gates, the *senatus* joined Bridei in showing Columba an appropriate measure of respect.

The extent of Bridei's kingdom is a matter of debate. It clearly included an area around the River Ness, but we cannot assume that this was the core of his realm. An early medieval king was usually peripatetic: he and his family, together with their entourage, typically moved around the kingdom throughout the year, utilising a number of sites as residences and ceremonial venues. The fort near Inverness may have been one of several strongholds used by Bridei on these periodic 'circuits'. Other sites on his itinerary perhaps lay further north in Caithness, or southward towards Atholl. A northerly expansion of his power is implied by *Vita Columbae* in the story of Cormac, a monk of Iona who desired to sail away on pilgrimage. The setting for this tale is one of Bridei's residences, the location of which is not described. Here, the king is asked by Columba to guarantee safe passage for Cormac and his fellow travellers in the seaways around Orkney. The request is made in the presence of an Orcadian *regulus* or 'kinglet', a ruler whose passive role indicates subservience to Bridei. Adomnán shows Columba treating the *regulus* in a dismissive, almost contemptuous manner as he pleads on behalf of the pilgrims:

> Commend them to the care of this *regulus*, whose hostages you hold, so that, if by chance their long wanderings should bring them to Orkney, they should meet with no hostility within his boundaries.[19]

The hostages would have been younger members of the Orcadian king's family, their safety dependent on his continuing loyalty to Bridei. This was common practice in political relationships between a powerful overking and his vassals. We have already encountered it in *Vita Columbae* in the story of Scandlán of Ossory, the young Irish prince held captive by Áed mac Ainmerech. Adomnán does not say if the Orcadian hostages were kept in chains like Scandlán or treated in a more dignified way, but they would have been under constant threat of harm. Bridei evidently complied with Columba's request by issuing an order to the *regulus*, for we learn that Cormac passed without hindrance through Orcadian waters. What this episode tells us is that Bridei's hegemony extended to Orkney, and that part of the archipelago recognised his authority. The *regulus* had presumably submitted to the overking after losing a battle or after seeking protection from enemies.

With a power-base on the River Ness and overlordship in Orkney it is likely that Bridei held the lands in between under his sway. This should mean that Easter Ross and Caithness lay within his hegemony. How far his rule reached westward is unknown, but he appears to have ventured west of Druim Alban at least once. An entry in the annals, under the year 558, records a clash between Pictish and Dál Riatan forces:

> Flight of the Scots before Bridei, Maelchon's son, king of the Picts, and the death of Gabrán, son of Domangart [20]

The location of Bridei's victory is not given, but it was possibly fought in one of the glen routes between the Pictish east and the Gaelic west. Gabrán, the father of Áedán, may have been among the casualties, if his death is not simply an unconnected event in the same year. If we could be sure Bridei was the aggressor, the battle would be evidence of his western ambitions, but the entry as it stands tells us little. His reputation as a strong ruler, implied by Bede's description of him as *rex potentissimus*, 'a very powerful king', must have been achieved through successful war-leadership, yet we have no record of his victories other than the entry for 558. Perhaps his reputation was won by the subjection of Orkney alone? There is, in any case, no warrant for assuming that his overlordship reached as far west as Dál Riata, or even south of the Grampians into Perthshire. *Vita Columbae* suggests that the monks of Iona in the late seventh century regarded Bridei as a ruler of northern Pictland. Based on this perception, we may cautiously identify him as a king of Fortriu, the ancient region roughly coterminous with Moray. This may have been his core domain or power-base, the area from which he drew the military resources that enabled him to become *rex potentissimus*.

Adomnán does not explicitly state that Bridei renounced paganism. The king may have been tempted by Christianity, but we cannot be sure that he went so far as to embrace it himself. Like other pagan rulers he would have been aware that baptism brought a number of status-enhancing benefits, not least of which was membership of an international religion whose priests used the language of imperial Rome. Christianity must have seemed sophisticated and exotic to a barbarian king who ruled on the outermost fringe of the known world. However, in the absence of a definitive statement from Adomnán, we cannot assume that Bridei became Christian. *Vita Columbae* consistently portrays him as the pagan king of a pagan people and there is no hint that missionaries from Iona steered him towards conversion. Even if his own view of Christianity was broadly favourable he would not have lightly dismissed the ancestral beliefs of his people. Nor could he have ignored the heathen clergy who plainly wielded considerable influence within his realm. We have already encountered these *magi* in the context of Columba's visits to Pictland. Their leader was Broichan, one of the most vivid characters in Adomnán's narrative.

The chief wizard

We first meet Broichan when Columba asks him to release a slave-girl, apparently a young Scot from Dál Riata. Adomnán calls Broichan a *magus* and assigns him a position of seniority at Bridei's court. He was the king's *nutricius*, 'foster-father', a role of special significance in early medieval society. A foster-father was both tutor and guide to the person in his care and could expect to receive an obligation of future loyalty. Broichan's high status is indicated by his proximity to Bridei. He was at the royal residence near the River Ness when Columba begged him, in the king's presence, to release the slave-girl, a request that he flatly refused.[21] Columba then walked out of the house and went down to the river where he picked up a small white pebble. This was the cue for a miracle of foresight involving Broichan who, at that very moment, was brought to the brink of death by a sudden seizure. The cold-hearted wizard had been taking a drink when an angel suddenly appeared, striking him so hard that the drinking glass shattered in his hand. Down at the riverside Columba had a vision of the incident and foresaw that he would be asked to intervene. Turning to his companions, he told them that Bridei 'will send two messengers hurrying out to us to call on our help for Broichan, and urgently, for he is dying.' This duly happened, and the saint sent two monks back to the royal fortress. There, in accordance with his instructions, they informed the king that Broichan would be healed by drinking water into which the white pebble had been dipped, but only if the slave-girl was first set free. When this condition was met, the ailing *magus* drank the water and was immediately restored to health. Adomnán adds an epilogue to the story, telling his readers that the pebble was afterwards kept in the royal treasury. How long it remained there he does not say, but the source of his information might have been a Pictish legend about a white stone with alleged healing powers, an object linked to Columba in local folklore around the River Ness. The tale as told in the *Vita* might even be based on an actual incident during one of Columba's visits to Pictland, its core elements embellished with the addition of a magical stone. Perhaps Broichan really did fall perilously ill but recovered so quickly that a supernatural explanation seemed appropriate?

Immediately after the story of the pebble comes another miracle-tale involving Broichan. Here we see the ungrateful wizard, now fully healed, boasting that he can conjure a storm to prevent Columba from sailing home via Loch Ness.[22] 'I have the power to produce an adverse wind and to bring down a thick mist,' he asserts confidently. Adomnán does not deny him this ability and seems content to portray him as a dangerous manipulator of Nature. Sure enough, a fierce gale rises over the loch and a thick fog shrouds the water as Columba prepares to embark. To reassure the anxious reader, Adomnán points out that even diabolic forces are part of God's purpose. 'One must not be surprised,' he writes, 'that such things happen occasionally by the art of devils – when God permits it – so that the wind and waves can be stirred up to a storm.' Columba boards the boat and orders his companions to hoist the sail. Then he utters a prayer and the wind changes direction to blow more favourably. At the lochside, the heathen *magi* can only watch in amazement as the saint's vessel speeds on its way. The crowd of Picts who have gathered to watch the saint's departure likewise witness the defeat of Broichan's demonic powers. In crafting this tale Adomnán referred to, and borrowed from, a famous *vita* of St Germanus written two hundred years earlier by Constantius of Lyon. Germanus, bishop of Auxerre, was a major figure in fifth-century Gaul and a leader in the fight against heresy. During a sea-voyage to Britain he was attacked by evil spirits who tried to impede him by stirring up mists and storms, but his prayers vanquished them. Adomnán drew a direct comparison with this incident in his story about Columba battling Broichan's sorcery on Loch Ness, noting that both saints had to contend with similar perils. Germanus, like Columba, was beset by supernatural forces capable of 'stirring storms and blotting out the daylight sky with a mist of darkness'. The two stories appear, in fact, to be identical. Is the incident described in *Vita Columbae* based on a real storm, albeit a natural one, that arose with terrible force on Loch Ness? Or is it nothing more than a slice of Gaulish hagiography transplanted to a Pictish setting?

The mystery of Taran

One of Columba's miraculous prophecies referred to a Pictish nobleman called Taran who was living in exile among the Scots.[23] Columba commended him to Feradach, a wealthy man on Islay. Although Adomnán does not say so directly, it is clear that Taran had sought help from Columba, hoping perhaps for sanctuary on Iona. Instead, he was passed on to Feradach, to 'live in his household as one of his friends'. Within a few days of his arrival on Islay the exiled Pict was murdered at the command of his host. Furious at this act of cruelty and treachery, Columba prophesied that Feradach would die before the year's end, adding that 'his name will be removed from the book of life'. When news of the prophecy came to Islay, Feradach scornfully dismissed it as an idle threat. In the autumn, however, the saint's foresight was proved true and Feradach succumbed to a fatal seizure just as he was sitting down to a feast.

This would be a fairly unremarkable miracle-tale were it not for the presence of Taran, a high-status Pictish exile, in a central role. The story's chronological setting is the late sixth century. Its geographical context is Islay, the large and temperate Hebridean island lying west of

Kintyre. In Adomnán's time the chief kindred of Islay was Cenél nÓengusa, 'Descendants of Óengus', who claimed as their eponymous forefather a brother of Fergus Mór, the legendary king of the Scots. Like the other principal *cenéla* of Dál Riata, Cenél nÓengusa seems to emerge in the seventh century. However, unlike the mainland kindreds of Cenél nGabráin ('Gabrán's kindred') and Cenél Comgaill, the descendants of Óengus have left barely a trace in the documentary record. Their literary insignificance might imply that they played only a minor role in the great events of the period, or, perhaps more likely, that their deeds went unrecorded by the annalists on Iona. Feradach, the man of wealth to whom Columba entrusted the fugitive Taran, may have been a sixth-century progenitor of Cenél nÓengusa or a client of its ancestors. Little more can be said of him beyond these vague guesses. Taran, on the other hand, is rather more interesting, chiefly because he had a namesake who was a contemporary of Adomnán. The later Taran was likewise a high-status Pict who appears to have gone into exile among the Gaels after being expelled from his homeland. Some historians wonder if this is actually more than coincidence and if the two Tarans are in fact one and the same. The mystery begins with two entries in the Irish annals, both of which originated on Iona:

> 697 Taran was expelled from his kingdom.
> 699 Taran went to Ireland.

The Taran referred to here was a Pictish king whose reign lasted four years from c.693. In the king-list of the Picts his patronym is *filius Enfidaig*, 'son of Ainftech'. The annalists noted the slaying of a man called Ainftech in 693, the approximate start of Taran's reign, but did not say why, where, or by whom he was killed. Drawing these scraps of information together we can, nonetheless, create a plausible historical context. This sees Ainftech and his son as participants in a Pictish dynastic struggle at the end of the seventh century. It has Ainftech's death in 693, at the hands of rivals, being followed almost immediately by Taran's seizure of the kingship. The scenario ends four years later with Taran's flight into Irish exile. If this is a fairly accurate reconstruction of events, Taran may have fled first to Dál Riata, staying there for a couple of years before seeking refuge further afield in Ireland. It is at this point that the two Tarans begin to converge, the one seeking a safe haven among the Gaels by entrusting himself to Columba, the other finding his own Gaelic refuge with the Irish at a time when Adomnán was abbot of Iona. To some historians, the convergence is too close to be coincidental. They prefer to see the earlier Taran of *Vita Columbae* as a fictional character, a precursor of his seventh-century namesake. The latter, they argue, fled to Dál Riata after his expulsion from Pictland to find sanctuary with Adomnán, who entrusted him to the care of wealthy laymen. Two years later, in 699, and presumably with Adomnán's help, this Taran crossed over to Ireland. The parallel sixth-century story is rejected as an example of 'historicising', of projecting current events back into the past. By this interpretation Adomnán parachuted the Taran of his own time into *Vita Columbae* to make him a contemporary of Iona's founder. The treachery of Feradach and his subsequent death can then be seen as a warning to the hosts of the later Taran, as Adomnán's way of reminding them of their duty of care: dire consequences awaited them if they dared to harm a fugitive who was under Iona's protection. Just as Columba's wrath had brought death to the treacherous Feradach, so too would doom fall heavily on anyone who betrayed Adomnán 's trust.

Overview: the Columban 'mission' in Pictland

In spite of Bede's claims to the contrary, there is no evidence that Columba was an 'Apostle of the Picts' who personally guided large numbers of them away from paganism. Adomnán placed a number of stories in Pictish settings, but, taken together, they do not look like episodes in a major evangelising mission. As it is likely that some came from Cumméne's book, we can probably infer that Iona's view of the 'Pictish mission' remained unchanged from c.640 to c.700. This view seems, in essence, to have regarded Columba as an occasional visitor to the northern Picts rather than as their evangelist. In the early eighth century, perhaps around the time of the Anglo-Pictish peace treaty in the second decade, Bede and his fellow Northumbrians obtained a different version in which Columba played a greatly enhanced part. This version was clearly intended to provide a northern counterweight to what was essentially an account of how Christianity arrived in southern Pictland not from Iona's 'Celtic' clergy but from Nynia, a more orthodox missionary who had undergone training at Rome. The entire tale had more to do with the Easter Controversy – a topic examined in the next chapter – than with Columba's real dealings with the Picts. We can therefore disregard it in favour of Adomnán's version which, as already noted, portrays Columba as a visitor rather than as a missionary in the lands east of Druim Alban.

This is not to deny that Columba did not play a key role in sowing the seeds of Pictish Christanity. Even Adomnán, who does not credit him with mass conversions, says that he founded monasteries in Pictland 'where today he is still honoured'.[24] Although these monasteries are left unnamed and unlocated by Adomnán, there is little doubt that they existed in his time. Columba may have been honoured at some of these places not because he had founded them in person, but because his disciples had done so in the years after his passing. In *Vita Columbae* his baptising of high-status families in Glen Urquhart and elsewhere would have established islands of the Faith in what was undoubtedly a sea of paganism. By converting members of the landed aristocracy rather than folk of low status he was targeting people who wielded power and influence at local level. He was therefore laying secure foundations on which his disciples and successors could build. That this was a deliberate, forward-looking policy on his part is nowhere implied in *Vita Columbae*, but seems rather to be hinted at by recent archaeological findings. Our gaze falls on a site at Portmahomack in Easter Ross where excavation has revealed a monastery founded perhaps in the second half of the sixth century and certainly flourishing in the eighth when it became a major centre of Pictish monumental stone carving. Given its location on a peninsula on the northern side of the Moray Firth, it is likely that its earliest secular patrons were subject to King Bridei whose hegemony, as we have seen, reached as far north as Orkney. It is even possible that the sixth-century evidence unearthed at Portmahomack relates to a monastery founded by Columba himself.[25] Less secure as a base for such theories is the legend promoted by the Pictish monastery at Deer in Buchan in which Columba and an otherwise unknown St Drostan appear as founders. The legend is unknown before c.900 and can probably be dismissed as ecclesiastical fiction. Even if Drostan existed – and we cannot be sure that he did – he would merely be one of a number of early saints with Pictish associations who may have been contemporaries of Columba. Any or none of these obscure figures might have been monks of Iona, but even such vague musing seems to run too far with the evidence.[26]

CHAPTER 7
Saint

The death of Columba

In late May 597, on a day of early summer, Columba travelled across Iona to visit a group of monks who were busy in the fields of the machair on the western side. He was seventy-five years old and already too infirm to undertake the journey on foot. He therefore went by cart and eventually came to a small knoll overlooking the fields. Climbing out, he stood on the low summit and addressed the monks, comforting them in their toil. His words are presented in *Vita Columbae* as a prophecy:

> My children, today is the last time you will see my face here at the machair.

This appears to be a borrowing from the Life of St Antony by Evagrius. Although not an exact copy, it is a fairly close adaptation of Antony's address to his disciples in his final days. 'My children,' Antony had said, 'hear your father's last words, for I think you will not see me again in this world.' Adomnán's paraphrasing of Evagrius does not make the account of Columba's parting speech untrue. The visit to the machair no doubt occurred, and it is likely that the venerable abbot, weighed down by age and infirmity, needed no prophetic vision to tell him that he would not see the western side of Iona again. Although the actual words he spoke may have differed somewhat from those quoted above, their sentiment was surely the same. The monks listening on the machair below the knoll were filled with great sadness. They wept as their aged mentor lifted his hands to bless the island of Iona and all who dwelt there.

When the community assembled in the monastic church on the following Sunday, 2 June, Columba was well enough to attend mass, but the service was to be his last. At the end of that week, on Saturday, he went about his duties as normal. Accompanied by his faithful attendant Diarmait, he visited a barn to bless the grain stored within. To Diarmait's dismay he ended the blessing with these words:

> I am very glad for the monks of my community, knowing that if I have to go away somewhere you will have bread enough for a year.

He then said that he knew death was only hours away and that the time of his passing had been revealed to him by God: 'For now my Lord Jesus Christ deigns to invite me, and I shall go to him when he calls me in the middle of this night.'

On hearing these words, Diarmait was stricken by grief and foreboding. Columba tried to console him as they left the barn to make their way back to the monastery. They paused to rest along the way and saw an old white horse approaching. This was the animal that carried pails of newly drawn milk from the cattle-pen. It came to the abbot and nuzzled him, before receiving his blessing. Columba and Diarmait next went up onto a small hill and stood there for a while. Together they gazed out over the monastery before coming back down to Columba's writing-hut where he worked quietly on a psalter. When evening came, they made their way to the church for vespers. After the service, Columba returned to his lodging and rested for a brief time before conveying to Diarmait his final words of guidance to the monks:

> I commend to you, my children, these my last words: Love one another sincerely and in peace. If you keep this course according to the example of the holy fathers, God who strengthens the good will help you, and I dwelling with him shall intercede for you. He will supply not only enough for the needs of this present life, but also the eternal good things that are prepared as a reward for those who keep the Lord's commandments.

They remained in the lodging until the ringing of a handbell summoned the community to the midnight service. Rising from his bed, Columba hastened out to join his monks as they made their way in the darkness, but he quickened his pace to enter the church before them. At the altar he knelt in prayer, alone in the night. In that very moment, so Adomnán tells us, the saint's form was bathed in a celestial light that filled the entire building. Some of the monks saw the heavenly glow as they drew near, but it quickly disappeared. Diarmait reached the door of the church, but the light was already gone and he could see little among the shadows. He had no lantern, so he carefully made his way inside, weeping as he went.

'Father, where are you?' he cried.

At the altar he found Columba lying on the floor. By then, the monks were slowly entering the church, some bearing lamps. Coming to the altar they saw Diarmait sitting on the floor with the old abbot's head cradled in his arms. They gathered around mournfully, knowing that the end was near. With Diarmait's help, Columba used his last strength to lift his right hand so that he could give his monks a final blessing. Then he died peacefully, with an expression of great joy and wonder on his face.[1]

So ends the account of Columba's passing. Much of it, we may guess, was derived from Cumméne's book. Many modern readers have felt deeply moved by the detailed descriptions of the saint's last days and of his final words to the Iona brethren. There is little need to doubt the overall accuracy and authenticity of Adomnán's account. Peering beneath the obvious hagiographical additions we are almost certainly being given a series of first-hand testimonies, most notably Diarmait's. These would have been preserved at the monastery as revered traditions passed by word of mouth to each new generation of monks. Some may have existed in written form before Cumméne and Ségéne began to collect stories about Columba in the second quarter of the seventh century. The tale of the founder's death was so precious to the community that Adomnán may have left Cumméne's account of it largely unaltered. His own amendments were most likely cosmetic, to make the earlier work conform to his own style. It is likely, for instance, that the words spoken by Columba in his final hours were too well known to be rewritten. Nevertheless, Adomnán did add some new material, primarily by reporting celestial visions seen on the night of Columba's death. One of these was a fiery pillar that rose up in the sky while a group of monks fished a river near Derry. Adomnán heard this particular tale directly, as a young man, from an eyewitness.

Columba's funeral was modest and austere. After death his body lay for some hours in the church until the time came for the morning hymns. He was then borne back to his humble lodging, accompanied by chants, so that the ceremonies could begin. These did not involve anyone from outside the monastic community. Even if news of Columba's passing had reached Mull, for instance, none of the people there would have been able to attend the funeral. Iona was cut off, for a great storm raged in the waters around the island and no boat could get through. The bad weather continued for the duration of the ceremonies which lasted for three days and three nights. Adomnán mentioned the storm in the context of a prophecy uttered by Columba himself, probably some years earlier, when he responded to a claim that the population of all the surrounding lands would wish to attend his funeral. Columba had dismissed the claim, foreseeing instead that Iona would be effectively removed from the world at that time: 'Only the monks of my own community will carry out my burial and perform the funeral duties.' As Adomnán pointed out, this meant that the inhabitants of Mull and other islands were unable to participate when the time came. What he does not say is whether the storm abated sufficiently for monks from nearby Tiree to take part. It thus remains a possibility that the esteemed Baithéne, who may have been prior of Mag Luinge at the time, was unable to attend his cousin's funeral.

After the third night, the tempest subsided and the waters around Iona became less perilous. By then, the rituals were over and Columba was committed to the earth. The simplicity of his burial was appropriate for one who placed high value on austerity and humility. His body was wrapped in white linen and laid in the ground, with the stone pillow from his lodging set beside the grave. There was no coffin, no elaborate tombstone. It is likely that the spot was marked by nothing more than a rough stone inscribed with a simple cross. Only the pillow of rock placed alongside it would have distinguished the founder's grave from those of his monks. Neither the whereabouts of the pillow-stone nor the location of the grave are known today. The abbey museum contains a cross-marked boulder discovered in 1870 and traditionally called 'St Columba's Pillow'. It appears to have been inscribed in the eighth century, but its claim to be the saint's pillow-stone is entirely spurious. It was found, in any case, at Cladh an Disirt which is too far from the monastery to be a likely burial-place for the founder. A better candidate is an area near the west door of the medieval abbey, where the tiny chapel known as St Columba's Shrine nestles against the abbey's west front. Even if the saint's bones did indeed lie in this vicinity, they did not remain forever undisturbed, nor were they destined to stay there in perpetuity. Thus, although the simple grave still existed in Adomnán's time, the cult that grew around Columba eventually required a tomb more suited to veneration. This was probably made in the eighth century or, at latest, in the early years of the ninth. It existed in 825 when Viking raiders searched for it during a raid on the monastery. According to a near-contemporary report they failed to locate it, for it had been secretly hidden in the ground, but they knew that it was adorned with precious metals.[2] It was evidently a richly decorated tomb-shrine, mounted near the altar of the monastic church on some kind of base or table which allowed the monks and their guests to view it. The description suggests that the shrine was a wooden coffin covered almost entirely with metal plates or sheets, some of which were of silver and gold. This is undoubtedly the 'shrine of Columba' mentioned by later writers in the context of division and distribution of his mortal remains.

Cult

Even in life, Columba was revered as a holy man of exemplary virtue. Although this aspect was greatly embellished by his seventh-century hagiographers, there seems little doubt that he was, to some extent, a living saint. That this was how his contemporaries perceived him is indicated by *Amra Coluim Chille*, the eulogy composed within a few years of his death by the Irish poet Dallán Forgaill. In discussing the provenance of this text in Chapter 1 we observed its similarity to praise-poems composed in honour of secular lords. It calls Columba *nia*, 'a champion', and portrays him as a great warrior who won victories over sin and temptation rather than over earthly enemies. In Dallán's verses Columba has not yet become the miracle-worker of later tradition, a figure endowed with supernatural powers, but is simply an exceptionally gifted Irishman who uses his talents well. If, as stated in the text, the poem was commissioned by 'King Áed', we should probably view it as a commemorative piece created by the high lords of Cenél Conaill for their saintly kinsman.[3] It might thus reflect the esteem in which Columba was held by his family back home in Donegal, just as the stories collected a generation later on Iona represent similar veneration by his spiritual kin.

It is evident from the *Amra* and from hagiography assembled by Cumméne and Adomnán that stories about Columba were circulating in both Ireland and Britain soon after his death.[4] We cannot assume that the majority of these tales were preserved solely in oral form until their systematic collection at Iona during Ségéne's thirty-year abbacy (623–52). On the contrary, many stories in *Vita Columbae* embellish a hagiographical core with so much circumstantial detail that it is hard to imagine their sources as anything other than eyewitness testimonies written down within a few years of the saint's passing.[5] It is nevertheless to the generation of Ségéne and Cumméne that we should credit the true beginnings of a formal cult of Columba. Cumméne's book of miracles, rather than *Amra Coluim Chille*, was the first real literary manifestation of the cult. That both works were swiftly and widely disseminated was largely due to the federation of churches and monasteries sharing common allegiance to the mother-house on Iona. As some of these had already been founded before Columba's death, the origins of the federation can be assigned to his lifetime. It is a striking testament to the energy of his successors, his abbatial heirs, that the Columban *familia* became the most influential ecclesiastical network in Ireland and northern Britain during the seventh and eighth centuries. To these abbots can be credited the parallel development of the saintly cult that grew swiftly around the founder's memory. A later part of this book will trace the history of the cult in greater detail, from its seventh-century beginnings to its sundry modern manifestations, but some aspects of the early development of the 'legend' of St Columba will be discussed in the present chapter.

Seventh-century abbots

In 597, the abbacy of Iona passed to Baithéne, Columba's cousin, a figure mentioned frequently in *Vita Columbae*. He may have been designated heir-apparent long before Columba's death. Adomnán describes him as the founder's *alumnus*, 'pupil', and indicates that he was second-in-command at Iona. A stint as prior of Mag Luinge on

Tiree had undoubtedly given Baithéne useful experience of running a monastery, but his tenure of the abbacy of Iona was too brief to allow him to leave his mark. He died after holding the post for only three years. What he accomplished in this short time is unrecorded, for the *vita* that commemorates him is essentially a book of miracles with minimal biographical data.[6] His successor was Laisrán, another of Columba's cousins, formerly in charge of the daughter-house at Durrow. Of Laisrán's abbacy we likewise know little beyond a traditional association with the Isle of Arran in the Firth of Clyde. Holy Island, just off Arran's eastern coast, was home to a religious community in early medieval times. Its history might be revealed by archaeological excavation, but, until such time, we are free to speculate about a possible connection between Laisrán and the old church of St Bride at Lamlash on the adjacent Arran shore. A carved stone cross of uncertain date, now positioned beside St Bride's, originated on Holy Island. However, it is the place-name *Lamlash* that draws our attention, for it appears to be the smaller island's original name. It is recorded in the fourteenth century as *Helantinlayshe*, more correctly *Helantmlaysche*, representing Gaelic *Eilean Mo-Laise*, 'My Laisrán's Isle'. If the saint in question is not one of several obscure Irish namesakes, we may tentatively identify him as Baithéne's successor.[7] This raises the possibility that monks of Iona settled on Holy Island during Laisrán's abbacy, thereby establishing a Columban foothold on the east side of Arran.

Laisrán died in 605 and was succeeded by Fergna, surnamed *Brit*, 'the Briton', in later Irish tradition. Fergna's ancestry is unknown, for neither Adomnán nor the annalists give his father's name. In one late text his ancestry is linked to Cenél Conaill, but this is almost certainly a fabrication.[8] His surname or epithet suggests that he had British blood, perhaps through a familial link with Alt Clut or with some other territory of the North Britons. Adomnán's statement that Fergna became abbot of Iona 'by the will of God' might represent acknowledgement of an unusual or unexpected succession. There can be no doubt, however, of Fergna's worthiness as a candidate. He had lived on Iona during Columba's abbacy and had borne witness to a miracle in the monastic church. At that time he was 'a young man of natural goodness'.[9] Later, as abbot, he may have overseen a rebuilding project at the monastery on Tory Island off the coast of Donegal. This Columban daughter-house in Cenél Conaill territory was plundered in

617, presumably by pirates, and rebuilt four years later. Although the date of its original foundation is unrecorded, its reconstruction fell within the final years of Fergna's abbacy, in which case he may have inspected the completed work in his role as head of the Columban *familia*. His death two years later saw the abbacy revert to Columba's kin in the person of Ségéne, a nephew of Laisrán. Under Ségéne's leadership the *familia* extended its influence to new lands and new peoples, bringing the cult of the founder to a wider circle of devotees. Ségéne emerges as one of the prime movers in the religious affairs of seventh-century Britain and Ireland. His long tenure of the abbacy saw Iona's first significant involvement in the Easter Controversy, an extremely divisive issue in which the towering figure of Columba played no small part, albeit a posthumous one. More will be said below on this important topic but, in the meantime, our gaze moves away from the Gaelic world to examine one of the key events of Ségéne's abbacy: the founding of Lindisfarne. The spotlight falls on three individuals who each played a key role: Ségéne himself, his subordinate Aidan and the Northumbrian king Oswald. Working closely together, these three brought the pagan English or 'Anglo-Saxons' of Oswald's kingdom into the Christian fold. More than this, they encouraged devotion to St Columba among a people whose path he had never crossed in life. Alongside this devotion came spiritual allegiance to Iona and a major foothold for the federation outside its Gaelic heartlands.

Oswald, Aidan and Ségéne

In the opening chapter of *Vita Columbae* Adomnán introduced his readers to St Columba's amazing powers of prophecy, adding that one aspect of this gift of foresight was a special ability to predict the military fortunes of kings. 'Some kings,' Adomnán wrote, 'were conquered in the terrifying crash of battle and others emerged victorious according to what Columba asked of God by the power of prayer.'[10] Thus was King Áedán's hard-fought victory over the Miathi attributed, at least in part, to the prayers of Columba and his monks. A more memorable example of this special ability was credited to Columba nearly forty years after his death, its sole eyewitness being the English king Oswald. An account of this posthumous miracle of prophecy came to Iona during Ségéne's abbacy, perhaps in 634 or 635, at the beginning of Oswald's reign. Oswald himself relayed the tale to Ségéne, with other senior members of the community in attendance. Also present was a young Irish monk called Failbe mac Pipáin, a future abbot of Iona, from whom Adomnán heard the story many years later.

Oswald is one of the most famous figures in early English history. He was much admired by Bede who portrayed him as a paragon of Christian kingship. In the *Ecclesiastical History* we see Oswald in a dual guise, as both strong war-leader and devout follower of Christ. He was a native of Bernicia, the more northerly of the two kingdoms that later became the unified realm of Northumbria. His father was Aethelfrith, the king who had defeated Áedán mac Gabráin at Degsastan in 603. After Aethelfrith's death in 616 or 617, his children fled in fear of his Deiran rival Edwin who immediately seized power in Bernicia. Bede tells us that Oswald and his siblings spent their youth 'living in exile among the Irish (*Scotti*) or the Picts where they were instructed in the faith as the Irish taught it and were regenerated by the grace of baptism'.[11] Here Bede uses the Latin term *Scotti* in its widest sense to embrace not only the Scots of Dál Riata but also the people of Ireland, their fellow Gaels. To Bede, as to many of his contemporaries, there was little to distinguish one group of Gaelic-speakers from another. Today we may find a distinction between 'Scots' and 'Irish' rather more useful, although we should be wary of envisaging two different ethnic groups. What Bede is telling us, then, is that Aethelfrith's children fled their homeland in childhood, some finding refuge with the Picts while others came to the Gaelic-speaking Scots of Argyll. All were baptised in exile by Irish priests, or by priests trained in the ways of Christianity 'as the Irish taught it'. We know of only one refugee who dwelt with the Picts: Eanfrith, perhaps Aethelfrith's eldest son, who later sired a child with a Pictish princess. The others came to Dál Riata, to Kintyre, where Eochaid Buide had succeeded his father Áedán as king. Oswald, a boy of twelve or thirteen when he left Bernicia, was among this group. There is little doubt that he received Christian baptism on Iona, perhaps during the abbacy of Fergna Brit.

In *Vita Columbae* we meet Oswald not as an exiled child but as a fully grown man in his early thirties. By then he was king of Bernicia, having succeeded his elder brother Eanfrith whose reign had been very brief. Eanfrith had returned from exile in 633 as soon as news of Edwin's defeat and death reached the royal courts of the Celtic North. He came back to Bernicia as a baptised Christian, but turned his back on the Faith to resume the pagan rites of his ancestors. He was slain a few months later on the orders of Cadwallon, a British king, whose army lay encamped in the lands of the northern English. Cadwallon had recently destroyed Edwin in battle. Now he added Eanfrith to his tally of royal victims before rampaging through Bernicia and Deira. His downfall came in 634 with defeat and death at the hands of Oswald in a decisive battle near Hadrian's Wall. Oswald's victory was undoubtedly achieved with assistance from Dál Riata, perhaps with troops loaned by his foster-family in Kintyre. Having disposed of Cadwallon, he claimed the kingship to become Bernicia's first Christian monarch. Not long after these momentous events, probably in 634 or 635, he travelled back to Iona to tell Abbot Ségéne that his victory had been achieved through the intercession of St Columba.

Adomnán presented Oswald's report to Ségéne as clear proof of Columba's divinely ordained power. The English king spoke of a vision that had entered his dream as he lay sleeping on the eve of battle. In the dream he saw Columba as a gleaming apparition towering over the encampment. Then he heard the saint's voice: 'Be strong and act manfully. Behold, I will be with thee.' Adomnán reminded his readers that these were the very words spoken by God to Joshua, the war-leader of the Israelites during the conquest of Canaan. The attribution of this Old Testament quote to Oswald may be genuine: it is possible that he had heard it in his youth, perhaps on Iona, while listening to a lesson on Christian kingship. If so, he may have felt so inspired by the words that he long remembered them. He told Ségéne that Columba spoke to him again, promising a great victory:

> This coming night go out from your camp into battle, for the Lord has granted me that at this time your foes shall be put to flight and Cadwallon your enemy shall be delivered into your hands and you shall return victorious after battle and reign happily.

On hearing this prophecy Oswald awoke from the dream. He then described it to his henchmen who responded with a pledge to abandon paganism if the prophecy came true. Taking Columba's advice, Oswald led his army on a night march to launch a surprise attack on the enemy. In the ensuing battle the Britons were utterly routed and Cadwallon was slain.

This sequence of events was also described by Bede, although without any mention of Columba. In Bede's version the soldiers under Oswald's command were already Christian. On the eve of battle they knelt *en masse* before a wooden cross set up by Oswald in the camp, joining him in prayer as he begged for God's blessing. This account and Adomnán's essentially tell the same story from different viewpoints. To Bede, the victory over Cadwallon was proof of Oswald's special status in the eyes of God. To Adomnán, it demonstrated Columba's continuing ability, even in death, to influence the fortunes of kings. Both writers were aware that the victory paved the way for the conversion of Bernicia, a process initiated by Oswald and accomplished by priests from Iona. Bede implies that the missionaries began to arrive shortly after the battle:

> Oswald, as soon as he had come to the throne, was anxious that the whole race under his rule should be filled with the grace of the Christian faith of which he had had so wonderful an experience in overcoming the barbarians. So he sent to the Irish elders among whom he and his thegns had received the sacrament of baptism when he was an exile.[12]

The 'Irish elders' were the senior clergy of Iona, whose chief during Oswald's reign was Abbot Ségéne. Bede had previously mentioned Ségéne in a slightly different context, as one of several recipients of a letter sent by the future Pope John IV to an Irish synod in 640. In Bede's extract from this letter Ségéne is listed as a 'priest' alongside key figures from Clonard, Movilla, Armagh and elsewhere. He next appears in the *Ecclesiastical History* as the abbot who answers Oswald's request for a Christian mission from Iona. Bede does not say how the request was made, whether by the king in person or via an intermediary, but we can infer from Adomnán that it led to a face-to-face discussion. It was most likely during the same meeting that Oswald told Ségéne of his vision on the eve of battle. The story of Columba's intercession on behalf of such a virtuous king would have profoundly moved the abbot and his monks. From Oswald's point of view it had the desired effect, for Ségéne appointed a Columban priest as the first bishop of Bernicia. This individual's name is unrecorded, but Bede describes him as a man of harsh disposition who failed to win the hearts of Oswald's pagan subjects. He apparently regarded the Bernicians as a stubborn, uncivilised people unwilling to accept the Christian message. Eventually he returned to Iona, having made little progress, and a new bishop was despatched in his stead. The replacement was Aidan, a man of wholly different character. Although not mentioned in *Vita Columbae*, Aidan received a glowing appraisal from Bede and was clearly held in high regard both in Bernicia and on Iona. From Oswald he received as his episcopal seat the island of Lindisfarne, also known as Holy Island. Its geographical setting closely mirrored that of Iona: just as the Hebridean isle is separated from Mull by only a mile of water so Lindisfarne lies a similar distance off the coast of Bernicia. The sea recedes twice daily to reveal a narrow causeway over which travellers can pass dryshod for a limited time. Like Iona, Lindisfarne was well suited to the needs of a religious community whose members desired isolation from the cares and temptations of the outside world. Both places were nevertheless not so remote from the centres of secular power that their clergy were unable to participate in the affairs of kings. Just as the abbots of the Hebridean monastery had easy access by land and sea to the political centres of Dál Riata, so too did the bishops of Lindisfarne maintain contact with their English royal patrons. In Lindisfarne's case the distance was so short that Bishop Aidan could see Bamburgh, the great citadel of Bernicia, simply by gazing southward from his window.

Through Aidan's teaching the memory of Columba came to be venerated among Oswald's people. The monastery on Lindisfarne became a daughter-house of Iona, a satellite of no lesser status than Durrow or Derry. Its first residents were Columban monks sent by Ségéne to serve Aidan in the early years of the mission, but these were eventually joined by young Bernician recruits. Aidan himself laboured tirelessly, travelling around the kingdom to preach the Word of God, often accompanied by Oswald as chief interpreter. After the king's death in battle in 642, Aidan served his successor Oswiu, but also cultivated a close friendship with King Oswine of Deira, a kinsman of Edwin. Aidan eventually died in 651 after nearly seventeen years as bishop of the northern English. He was buried on Lindisfarne, bequeathing to his successor a flourishing monastery sustained by good relations with local secular elites. His only fault, in Bede's view, was his adherence to certain religious customs practised by the Columban *familia* and regarded with disapproval by the majority of churches in Western Christendom.

Iona and the Easter Controversy

The previous section mentioned a letter sent from Rome in 640 to an Irish synod whose members included Abbot Ségéne. It was written by pope-elect John in reply to a letter sent by the synod in June or July of the same year. The letter from Ireland had been addressed to Pope Severinus whose tenure of the papacy lasted barely two months. John's succession to the vacant papal chair was delayed until December, but, in the interim, he realised that no response had been sent to the Irish. He resolved to deal with the matter himself, the resulting letter being the one mentioned by Bede. One of the topics he addressed was an important point of disagreement between the papacy and a substantial number of churches in Ireland and Britain. The abbots and bishops who led these churches were, according to John, 'befogged by blindness', chiefly on account of their stubborn refusal to abandon certain outmoded practices. Most serious of all was their failure to adopt a revised method for choosing the correct Sunday on which to celebrate Christ's Resurrection. They clung instead to an older method which, according to John, amounted to a rejection of 'our Easter in which Christ was sacrificed for us' because it relied instead on a belief that the Resurrection should be celebrated 'on the fourteenth day of the moon'.[13] In these few words, John went right to the heart of what historians now call the Easter Controversy, a dispute that would soon cause much bitterness and ill-feeling among religious communities across the British Isles. Iona took a central position in the unfolding sequence of events, as did her daughter-house on Lindisfarne. Even Columba himself was summoned, posthumously, to play a significant role.

To the eyes of a layman in our enlightened modern era the method by which the date of Easter Sunday is calculated each year might seem a trivial point of debate. In the seventh century it was viewed as a subject of grave importance. Bishops and abbots all over Europe believed that choosing the correct Sunday for the paschal celebration was absolutely vital. So did the Pope. The problem for the papacy was one of conformity, for many churches in the British Isles used a method of paschal reckoning long since abandoned by Rome and the rest of Western Christendom. This sometimes led to Easter being celebrated on different Sundays in, for example, Ireland and Italy. Although the two methods often converged in selecting the same

Sunday, the years in which they failed to coincide highlighted the difference. By 600, the Easter Controversy was becoming a major source of concern for Rome and, as the century progressed, it grew into a serious dispute. Some contemporary observers began to see it as a test for the authority of the Pope, although dissent was not what the non-conforming clergy of Britain and Ireland intended by their unwillingness to change. They, for their part, remained steadfast in their loyalty to the Holy See. All the same, they felt reluctant to discard traditions bequeathed to them by illustrious predecessors. On Iona, for instance, conformity with Rome would have meant abandoning paschal customs handed down by St Columba himself.

Refusal to accept reform was not the only issue at stake. An additional problem was the form of tonsure worn by clergymen in Britain and Ireland. The two issues were, in fact, bound together in what the papacy and its supporters saw as twin aspects of an intransigent, insubordinate attitude. Whereas most male clerics in Western Christendom cut their hair in the Petrine Crown, 'Crown of St Peter', a style familiar to modern eyes as the usual tonsure of a medieval monk, their brethren in Britain and Ireland had long favoured a different custom. This involved shaving a band of hair across the middle of the scalp, from ear to ear. It seems to have been unique to the British Isles and may have had pre-Christian origins among the pagan priesthood. When the Easter Controversy arose in the seventh century, the style of tonsure was seen as a visible statement of belief and practice. Conformity with Rome on paschal reckoning went hand in hand with adoption of the Petrine Crown. Any British or Irish cleric who still wore the 'Celtic' tonsure was judged to be an adherent of similarly traditionalist views on Easter.[14]

Iona was not alone in adhering to the old ways. Nearly every church in Ireland entered the seventh century in non-conformity with Rome. Pressure from both the papacy and a home-grown reformist movement led eventually to formal rejection of 'Celtic' practices by an Irish synod. The decision was essentially a response to a letter from Pope Honorius I (625–38) in which he pleaded with the Irish churches to fall into line. Although the letter has not survived, its main points were summarised by Bede in the *Ecclesiastical History*. From Bede we learn that the Pope urged the Irish clerics 'not to consider themselves, few as they were and placed on the extreme boundaries of the world, wiser than the ancient and modern Churches of Christ scattered throughout the earth'. The synod that assembled to consider the matter was held c.630 at Mag Lene in Southern Uí Néill territory.[15] It was essentially a southern Irish gathering whose decree had no remit in the North. Conformity with Rome continued to be rejected by major northern churches such as Bangor, Movilla, Nendrum and Armagh. Iona and her satellites also kept faith with Celtic custom, not least as a mark of loyalty to the teachings of Columba. The difference of opinion between northern and southern Ireland was mirrored in Britain where the division had a more ethnic aspect. Here, the main advocate for 'Roman' paschal reckoning was the archbishopric of Canterbury in the southern English kingdom of Kent. Canterbury's archiepiscopal see had been founded in 597 by St Augustine, a monk sent from Rome by Pope Gregory the Great to evangelise the pagan English and to bring the Christian Britons into conformity on the matter of Easter. The mission achieved success in the first of these goals, for the Kentish king and his people eagerly accepted baptism. Bishoprics subject to Canterbury were subsequently founded at London and Rochester. In the British kingdoms of the north and west, however, a long-established native clergy saw no reason to recognise Augustine's authority over their own bishops. Like their peers in Ireland and Argyll they preferred to follow the 'Celtic' practices of their forebears but they agreed to meet Augustine to hear his arguments. The meeting began with an unfortunate misunderstanding which arose when the British bishops entered the room. They expected Augustine and his companions to stand as a mark of courtesy and were deeply offended when he remained in his seat. Antipathy between the two sides increased when the Britons rejected the case for reform, their intransigence prompting an angry tirade from Augustine. To him, and to his superiors at Rome, this stubborn adherence to Celtic custom seemed almost heretical.

The case for reform made little headway among the Britons. Rome instead devoted her energies to Christianising the English and to raising among them an indigenous clergy who practised the 'correct' method of Easter calculation. Canterbury's influence continued to expand in the southern English kingdoms after Augustine's death in 604, coming north to Deira in the 620s during the reign of King Edwin. In Ireland, at around the same time, the reformers gained their great victory at the synod of Mag Lene. So significant was the synod's decision that its repercussions were felt even among some northern Irish churches where, inevitably, the case for conformity began to be heard. A certain Cummian, probably based at Clonfert in County Galway, forcefully expressed his views on the paschal issue in a letter to Abbot Ségéne. This was addressed also to Beccán, a hermit, a figure we can cautiously identify as Beccán mac Luigdech who composed two poems in praise of Columba. To Cummian, a fervent advocate of reform, there were no grounds for defence in what he called 'the traditions of the elders' and a 'back-to-front ordering' of Easter dates. Echoing, no doubt, a view prevalent in Rome and Canterbury, he described the Celtic traditionalists as 'an insignificant group of Britons and Irish who are almost at the end of the world and, if I may say so, but pimples on the face of the earth'.[16] Beccán's reaction to the letter is unknown: if he has been correctly identified as the eulogist of Columba, he may have continued to follow Iona's guidance on paschal custom. Ségéne apparently remained unmoved by Cummian's words, hence his later inclusion among the recipients of John's epistle in 640.

It was against this background of debate and uncertainty that the monastery on Lindisfarne was founded as a Columban daughter-house. The timing no doubt seemed advantageous to the senior clergy on Iona, for Oswald's request for a bishop gave the Celtic traditionalists a valuable foothold in England. Canterbury had already tried to impose its authority among the northern English by appointing one of its own priests, Paulinus, as the first bishop of York during Edwin's reign, but the attempt had proved short-lived. Paulinus fled back to Kent after Edwin's death in 633 at the hands of Cadwallon. Into the vacuum stepped Aidan, arriving in Bernicia in the wake of Oswald's victory in 634, bringing the practices of Iona to lands formerly under the spiritual authority of Canterbury's emissary at York. Oswald's kingdom thus received the paschal reckoning of the northern Irish and Dál Riatan churches, together with the Celtic tonsure and other traditionalist customs. When Edwin's former heartland of Deira also fell under Oswald's sway, those English communities who had already received baptism from York's 'Roman' priests became spiritually answerable to Aidan. The Lindisfarne bishopric was not, however, Ségéne's only venture into territory regarded by the Romanists as their own. In 635, around the time of the Bernician mission, he founded a monastery on *Rechra*, now Lambay Island, 3 miles off the coast of County Dublin. Although Lambay lay within the Southern Uí Néill hegemony, it was made available to Ségéne because his Cenél Conaill kinsman, Domnall mac Áeda, at that time held the high kingship of

Tara. Like Durrow, the new monastery represented a foothold of the Columban *familia* in the Irish midlands, an area where the recently reformed southern clergy had major interests.

Ségéne died in 652, outliving Bishop Aidan by one year and King Oswald by ten. To these three devotees of St Columba we can credit the Christianising of Bernicia and the founding, at Lindisfarne, of one of the great monasteries of early medieval Britain. None of this trio witnessed the inevitable climax of the Easter Controversy: a face-to-face confrontation between Iona and the Romanists to decide, once and for all, the future direction of Northumbrian Christianity. This came in 664, twelve years after Ségéne's passing, at a time when Cumméne held the abbacy of Iona. By then, the daughter-house on Lindisfarne headed its own *paruchia* of satellites, at places like Old Melrose in Tweeddale, Coldingham on the Berwickshire coast and Lastingham in North Yorkshire. Although these tended to follow 'Celtic' practice, not all of their personnel felt comfortable with their leadership's continuing resistance to paschal reform. Some Northumbrian-born monks and nuns had, in any case, been trained in the Romanist tradition, learning their craft in southern English kingdoms whose churches answered to Canterbury. Within Northumbria the reformers secured a major foothold at Ripon in Deira. This monastery, endowed in 658 by Alchfrith, eldest son of Oswald's brother and successor Oswiu, was originally founded as a Lindisfarne satellite. Alchfrith was subsequently persuaded to the Roman cause by Wilfrid, a Northumbrian monk who had studied at the Holy See as well as in Frankish Gaul. When Alchfrith asked the Ripon monks to abandon their Celtic practices, they refused and were ordered to leave. Their abbot was replaced by Wilfrid, an appointment that would soon prove disastrous for Iona's interests.

Resolution of the divisive Easter issue was eventually demanded by King Oswiu and his second wife Eanflaed, a daughter of Edwin of Deira. Oswiu, like Oswald, had been converted to Christianity on Iona. Queen Eanflaed, by contrast, had received baptism from Paulinus of York during her father's kingship. Although Paulinus had fled Northumbria in 633, his deacon James had stayed behind to continue the Canterbury mission, becoming an influential figure at the royal court after Eanflaed's marriage to Oswiu c.643. With two different systems of paschal reckoning being used at the very heart of the Northumbrian kingdom a bizarre situation arose whenever the calendars failed to coincide. In some years the king and queen celebrated Easter together, but in others they observed their rituals separately, on different Sundays. This no doubt seemed awkward enough, but the final straw may have come when the traditionalist monks were expelled from Ripon, a deed which surely demonstrated to Oswiu that the controversy had turned into a crisis. To him and his queen the solution seemed clear: all clergy in the kingdom must agree to follow a single method of paschal reckoning. So, in 664, he summoned the ecclesiastical elite to a synod where each side could argue its case. The chosen location was Whitby on what is now the coast of North Yorkshire. Here, on a headland now occupied by the ruined medieval abbey, stood a monastery where monks and nuns lived in two separate communities. It was led by Abbess Hild, a member of the Deiran royal family, whose own early experiences of Easter had been observed according to the Roman custom favoured by her kinswoman Queen Eanflaed. Hild's observance had changed at the age of thirty-three when Bishop Aidan offered her the abbacy of Whitby, an appointment that obliged her to adopt the customs of Iona. At the synod in 664 she chaired the proceedings as host without taking a major role in the discussions, although her sympathies lay with the traditionalists. Also present in a neutral role was Cedd, a Northumbrian-born bishop of the East Saxons and a former disciple of Aidan at Lindisfarne. Like Hild he had a personal preference for Celtic practice, but was not called upon to voice his opinion, his main role being to act as interpreter between the English and Gaelic delegates. King Oswiu, too, attended the gathering, together with Alchfrith his son.

The reformists were represented by Wilfrid of Ripon as chief spokesman. Alongside him stood his Frankish mentor Agilbert who at that time was bishop of the West Saxons, together with James the Deacon and the queen's chaplain Romanus. Chief advocate for the Celtic side was Bishop Colmán of Lindisfarne, a less forceful orator than his superiors on Iona might have wished for at such a crucial time. Oswiu regarded Colmán with great affection, but felt obliged to refrain from intervening on his behalf. The king and all others who were present knew that the fate of the Columban mission in Northumbria not only hung in the balance, but rested on the shoulders of one man. The weight of so much responsibility must have been daunting to Colmán, who seems to have been a person of humility and gentleness. In the ensuing debate he made an earnest defence of his position, but, in the end, he was no match for the eloquent and combative Wilfrid. Their robust exchange of views was reported by Bede in our only surviving account of the proceedings. We learn that the climactic moment came when Wilfrid questioned what he saw as Colmán's elevation of Columba's authority over that of the Pope, the heir of St Peter. Colmán had previously argued that the paschal reckoning of 'our most reverend father Columba and his successors' was based on ancient wisdom reaching back nearly four hundred years. Moreover, the holiness of Iona's founder and the abbots who followed him was surely confirmed by the miracles attributed to them. 'And as I have no doubt that they were saints,' Colmán added, 'I shall never cease to follow their way of life, their customs, and their teaching.'[17] This elicited an astonishing response from Wilfrid:

> So far as your father Columba and his followers are concerned, whose holiness you claim to imitate and whose rule and precepts (confirmed by heavenly signs) you claim to follow, I might perhaps point out that at the Judgement, many will say to the Lord that they prophesied in his name and cast out devils and did many wonderful works, but the Lord will answer that He never knew them.

Perhaps to make amends for this barely-concealed scorn of Iona's revered founder, Wilfrid backtracked slightly in his final words on the matter of Easter. He nonetheless delivered a stunning *coup de grace*:

> And if that Columba of yours – yes, and ours too, if he belonged to Christ – was a holy man of mighty works, is he to be preferred to the most blessed chief of the apostles, to whom the Lord said: 'Thou art Peter and upon this rock I will build my Church and the gates of Hell shall not prevail against it, and I will give unto thee the keys of the kingdom of Heaven'?

To this the bishop of Lindisfarne had no answer, but King Oswiu looked at him and said:

> 'Is it true, Colmán, that the Lord said these words to Peter?'
>
> 'It is true, O King', said Colmán.
>
> 'Have you anything to show that an equal authority was

> given to your Columba?'
>
> 'Nothing,' Colmán replied.

Then Oswiu addressed Colmán and Wilfrid together: 'Do you both agree, without any dispute, that these words were addressed primarily to Peter and that the Lord gave him the keys of the kingdom of Heaven?' When the two adversaries both answered 'Yes', the king felt able to make his decision, having now concluded that the commands of the Holy See could no longer be denied. Papal authority came directly from God, who had bestowed it on St Peter. To Oswiu this seemed to put the matter beyond doubt, for Peter was the doorkeeper of Heaven and the chief of the saints.

> 'Then I tell you,' said the king, 'since he is the doorkeeper I will not contradict him; but I intend to obey his commands in everything to the best of my knowledge and ability, otherwise when I come to the gates of the kingdom of Heaven there may be no one to open them because the one who on your own showing holds the keys has turned his back on me.'

So ended the Synod of Whitby. So, too, ended Iona's mission in Northumbria. The daughter-house on Lindisfarne, together with its satellites throughout the kingdom, ceased to be members of the Columban federation. All churches and monasteries in lands subject to Oswiu were ordered to bring their paschal reckoning into line with Canterbury and Rome. Their clergy, too, were forbidden to tonsure their hair in the Celtic style. Any who refused to adopt these rules were no longer welcome and had to leave. Among those who accepted reform were Abbess Hild, who returned to the Easter customs of her childhood, and Bishop Cedd, the interpreter. But Colmán himself remained faithful to the teachings of Columba. Returning to Lindisfarne he gathered those who wished to retain the Celtic tradition – including some thirty English monks – and departed from the kingdom. The travellers made their way to Iona where, we may assume, Colmán gave a full report of the synod to Abbot Cumméne. The latter can only have been bitterly disappointed, regardless of whether or not he privately expected the outcome. Erosion of his influence in Northumbria in a practical sense had probably been happening for many years, but the synod dealt a serious blow to Iona's prestige.

Colmán, meanwhile, still accompanied by many of his former monks from Lindisfarne, journeyed on to the west of Ireland. He came to the little isle of Inishbofin off the coast of Connemara and founded there a monastery, essentially a daughter-house of Iona and a new addition to the Columban *paruchia*. Bede tells of a conflict that swiftly arose among the brethren there, a petty internal dispute over the gathering of the harvest. The English monks felt aggrieved at having to do all the hard work on the island while their Irish colleagues roamed freely on the mainland.[18] Colmán dealt with the problem by establishing a separate monastery for the English at *Mag eo*, 'Plain of the Yew Trees', now the village of Mayo in the county of the same name. The Northumbrians thrived in their new abode, building its reputation so high that it attracted more of their compatriots from Britain. It continued to flourish as a colony of English monks, hence the name by which it came to be known in later Irish chronicles: *Mag nEo na Sachsan*, 'Mayo of the Saxons'. Its abbot continued to acknowledge the spiritual authority of Iona.

The settlement at Mayo was still in its infancy when, in February 675, its venerable founder Colmán passed away. By then, barely ten years after the synod of Whitby, Colmán's former patron King Oswiu was also dead. So, too, was Abbot Cumméne. Iona was now led by Failbe, whom we have already encountered in his earlier guise as a young monk during Ségéne's abbacy. Like his predecessor, Failbe had been a disciple of Ségéne and remained faithful to the old policies on Easter and the tonsure. The Columban federation thus entered the final quarter of the seventh century in stubborn resistance to reform. But for how much longer could the traditionalists hold their ground? From Durrow to Derry, from Tiree to the churches of Pictland, a wind of change was rising up around the daughter-houses of Iona. Even at the mother-church the old ways were increasingly being questioned and, in 679, the abbacy passed to a man whose views were less deeply rooted in the past.

Adomnán

As our best source of information on St Columba we have already encountered Adomnán many times in this book, usually in his literary guise as a hagiographer *par excellence*. Fleeting glimpses of his personality appear in *Vita Columbae*, but at no point in his narrative does he pause to say much about himself. Turning elsewhere, we find remarks on his character in Bede's *Ecclesiastical History* and in a handful of annal entries reporting his achievements, but few other contemporary references survive. During the tenth century an anonymous author composed, in Irish, a hagiographical work purporting to describe key events from Adomnán's career. This carries the title *Betha Adamnáin*, 'Life of Adomnán', but it contributes almost no worthwhile biographical information. It differs from a conventional *vita* in omitting the subject's parentage and childhood. Instead, it concentrates on his dealings with various Irish kings, portraying him as a forceful figure endowed with powers of prophecy. Although many of these kings seem to have been alive in Adomnán's time, his confrontations with them look suspiciously like fictional episodes created long after his death. Analysis of the *Betha* suggests that its author sought to transplant the political circumstances of the tenth century into a historical setting of c.700. He was clearly an advocate for the Columban federation and presumably lived at one of its monasteries in Ireland sometime after 950. It seems likely that his abode was Kells in County Meath and equally likely that the *Betha* was composed there in the early 960s.[19] Parts of the narrative relate to events in northern Britain and, in one instance, to a historically attested Pictish king who died in 694. As it is unlikely that such material derives from Irish texts, we should assume that it came from Iona and might therefore be authentic. With access to more or less reliable information about the late seventh and early eighth centuries, the author of the *Betha* cannot have been ignorant of true history, but instead chose to present it as the backdrop to an artificial narrative pertaining to his own era. As one modern scholar has observed of the *Betha*: 'kings of Adomnán's day stand for their tenth-century counterparts'.[20]

What we know of the real Adomnán comes not from pseudo-biography of the tenth century but from *Vita Columbae*, the annals and a few other sources. Among the latter is the *Aberdeen Breviary*, a sixteenth-century Scottish compendium of hagiographical fragments, in which unique material – some of it presumably from Iona – is preserved. Although parts of this material are likely to be factual, the difficulty arises in distinguishing these from the fictional parts, a task not made easier by the lateness of the surviving text. In addition to the *Breviary* we have a text of a rather different character: *Cáin Adamnáin*,

'Adomnán's Law'. This is of particular relevance to the history of the Columban federation and will be described in greater detail below.

By drawing together the scattered data on Adomnán we can construct a broadly coherent picture of his life and career. In *Vita Columbae* he refers to *nostrum Scotiam*, 'our Ireland', from which we can deduce that he was an Irishman by birth.[21] Pinpointing his district of origin is rather more difficult. Material added to the original text of *Cáin Adamnáin* in the eleventh century but drawn from a lost earlier work identifies his father as Rónán, son of Tinne of Cenél Conaill, and his mother as Ronnat of the neighbouring Cenél nEndai. Adomnán's parentage on both sides therefore makes him a native of Donegal. His traditional association with the monastery of Raphoe, in Cenél nEndai territory, suggests that he may have been raised among his mother's people, a not unusual occurrence in early medieval Ireland.[22] Raphoe itself, like *Cáin Adamnáin*, will be discussed further below.

The early phases of Adomnán's ecclesiastical career are undocumented but were probably spent in one or more Irish monasteries. It has been suggested that Durrow was one of these, on the basis that he mentions the place several times in *Vita Columbae*, but this is not a necessary deduction. Given his Donegal origins, a northern monastery might seem a better candidate, but, again, it is no more than a vague inference. At some point he arrived on Iona and was eventually selected as Abbot Failbe's successor, possibly by Failbe himself. In 679, at the age of fifty-two or thereabouts, he became the tenth abbot. As head of the Columban federation he immediately became an important figure not only in ecclesiastical circles but in the political affairs of Ireland and Britain. Subsequent events would show that he was more than capable of handling these responsibilities. Like Columba, he was not afraid of stepping into the world of kings if the interests of Iona and her *familia*, or those of his friends and patrons, required his intervention. The first of his achievements – or the first of which we have any knowledge – resulted from such a venture into the secular sphere. This occurred in 686, within a year of the Battle of Dun Nechtáin, one of the most important events of the seventh century. The battle was a great victory for the Pictish king Bridei, son of Bili, over a Northumbrian army led by King Ecgfrith, a son of Oswiu and nephew of Oswald. Ecgfrith's successor was his half-brother Aldfrith, a deeply religious man of Irish upbringing who had studied as a monk on Iona. Aldfrith's accession to the kingship restored, to some extent,

Iona's relations with the northern English, even if the favoured position relinquished at Whitby in 664 was now gone forever. The main purpose of Adomnán's visit in 686 was to ask for the release of captives taken by Ecgfrith in a raid on Ireland two years earlier. Ecgfrith's forces had directed their assault on Brega, a midland kingdom under the overlordship of the Southern Uí Néill, and had wreaked much devastation there. Adomnán went to Northumbria not so much as an Irish cleric on a humanitarian mission but as a high-status ambassador acting on behalf of the Southern Uí Néill.[23] His task would have been eased considerably by his previous contact with Aldfrith during the latter's sojourn on Iona, but a successful outcome was by no means guaranteed. The ensuing negotiations eventually secured freedom for the Irish prisoners whom Adomnán escorted back to their homeland. Before he left Northumbria he visited the monastery at Jarrow where, we may be fairly certain, he met the adolescent Bede.

Adomnán travelled to Northumbria again, in 688. This second visit was reported in some detail by Bede, who was in his mid-teens at the time. Its primary purpose may have been social rather than political and perhaps followed an invitation from King Aldfrith. While availing himself of the hospitality of the Northumbrian court, Adomnán visited a number of churches around the kingdom. He may have gone to these places informally, as a tourist and royal guest rather than in an official capacity, but Bede portrays the tour as an information-gathering exercise by one of the chief practitioners of the Celtic Easter. Bede implies that Adomnán made only this one visit to Northumbria and omits any mention of the liberation of Ecgfrith's captives. We know from Adomnán's own words in *Vita Columbae* that he did, in fact, make two visits, but Bede's omission of one of these need not surprise us. The account in the *Ecclesiastical History* was tailored to Bede's specific objectives with regard to the Easter Controversy, an issue in which he invested much of his literary energy. Many of his contemporaries in the Northumbrian clergy also regarded the topic as vitally important, but few, perhaps, were quite so zealous as he in voicing their opinions. In Bede's view, Adomnán came to Aldfrith's kingdom for no other reason than 'to see the canonical rites of the church'. The visit, he tells us, proved to be quite educational for the abbot of Iona:

> He was earnestly advised by many who were better instructed than himself that he, in company with a very small band of followers, living in the remotest corner of the world, should not presume to go against the universal custom of the Church in the matter of keeping Easter and in various other ordinances. He altered his opinion so greatly that he readily preferred the customs which he saw and heard in the English churches to those of himself and his followers.[24]

Notwithstanding Bede's well-merited status as our most valuable source of information on early English history, his remarks on the outcome of Adomnán's sojourn in Northumbria surely distort the truth. It seems barely credible that the leader of the Columban *familia*, one of the most senior figures in Western Christendom and a man whose wide circle of contacts extended beyond the British Isles, would not already have spent much earnest thought and many hours of discussion on the paschal issue before even setting foot in Aldfrith's realm. It is highly unlikely that a tour of Northumbrian monasteries would have influenced or altered his opinions. For Adomnán, the most important voices in the matter of Easter observance were not the reformed English clergy at Jarrow but his own community on Iona. Thus, although he may have nurtured a personal preference for Roman customs in the 680s, the notion that this was sparked by conversations with his Northumbrian hosts can be disregarded. Bede went on to describe Adomnán returning to Iona where he tried, unsuccessfully, to bring about reform. The other Columban churches in Britain also stood firm, so Adomnán withdrew to Ireland where, according to Bede, 'he restored nearly all who were not under the dominion of Iona to catholic unity, teaching them to observe Easter at the proper time'. This version of events is not reflected in other sources and immediately invites our scepticism. In *Vita Columbae*, Adomnán indicates that he continued to reside on Iona after his return from Northumbria. He leaves us in no doubt that he remained there throughout the final decade of the seventh century. The annalists tell us that he went to Ireland in 692, but this was only a visit, not a permanent relocation, and he came back to Iona afterwards. He presumably travelled to his homeland in his capacity as head of the Columban federation to meet with senior clergy at the daughter-houses and to receive their tribute-payments. We can probably assume that he undertook this journey on more than one occasion in the period after his Northumbrian visits. Bede's notion of a permanent withdrawal to Ireland is little more than propaganda designed to exaggerate the differences of opinion on Iona over the Easter issue. It suited Bede's purposes to imagine an acrimonious schism between the community's stubborn traditionalists and their newly enlightened abbot. Likewise, the idea that Adomnán brought paschal reform to Irish churches outside the *paruchia* – but not to those within it and therefore under his authority – can be dismissed for similar reasons. Again, Bede wanted his readers to believe that Iona and its recalcitrant satellites were left standing alone against a tide of reform that swept Ireland in the wake of Adomnán's 'conversion' by persuasive English clerics. In truth, Adomnán's own stance on Easter was rather more complicated. He undoubtedly adopted a reformist view at some point in his abbacy, but retained a strong devotion to the traditions handed down by his predecessors as well as a deep admiration for Columba. Like Iona's first abbot he was a charismatic, strong-minded individual who could, perhaps, have imposed his personal beliefs on those who looked to him for guidance and leadership. But he was wise enough to perceive that a head-to-head confrontation with the traditionalists was not the best way forward. He surely did not want Iona to become a venue for the kind of vitriolic debate seen at Whitby in 664, nor did he wish to see the Columban federation break asunder into two factions. Dissension and division would have robbed the *paruchia* of its status as the premier ecclesiastical power in Ireland and northern Britain, a position that was already being challenged by rivals.

In writing a 'Life' of St Columba, Adomnán had as one of his purposes the elevation of Iona to a position of pre-eminence among the churches of Gaeldom. *Vita Columbae* can thus be seen as ecclesiastical propaganda crafted by its author to fit the particular circumstances of his own time. In the final quarter of the seventh century the matter of Easter was obviously of major concern in many parts of the British Isles and we have already examined some aspects of Adomnán's role in it. Another pressing issue, perhaps of no less importance to him, was the increasing influence of the clergy of Armagh and their encroachment on Columban interests in Ireland.[25] Armagh's claim to have been founded by St Patrick in the fifth century gave it an aura of antiquity and, in the eyes of its own clergy, an air of seniority. Kildare in Munster promoted a similar claim to national primacy on behalf of its founder St Brigid whose death c.524 placed her a couple of generations before Columba. As the seventh century progressed, both Armagh and Kildare sought to build monastic federations of their own in rivalry with, or in imitation of, the extensive *paruchia* led by Iona. One aspect of this strategy was the dissemination of promotional literature in the form of a 'Life' of the founding saint and it is no surprise that *vitae* of Patrick and Brigid appeared in the century's middle decades. Armagh seems to have been more successful in these ventures, while Kildare's hopes of becoming the most powerful ecclesiastical centre in Ireland began to dwindle. Eventually the contest became a two-horse race between the Columban and Patrician federations, with the former being portrayed in the latter's hagiographical literature as intruding on Armagh's rightful hegemony. It is worth noting that Armagh was swayed by the arguments for paschal reform during the last quarter of the seventh century and adopted the Roman Easter at some point in the 680s.[26] The heirs of Patrick, in seeking ecclesiastical primacy in Ireland, may have regarded conformity with Rome as a useful stepping-stone towards this goal. Later, in the early 690s, they tried to curry favour with the Southern Uí Néill during the latter's tenure of the kingship of Tara, but this tactic came to nought when, in 695 or 696, the sovereignty reverted to a northern king from Cenél Conaill. With a kinsman of Iona's abbot once more holding the high-kingship of Ireland, the ambitions of Armagh were temporarily curtailed and, as the seventh century drew to a close, the Columban federation's claim to pre-eminence was hard to deny. As if to hammer home the point, Adomnán used his authority to summon the kings and senior clerics of Ireland as witnesses to his greatest achievement.

The Law of Innocents

The year 697 marked the first centenary of Columba's death. It was no coincidence that Adomnán chose the same year in which to issue a major piece of ecclesiastical legislation: *Lex Innocentium*, 'The Law of Innocents'. This was noted by the annalists on Iona:

> Adomnán went to Ireland and gave the Law of Innocents to the peoples.

Rather surprisingly, we find no reference to the Law in *Vita Columbae*. From the annalists we learn only that it was proclaimed in Ireland in 697. Twenty-five years later they referred to it again in another brief entry:

> 727 The relics of Adomnán are brought over to Ireland and the Law is renewed.

The details of the Law are preserved in two late manuscripts written, respectively, in the fifteenth and sixteenth centuries. Both contain what is clearly an embellished version – probably compiled c.1000 – of an earlier text whose core reaches back to the seventh century.[27] In medieval Ireland the *Lex Innocentium* was known as *Cáin Adamnáin*, 'Adomnán's Law' to distinguish it from other *cana* or clerical laws such as *Cáin Patraicc*, 'Patrick's Law', and *Cáin Domnaig*, 'The Law of Sunday'. Unlike the large body of traditional secular law that had arisen over many centuries of social interaction, the *cana* were new laws crafted by the clergy to deal with specific moral and religious issues. They were aimed primarily at kings who, in turn, were expected to impose the legislation throughout their kingdoms. The Law of Innocents was thus a royal as well as an ecclesiastical law. Its main purpose was to place an obligation on the secular elite to protect women, children and members of religious orders from the perils of war. Adomnán felt strongly that such 'innocents' should be given immunity not only from marauding soldiery but also from the duties of military service. To ensure the widest possible application of the Law he summoned an array of kings, abbots and bishops to a great gathering – no less than a synod – at the monastery of Birr in County Offaly. Iona's royal patrons in Dál Riata were represented by Eochaid, great-great-grandson of Áedán mac Gabráin, while from Pictland came a king and a bishop. Not all those who were invited turned up in person but even those who participated *in absentia* agreed to abide by the Law. In so doing, they effectively stood as guarantors of its clauses within their own areas of jurisdiction. It is interesting to note, given our earlier discussion of rivalry between the Columban and Patrician *familiae* for the primacy of Ireland, that the list of guarantors is headed by the bishop of Armagh. Columba himself is not mentioned in the surviving versions of *Cáin Adamnáin*, but it is more than likely that he was presented in 697 as the patron of the Law.[28]

Transgressions of the Law were punishable by a range of penalties, ranging from gruesome mutilation in the most serious cases to fines payable to Iona for the rest. Protection of non-combatants, then, was the primary objective of *Lex Innocentium*, but it was not otherwise concerned with the routine business of warfare. It was certainly not designed to restrict the military activities of kings, nor did it try to advocate peace as a realistic alternative. Adomnán himself sprang from a powerful family, the Cenél Conaill, which owed its wealth and status to success on the battlefield. He was not so much a pacifist demanding an end to organised violence as an idealist seeking to limit its worst excesses to those who willingly engaged in it. His law sought an exemption for those members of society who might otherwise find themselves unwittingly caught up in conflict. To what extent he succeeded is hard to discern, although the annal for 727 suggests that *Lex Innocentium* retained sufficient force eighteen years after his death to justify renewal. By the ninth century, when an embellished version of the original text began to take shape, fines levied under its clauses were no longer payable to Iona but to Raphoe in eastern Donegal, the church there having by then claimed Adomnán as its founding saint. It was in the same century, moreover, that Iona began to lose her primacy within the Columban federation, a process we shall examine more closely in Chapter 8.

Ecgbert, Naiton and Iona

Adomnán died in 704. The following year the Easter Controversy again came to the fore when the two methods of paschal reckoning failed to coincide. Bede felt relieved that Adomnán was spared the ordeal of witnessing the observance of yet another incorrect Easter Sunday by those on Iona 'who would not follow him in the truth'.[29] Whether this image of a split between traditionalists and reformers was a true reflection of the prevailing mood at the monastery in 705 we cannot say. It is all too easy, however, to take Bede's implication of division and bitterness at face value, especially when the annals present a confused picture of the abbacy in the wake of Adomnán's death. Thus, although an eighth-century list of abbots appears to show a normal pattern of succession, the annalists give a rather more complicated sequence. According to the abbatial list, the next four abbots after Adomnán were Conamail, Dunchad, Dorbbéne and Faelchu. Our expectation would be that each became abbot on the death of a predecessor, but this does not seem to have happened. According to the annals, Dunchad became abbot in 707, three years before Conamail's death, and was still alive in 713 when Dorbbéne held the abbacy for a mere five months before dying in the autumn. Dunchad lived on until 717, a year after the annalists state that Faelchu 'received the chair of Columba'. Historians are in doubt as to what was really happening on Iona at this time. Some adopt what we might call a 'Bedan' view by envisaging a schism between the reformists and traditionalists, each faction electing its own abbot. Others wonder if the apparent duality might simply indicate the resignation of elderly men who, although still living, became too infirm to perform their duties. A third option is to step back from the tangled web of data and acknowledge that we have little hope of unravelling the truth.

Among the uncertainty of these years one event stands out above the rest. It was noted by the annalists, without comment or fanfare, in an entry for 716:

> Easter was changed in the monastery of Iona.

Additional information is given by Bede, who wrote that 'the monks of Iona accepted the catholic ways of life under the teaching of Ecgbert, while Dunchad was abbot, about eighty years after they had sent Bishop Aidan to preach to the English'.[30] Ecgbert, a Northumbrian, had come to Iona in 716 to serve as bishop. Within the Columban federation a bishop had always been subordinate to the abbot of the monastery where he resided, this being a common feature of Celtic ecclesiastical organisation. This was not the case in Ecgbert's homeland, nor indeed in those Celtic areas where paschal reform had already introduced modernising influences. Prior to his appointment as Iona's new bishop, Ecgbert had spent much of his career in Ireland, mostly at the unlocated monastery of *Rathmelsigi* which – like Mayo – had long attracted English monks. In 697, he witnessed the promulgation of the Law of Innocents at Birr and was undoubtedly among Adomnán's circle of close contacts. Since he came to Iona as a convert to the Roman Easter and to the Petrine tonsure, we may assume that he was not invited there by the traditionalists. If, as seems likely, the invitation came from Abbot Dunchad, we can be fairly sure that these two shared similar views and hoped to work together in bringing about reform. The Easter issue was resolved in the year of Ecgbert's arrival, but in September the abbacy passed to Faelchu and nothing more is heard of Dunchad until his death in 717. In the following year, the Crown of St Peter was adopted as the normal tonsure on Iona and, when this happened, Ecgbert perhaps felt that the main objective of his episcopate had been achieved. He remained on the island to the end of his days, dying there in 729 at around ninety years of age.

Iona's adoption of the Roman Easter would have persuaded other Columban monasteries to follow suit. Although the sources do not say that the entire *paruchia* embraced reform, it seems safe to assume that this is what happened during the remaining months of 716 and into the following year. It is possible, in any case, that some Irish satellites had already adopted Roman practice months or even years earlier, their abbots choosing to act independently of Iona on this crucial issue. Before the end of 717 it is likely that every Columban daughter-house in Britain and Ireland had abandoned the old paschal tradition. Intriguingly, however, the annals contain the following entry under that year:

> Expulsion of the community of Iona across Druim Alban by King Naiton

This event, although devoid of context, is usually interpreted in light of the Easter Controversy. Naiton, previously mentioned in Chapter 6, was a Pictish king whose correspondence on ecclesiastical reform with the Northumbrian cleric Ceolfrith, abbot of Jarrow, was reported in detail by Bede. At that time, many Pictish churches still belonged to the Columban *paruchia* and were answerable to Iona, but Ceolfrith convinced Naiton of the need to bring them into conformity with Rome. Historians usually date the correspondence between the two men to c.710–15, before the reform of Iona in 716 and Ceolfrith's death in September of the same year. As a measure of his conversion to the Roman way of doing things, Naiton invited Northumbrian craftsmen to Pictland to build a stone church dedicated to St Peter. His expulsion of the Columban clergy is often assumed to mark a similar break with the past. However, we should note that the annalists date the expulsion *after* Iona's adoption of the Roman Easter. We cannot simply assume that the expelled clerics were stubborn Celtic traditionalists who attempted to retain their old customs in Naiton's kingdom. In fact, there is every reason to believe that the Columban satellites in Pictland followed Iona's example in 716 and swiftly abandoned the old method of paschal reckoning. Naiton undoubtedly had good reason to take the drastic step of sending the Columban clerics away, but it was not necessarily related to the reforms he and Ceolfrith had previously discussed.[31]

CHAPTER 8
Paruchia and *Familia*

Eighth-century Ireland

Faelchu, the thirteenth abbot of Iona, was in his seventies when he succeeded Dunchad and over eighty at his death in 724. It appears that he was assisted in the final two years of his abbacy by a monk called Feidlimid who perhaps handled the main burden of administrative duties.[1] Faelchu was succeeded by two abbots named Cilléne, the second of whom bore the surname *Droichtech*, literally 'bridge-builder', a Gaelic equivalent of Latin *pontifex*. In one obscure text Cilléne Droichtech is said to have visited Ireland bearing relics associated with Adomnán.[2] The same visit seems to be recorded in an annal entry for 727 which tells us that Adomnán's relics were taken to Ireland for a renewal of *Lex Innocentium* before their return to Iona in 730. The relics presumably accompanied Cilléne Droichtech as he toured the Irish satellites of the Columban federation in his capacity as chief abbot. It is likely that he levied tribute-payments from each church and monastery as a contribution to the running costs of the mother-house and towards his own expenses as head of the *familia*.[3] The source that mentions his visit to Ireland refers to his intervention as a peacemaker between the rival northern kindreds of Cenél Conaill and Cenél nEógain. According to the annals, these two fought a battle in 727, an event which appears to provide a context for Cilléne's alleged peace-making role. If he really did intervene in the dispute, he was continuing a tradition of Iona's involvement in Cenél Conaill affairs reaching back to the era of Druim Cett.

Cilléne Droichtech died in 752, the centenary of the passing of Ségéne. Both men had held the abbacy of Iona for more than a quarter of a century, the former for twenty-six years, the latter for twenty-nine. Each witnessed a number of significant political and ecclesiastical events during his lengthy tenure. In Ségéne's period of office, these events mostly took place in Britain. In Cilléne's, the focus switched to Ireland, where a fierce contest for the overkingship of the Northern Uí Néill was mirrored by renewed rivalry between the Columban *familia* and St Patrick's successors at Armagh. We have noted the later tradition of Cilléne's intervention in a war between Cenél Conaill and Cenél nEógain c.727–30. Whatever truce or treaty he negotiated at that time was subsequently breached and three battles were fought in successive years. In 734, the Cenél Conaill ruler Flaithbertach relinquished the overkingship, either voluntarily or by coercion, before retiring to a monastery. He was the last of his kindred to hold Northern Uí Néill supremacy, which quickly passed to his Cenél nEógain rival Áed Allan. Just as Cenél Conaill kings had long enjoyed a symbiotic relationship with kinsmen on Iona, so now the newly-dominant Cenél nEógain forged a similar bond with the abbots of Armagh. It is surely no coincidence that Áed Allan's first year as northern overking saw the proclamation of *Lex Patricii* (*Cáin Patraicc*), 'Patrick's Law', a new piece of ecclesiastical legislation issued at Armagh but disseminated throughout Ireland. This theoretically placed the clergy of every Irish church and monastery under Armagh's protection and, in so doing, bolstered the Patrician federation's claim to national primacy.[4] There is little doubt that it was drafted in imitation of, and in competition with, the *Lex Innocentium* of 697. Áed Allan's pro-Patrician stance became even more apparent a year or two later when the abbot of Armagh was angered by an assault on one of his churches by a band of men from the Dál Fiatach people of Ulster. He complained to Áed, who duly responded by defeating the Dál Fiatach in battle and beheading their king. In 737, Áed arranged a meeting on neutral territory with the powerful southern ruler Cathal mac Finguine, king of Munster, at which Cathal apparently accepted the terms of Patrick's Law, thereby implicitly acknowledging Armagh's authority over the churches of his kingdom. The reaction of the Columban federation to these developments can only be guessed at. Abbot Cilléne Droichtech might not have felt cheered by the growing ascendancy of Cenél nEógain, still less by the fate of the former Cenél Conaill king Flaithbertach. The latter, after losing or surrendering the overkingship, withdrew from secular life to become a monk at Armagh. We would probably have expected him to retire to a monastery within his own lands, to a satellite of Iona in Columba's old homeland of Donegal. The location of his new residence suggests an element of coercion, presumably by Áed Allan, as well as a symbolic victory for the heirs of Patrick.

The slaying of Áed Allan in 743, in battle with the Clann Cholmáin branch of the Southern Uí Néill, severely dented Cenél nEógain ambitions. It gave Iona an opportunity to realign its Irish interests in the wake of Cenél Conaill's decline. Ten years after Áed's demise we hear of a new ecclesiastical law being proclaimed by the Clann Cholmáin ruler Domnall Midi, paramount king of the Southern Uí Néill. This was issued as *Lex Coluim Cille*, 'The Law of Columba', and, although its clauses are unknown, it plainly represented a resurgence of Iona's influence and the acquisition of a new royal patron for the *familia* in Ireland.[5] Whatever specific aspects of morality or behaviour it covered, the Law would have ensured tangible benefits for both parties in the new alliance via obligatory payments from religious and secular communities. In this regard it would have been similar to *Lex Innocentium* or *Lex Patricii*, both of which demanded fines from transgressors and gifts of tribute from others.[6] The bond between Iona and Clann Cholmáin was further strengthened by Domnall's burial at the Columban daughter-house of Durrow in 763. In the following year a curious incident was noted in the annals: a pitched battle between Durrow and the neighbouring monastery of Clonmacnoise, the respective forces being led by rival princes of Clann Cholmáin. The conflict may have originated in dynastic strife rather than because of some disagreement between the monasteries but Durrow's favoured position among the Southern Uí Néill perhaps aroused jealousy and resentment at Clonmacnoise. We need not envisage a melee of spear-wielding monks but rather a battle involving warriors attached to the lay communities who resided at most major Irish monasteries. These men would have been indistinguishable from the armed retinues of the two competing princes. Both Durrow and Clonmacnoise probably housed a fairly large number of weapon-bearing dependents whom the abbots could summon to military service. If, as stated by the annalists, Durrow lost two hundred men in the battle, we can envisage a force of at least twice this number being available to the abbot. The monastery may have sent a contingent of similar size twelve years later, in 776, when its forces fought alongside Clann Cholmáin against enemies from Munster.

Cilléne Droichtech's lengthy headship of the Columban federation ended with his death in 752. His successor Sléibíne renewed *Lex Coluim Cille* during a visit to Ireland five years later. The next known renewal of the Law came in 778 in a joint proclamation by the southern overking Donnchad, son of Domnall Midi, and Abbot Bresal. Although the Law of Patrick was also renewed in this period, in 767, the strong friendship between Iona and Clann Cholmáin seems to have denied Armagh its claim to primacy through to the end of the century. In the early 800s, however, the situation began to change. A new distribution of secular and ecclesiastical power emerged with the transfer of political supremacy back to the North in the person of Áed Oirdnide of Cenél nEógain. In 804, Áed reaffirmed his family's old alliance with Armagh at a major synod and sponsored a renewal of the Law of Patrick two years later. His antagonism towards the Columban federation was displayed more openly in 817 when he ordered the murder of the abbot of Raphoe. Some historians suggest that the killing was undertaken in revenge for the death of Áed's brother in a battle against Cenél Conaill but, if so, it was a particularly cruel deed. A furious Columban leadership laid a curse on Áed, effectively excommunicating him, but such pronouncements had no remit among his Armagh allies. By then, in any case, the position of Iona within her own *paruchia* was already changing.

Kells and Dunkeld

The final decade of the eighth century heralded the first major phase of Viking raids on the British Isles. Iona was targeted at least once in the 790s and again in 802 when it was set on fire. In 806 another attack claimed the lives of 68 monks. The monastery's collection of high-status artefacts, many adorned with gold and silver, was an irresistible lure while its exposed position on a small Hebridean island left it pitifully vulnerable. Meanwhile, in Northumbria, the former Columban daughter-house on Lindisfarne had the dubious distinction of suffering the earliest recorded raid by a Viking force anywhere in the British Isles. Of the Irish satellites Lambay off the Dublin coast was the first to be assailed, in 795. Those further inland were less exposed and, in many cases, could rely on local secular powers to confront marauders. No such protection was available for any settlement –

religious or secular – whose remoteness left it beyond the reach of friendly patrons who might otherwise come to its defence. The raid on Iona in 806 would have highlighted this point to survivors of the slaughter. They nevertheless chose to stay on the island rather than leave it and relocate elsewhere. This fact is worth keeping in mind when we consider the annal entry for the following year:

> 807 The building of the new monastery of Colum Cille in Kells

The head of the Columban *familia* at that time was Cellach who had succeeded to the abbacy of Iona in 802. It is sometimes assumed that he ordered the construction of the monastery at Kells because of concerns about the Viking presence in the seaways, especially with regard to the vulnerability of his community's most treasured possessions. Kells has therefore been seen primarily as a refuge for those among the Iona brethren who regarded the island as too dangerous. The flaw in this assumption is that there was no simultaneous abandonment of Iona. What appears more likely is that Cellach took a course of action that his recent predecessors must also have contemplated: to gradually transfer the headquarters of the Columban *familia* to Ireland. Anxieties over the ambitions of Armagh, rather than fear of Viking raiders, may have been the main factor in Cellach's decision. He and his peers among the senior clergy on Iona perhaps felt that the interests of the federation would be best served from a base on the Irish mainland.[7] Kells, known in Gaelic as *Ceanannas Mór*, 'head abode' or 'chief residence', is in the Irish midlands, in the modern county of Meath. In 807 it lay in territory subject to Clann Cholmáin, the Southern Uí Néill dynasty whose kings had been favourable to Iona's interests in the eighth century. Although the dominance enjoyed by Clann Cholmáin had begun to shift northward by c.800 the dynasty still wielded great influence among its neighbours. Kells had probably been granted to the Columban *familia* at the height of Clann Cholmáin power, perhaps as a gift by King Donnchad before his death in 797.[8] Later tradition dated the grant slightly later, to 804, but the source may be unreliable. Lacking a precise chronology we can only guess that construction of the new monastery began in 807 and was completed, according to the annals, by 814. In that year, Cellach relinquished the abbacy of Iona and retired to Kells. Diarmait his successor stayed on the island, apparently to the end of his days, but resigned as abbot in 831. It was during Diarmait's abbacy that Viking marauders butchered a brave monk called Blathmac for refusing to reveal the location of Columba's ornamented tomb. After this, as far as we can tell, Iona ceased to be a target for the next fifty years. Moreover, by c.830, the Scandinavians who had previously arrived in the Hebrides as pirates were now settling as immigrants. Mingling and intermarrying with the natives, many of them adopted Gaelic speech and the Christian religion. By 825, when Blathmac suffered bloody martyrdom on Iona, it is likely that folk of Scandinavian stock were already venerating Columba on neighbouring islands.

The Book of Kells

In 1007, according to an entry in the *Annals of Ulster*, an object known as the 'Great Gospel of Colum Cille' was stolen from the monastic church at Kells. It was found some two and a half months later, buried in the earth and denuded of its gold fittings. This gospel-book is generally assumed to be the one now referred to as the Book of Kells, a magnificent example of early medieval craftsmanship preserved in the library of Trinity College, Dublin. Many of its pages are decorated with brightly coloured pictures and patterns reflecting a blend of Irish and Anglo-Saxon artistic styles. Analysis of the text and decoration points to c.800 for the date of composition, but a place of origin is harder to identify. The Columban monastery at Kells was built in the early ninth century and it is possible that the gospel-book was an early product of the scriptorium there. Alternatively, the volume may have been created on Iona before being brought to Kells after the first Viking raids on the island. Another possibility is that it was created on Lindisfarne and taken from there to Kells directly or via Iona. What is not in doubt is that the Book of Kells has no connection with Columba's time. The name bestowed on it in the *Annals of Ulster* – if it is indeed the same object as the 'Great Gospel of Colum Cille' – suggests rather that it was a prized possession of the Columban federation and not a relic of the founder.

Attacks on religious sites formed only one part of a wider, more sustained pattern of Scandinavian aggression which continued long after the oldest colonies became Gaelicised and Christianised. Raiding forces often penetrated far inland to wreak havoc across huge swathes of territory, especially when their leaders had political ambitions. The coastal skirmishes of the late eighth century gave way to large, set-piece battles in the ninth as Viking warlords strove to establish kingdoms of their own. By c.870, a large part of what is now eastern England lay under Scandinavian rule, as did many districts on the outer fringes of northern Britain. Orkney and Shetland were completely overrun and still preserve features of their 'Viking' heritage today. Meanwhile, in Dál Riata, the Scots faced difficulties not only from Scandinavian predators but from indigenous ones too. Although the sources give few details, it would appear that the old Gaelic-speaking kingdoms of the west had fallen under Pictish overlordship in the late eighth century, their leading *cenéla* acknowledging the rule of kings whose centres of power lay in what is now Perthshire. This political relationship gradually led to cultural exchanges across Druim Alban and to movements of people between Pictland and Dál Riata. From 800, as the Viking threat increased, an eastward migration of high-status Scots from the exposed western coastlands brought Gaelic speech to the upper tiers of Pictish society and, by some process we cannot yet identify, sent the Pictish language into terminal decline. Old ethnic and linguistic divisions began to fade and, by the middle of the ninth century, the Picts and Scots were merging together as one people. Political relationships between the two groups in this period are not easy to discern, partly because the sources frequently oversimplify the picture by presenting 'Picts' and 'Scots' as two homogeneous ethnic blocks. In reality, the situation is likely to have been much more fragmented and complicated, with some Dál Riatan elites continuing to acknowledge Pictish overlords while others did not. The Picts themselves were not a single political entity and still comprised at least two overkingships – a northern and a southern – divided by the eastern arm of the Grampian Mountains. What does not seem in doubt is that a Pictish overking was slain alongside his Dál Riatan vassal or ally in a great battle against Vikings in 839. This seems to have been a catastrophe with far-reaching consequences, not least of which was a period of dynastic strife involving rival claimants to one or more Pictish overkingships. The ensuing years saw a series of bitter contests as various competitors jostled for power. Where these men originated and where they played out their conflicts are questions that remain unanswered, but, by c.848, a new southern Pictish overking had emerged in the shape of Cináed mac Ailpín. Cináed may have arisen in the West, among the Scots of Dál Riata, and he was evidently a Gaelic-speaker. His name and his father's name look Pictish, but such an observation might be irrelevant or anachronistic in an era when ethnic identities were undoubtedly blurring. Whoever he was and wherever he came from, Cináed established his main centre of royal power in Perthshire, at Forteviot in Strathearn. He also exerted authority over some part of Dál Riata, perhaps in the Cenél nGabráin heartlands of Kintyre, for a later genealogical tradition linked him to this kindred. The connection, if it has historical merit, may explain his close association with Iona and her abbots, and with his nurturing of the cult of St Columba in his eastern domains.

Today, the impressive edifice of Dunkeld Cathedral stands on the site of a Pictish royal church selected by Cináed as a focus for patronage. Here he developed a saintly cult devoted to Columba, sanctifying the site by bringing bones and other relics from Iona. The project was undertaken in conjunction with Abbot Indrechtach, head of the Columban *familia*, who ordered Columba's grave to be opened and a portion of the venerable bones removed. Some went east to Dunkeld, some to Kells, while the rest remained in their tomb-shrine or reliquary. The redistribution was noted by the annalists:

> 849 Indrechtach, abbot of Iona, came to Ireland with the relics of Columcille[9]

A couple of interesting observations can be made about this event. First, although geography makes Kells seem slightly less vulnerable than Iona, it still lay within a day's march of the coast and would have been an easy target for seaborne raiders. Clearly, the relics that arrived in 849 were not sent there for reasons of safety. Nor were they accompanied by a mass exodus of Iona's inhabitants. It is far more likely that Indrechtach brought relics to Kells because it was becoming the new headquarters of the Columban federation. The great gospel-book now known as the Book of Kells also probably arrived at this time, perhaps from the library on Iona. If so, then other precious volumes no doubt accompanied it, together with much else that was valuable and portable. The old island monastery was not, however, totally denuded of her possessions. Life went on for those monks who chose to stay behind. To continue their duties and rituals on even a basic level they would have needed books, vestments and vessels for mass, together with tools for farming and other labours. They also required leadership, and this was provided by the continuing presence of an abbot who remained – for a while longer – the head of the *familia*. The mantle of leadership had not yet made the final move across the Irish Sea. Kells, although now earmarked as the new headquarters, was not yet the permanent residence of the federation's most senior cleric. Just as Cellach, the builder of Kells, had continued to dwell on Iona so also did Indrechtach regard the island as his home, even while endowing the Meath monastery with relics. Indrechtach was the first abbot of Iona to be described by the annalists as Columba's *comarba*, 'successor', a title rendered in Latin as *heres*. Tragically, the entry which accords him this title notes his slaying by English assailants while on a journey in Britain. The place of his martyrdom is unknown, but he may be the 'St Indract' venerated and reputedly entombed at Glastonbury Abbey in Somerset.[10]

Another transfer of relics to Ireland occurred in 878 during a period when Iona again became a target for raids. Among the items that left on this occasion was the portable shrine of Columba – a reliquary containing some of his bones. Its removal must have been hugely symbolic for it bore away almost the last of the founder's mortal remains, most probably to Kells. Even then, there was still no complete abandonment of Iona. The monks who lingered maintained the ancient link with the Hebridean zone, an area whose population was increasingly adopting a hybrid Gaelic-Scandinavian identity.

Comarba

In 880, the abbacy of Iona passed to Flann, son of Maelduin, who held it for eleven years. He was the last to lead the Columban federation from the ancient mother-church. With his death in 891 the headship finally moved to Ireland, never to return to its original home. Rather remarkably, Flann was succeeded as 'abbot of Iona' by none other than the abbot of Armagh. Given the long-standing rivalry between Armagh and Iona, it might seem strange that the head of the Patrician *familia* should be appointed *comarba* or 'successor' of Columba, but the appointee's blood and ancestry seem to have swung the nomination in his favour. A list of Patrick's successors preserved in the Book of Leinster says that the new Columban *comarba*, Máel Brigte mac Tornáin, sprang from Cenél Conaill. He was thus a member of the royal kindred to which so many Iona abbots had belonged. To the same information was added a note or gloss implying that kinship was indeed the key factor in the *hoentad* or 'union' of the two federations.[11] Beyond this we know nothing of the circumstances behind the appointment. It would be interesting to learn, for instance, whether the impetus came from Iona or from Armagh, and to which *familia* Máel Brigte's personal allegiance lay. What does not appear to be in doubt is that the Columban hierarchy regarded the Cenél Conaill ancestry of the new *comarba* as more important than his recent career path. Notwithstanding his Armagh connections, Máel Brigte maintained a symbolic link with the Columban past by adopting the title *abb Iae*, 'abbot of Iona', in spite of his choosing to dwell in Ireland. Nevertheless, the physical separation of a monastic federation's headship from the founder's principal church was unprecedented. It was an odd situation, but one that was made easier by the removal of Columba's bones from Iona to Ireland.

Máel Brigte led the unified Patrician and Columban federations for more than thirty years, perhaps from his old abbatial seat at Armagh. After his death in 927, the two *familiae* uncoupled once more, each appointing its own individual *comarba*. Cenél Conaill leadership of the Columban network was maintained by the appointment of Máel Brigte's cousin Dubthach whom the annalists describe as 'successor of Colum Cille and Adomnán'.[12] As Dubthach is nowhere given the ancient title 'abbot of Iona', his appointment might mark another significant break with the past: a separation of the *comarba* from the office of *abb Iae*. The latter still continued, but its incumbent was no longer the head of the federation. Thus, in the time of Dubthach's successor, the annalists noted the death of an Iona abbot who was not simultaneously *comarba* of the *familia* as a whole. By then, the federation's headquarters already lay at Kells. It is worth reminding ourselves again, with regard to the choice of site, that Kells was by no means a safe haven for the Columban community's leadership nor for its most treasured possessions. The monastery was raided by Vikings in 920, when monks were slaughtered, and again in 951 when several thousand inhabitants were captured as slaves. Further attacks came in 969 and 970, on both occasions by Scandinavian and Irish warriors raiding together. Although the participation of Irish forces in a raid on a religious site might seem unsettling to modern eyes, the Kells brethren were no strangers to aggression from their own countrymen.

In spite of relinquishing its role as the federation's headquarters, Iona still retained special status as the ancient mother-church. Pilgrims still visited the island, some to live among the remaining brethren as penitents. The famous Viking warlord Anlaf Sihtricsson, surnamed *Cuarán*, 'Sandal', came there to spend his final years in atonement for past sins. He died on Iona in 980, having presumably received forgiveness for leading the raid on Kells ten years earlier. Anlaf's choosing to dwell on Iona did not, however, mark a more general change of attitude among the Vikings. In a raid on the island six years after his death, the abbot and fifteen elders were killed. By a gruesome coincidence, a raid on Dublin in the same year claimed the life of the head of the *familia*.[13]

In 989, the Columban and Patrician federations were once again united under a single *comarba*, this being the aged Dub-da-leithe, abbot of Armagh. Unlike Máel Brigte, who had held the dual headship sixty years earlier, the new incumbent was not of Cenél Conaill blood. The annalists added the curious information that the appointment was approved by *fer nErenn & Alban*, 'the men of Ireland and Scotland'. At that time, the Gaelic-speaking kingdom of Scots and Picts, forged by Cináed mac Ailpín in the 840s, had acquired the name *Alba*. The 'men' of Alba who sanctioned the appointment of St Patrick's *comarba* to the headship of both *familiae* were presumably the leading Columban clergy of the Scottish kingdom, specifically the *seniores* at Iona and Dunkeld. By then, of course, Dunkeld was already yielding power and influence in Alba to St Andrews, a Pictish monastery on the Fife coast that was rapidly becoming the premier royal church for Cináed's descendants. Dub-da-leithe's appointment should probably be seen in the light of Armagh's quest for ecclesiastical primacy in Ireland, an ambition sustained after his death in 998. The two federations divided again and each appointed its own successor to Dub-da-leithe but, as before, the new Columban *comarba* was a high-ranking monk of Armagh.

The early years of the eleventh century saw the Columban *familia* maintaining its links with the Clann Cholmáin dynasty of the Southern Uí Néill at a time when both were losing ground to rivals. Brian Bóruma, the powerful ruler of Munster, took the high kingship of

Ireland and held it until his death at the battle of Clontarf in 1014. Just as his supremacy pushed the Southern Uí Néill aside, so also did his close friendship with Armagh give the Patrician federation the primacy it had sought for so long. After Brian's death, the ecclesiastical authority of the successors of St Patrick remained a potent force throughout the whole of Ireland. Thus, when an ambitious abbot of Clonard – the *comarba* of St Finnian – boldly claimed the headship of the Columban *familia* in the 1040s it was not Kells but Armagh that put him in his place. Nor was his claim cast out by word or letter or deliberation of a synod: it was forcefully extinguished on a battlefield in Meath by military forces of the Patrician federation.[14] In this period the headship of the Columban churches appears to have become an almost hereditary position, with instances where it passed to the son of a previous holder of the post. This would not have seemed strange to eleventh-century eyes, for celibacy was no longer a requirement of high monastic office as it had been in earlier times. Thus, while Ségéne, Adomnán and other great names among the successors of Columba had maintained a chaste existence, the same cannot always be said of those who followed them in the headship after it moved to Kells. It would appear that a Columban *comarba* of the eleventh and twelfth centuries was not even required to be in holy orders. How this change came about is unknown, but it seems to reflect a wider pattern of secularisation among the Irish ecclesiastical elite at a time when co-operation between kings and senior churchmen was perhaps much closer than it had been hitherto.[15] One drawback of any hereditary system is a son's expectation to follow in his father's footsteps, and bitter disappointment if his path is blocked and the succession denied. Hostility and envy often arise in such circumstances and might have been catalysts for a shocking incident that occurred in 1070, when a son of the Columban *comarba* murdered the abbot of Iona. Perhaps the killer had been a candidate for the Iona abbacy who, having been pushed aside, vented his frustration on the new appointee?[16] Whatever its precise circumstances, the tragedy confirms Iona's continuing importance in the federation's hierarchy, if only as a stepping-stone on the career paths of ambitious men.

Nonetheless, it is clear that the old monastery was now subordinate to Kells. As the eleventh century progressed, it seems also to have been overtaken in importance by Durrow. This shift in status within the *paruchia* was inevitable in an era when major Irish monasteries were amassing great wealth and power. Iona had no hope of attaining a similar level of prosperity. At Kells, for instance, the acquisition of new lands for the monastic estate seem to have been the main preoccupation of the abbot and his *seniores* in the eleventh and twelfth centuries. Other projects may have seemed less pressing, especially those that drew the abbot's attention further afield. Thus, we see little evidence that a typical Columban *comarba* in this period made regular visits to the churches of the *paruchia*. He was probably too busy with matters nearer home, not least with the fallout from political instability in the Irish midlands. At Kells it is possible that many of the religious duties formerly undertaken by the abbot were now delegated to the Céli Dé, a group of monks who lived in the monastery's hermitage as a sub-community.[17] Céli Dé, 'Clients of God', was the name given to a reformist movement that originated in southern Ireland in the eighth century. Its devotees sought a return to the old monastic ideals of austerity, discipline and prayer. Their views appealed to those who wished to turn back the clock to an age when the respective interests of secular and ecclesiastical elites were more clearly defined. At what point they formed a sub-community among the brethren at Kells is unknown, but they were already on Iona by 800 and at Dunkeld fifty years later. The Céli Dé who dwelt at Kells may have viewed the expansion of the monastery's business interests with disdain, especially in the twelfth century when it operated its own market. To the pious, austere inhabitants of the hermitage the rest of the monastic precinct must have seemed, at times, less like a religious centre and more like a venue for commercial transactions. It would not be inaccurate to describe twelfth-century Kells as a kind of urban settlement, a monastic 'town'.[18] With its abbot seemingly immersed in running his vast estate, and with the surrounding lands so beset by warfare that the monastery was repeatedly attacked and burned, Kells was becoming increasingly unsuited to its leading role among the Columban churches. A new *comarba* was plainly required, and a new headquarters for the federation.

Derry

The prominence accorded to Kells by the sources tends to obscure our view of what was happening elsewhere in the Columban *paruchia*. Durrow's location in the Irish midlands meant that it was affected, to some extent, by the same political instability that affected Kells. We thus know something of Durrow's history in the ninth to twelfth century, just as we know a few facts about Iona and Dunkeld in the same period. Of other Columban settlements we receive occasional snippets of information from the annals, but the overall picture remains dominated by Kells until c.1100. It is around this time that the focus begins to shift north, to Columba's own likely foundation at Derry. Hitherto, the annalists have given us occasional obituary notices for Derry clergymen without adding much about the monastery's role in relation to wider patterns of religious and secular events. Not until the end of the eleventh century do we start to gain a clearer idea of what was happening there.

Derry had long lain under the patronage of Cenél Conaill, a relationship that apparently continued into the late 1000s when the rival kindred of Cenél nEógain once more regained the northern supremacy. Cenél nEógain, as we have already observed, had been the main royal patrons of Armagh from the late eighth century. Three hundred years later, the Cenél nEógain king Domnall mac Lochlainn began to develop a close association with Derry by drawing it away from Cenél Conaill, whom he brought under his overlordship in the early 1100s. Domnall may have been hoping to boost Derry's profile when he nominated it as the principal church of a new episcopal diocese based on Cenél Conaill territory, but, if so, his hopes were dashed when Raphoe was chosen instead. This was one decision of a national synod where a major reorganisation of Irish churches was agreed by delegates from all over the country. This important gathering, convened in 1111, was held at Rath Breasail in modern County Laois. It led to fundamental changes that were considered necessary to bring Ireland into line with current ecclesiastical developments in England and on the Continent. The synod effectively ended the old monastic structure of the past by dividing Ireland into episcopal dioceses. Some twenty-four were created, each under the authority of a bishop who was no longer answerable to the abbot of a powerful monastery. The dioceses were grouped under two archbishoprics, a northern one centred on Armagh and a southern one centred on Cashel in Munster. There can be no doubt that the reorganisation marked another triumph for the Patrician federation which could now claim unchallenged leadership of all northern Irish churches. Its *comarba* at that time was Cellach, a dynamic figure who had previously united the roles of abbot and bishop of Armagh to himself. The Synod of Rath Breasail not only confirmed him as archbishop of the north but also placed him above his Cashel counterpart in status, thereby giving his *familia* the prize it had always sought: ecclesiastical primacy across the whole of Ireland. But the Columban federation – Armagh's old rival in the contest for primacy – was soon to gain from these developments. In 1137, Cellach's successor as *comarba* of Patrick and primate of all Ireland resigned from his post. Before giving up his chair, he chose as his replacement Gilla Mac Liag, the abbot of Columban Derry.[19]

Prior to attaining the archbishopric of Armagh, Gilla Mac Liag had not been accorded the rank of bishop. Domnall mac Lochlainn's efforts to make Derry an episcopal centre for the Cenél Conaill lands had ultimately come to naught at Rath Breasail when Raphoe was selected instead. After Domnall's death Derry had therefore remained a monastery, its brethren still led by an abbot rather than by a bishop. Under the national reorganisation it was placed under the bishop of Cenél nEógain whose seat lay at Maghera 25 miles eastward. However, Derry's star began to rise after 1137 when its former abbot Gilla mac Liag became archbishop of Armagh and nominal head of the entire Irish Church. The image of Kells, by contrast, seems to have been tarnished by its commercial interests, by the secularisation of its senior clergy and by the political instability of its region. Although the Columban churches had continued to regard Kells as the hub of their *familia* throughout the tenth and eleventh centuries, their allegiance to its abbot could no longer be taken for granted. Visitors were no doubt dismayed by what they saw there. The federation may have demanded a change of leadership and, in 1150, a new abbot was appointed at Derry with the title *comarba Coluim Chille*. It is possible that he took the title upon himself, without seeking a mandate from the rest of the *familia*, knowing that he could count on powerful support from a former Derry abbot in the person of Archbishop Gilla mac Liag.[20] The new *comarba*, Flaithbertach Ua Brolcháin of Cenél nEógain, had no genealogical link to Columba's kindred of Cenél Conaill nor to their southern cousins who had long been the royal patrons of Kells. Flaithbertach came from a different kin-group, and was also possibly the son of an earlier bishop of Armagh. The appointment of such a man as head of the Columban federation signalled another break with the past.

Whether or not any other churches of the Columban *paruchia* played a role in relocating the headship away from Kells is hard to judge. Those in the north presumably acknowledged Flaithbertach's status after he made an effort to visit them between 1150 and 1153. The Columban churches further south may have been slower to follow suit, their tardiness perhaps nudging the Archbishop of Armagh to intervene. In 1158, Gilla mac Liag convened a synod which decreed that every Columban church in Ireland must recognise Flaithbertach as 'arch-abbot'.[21] The same gathering also gave the *comarba* special status by giving him the same kind of authority over his geographically dispersed federation as that exercised by a bishop within a defined territorial diocese. Although the Columban *paruchia* already included two recently-created episcopal sees at Kells and Raphoe, these can probably be seen as subordinate to the abbot of Derry after 1158. In the ecclesiastical hierarchy envisaged by Gilla mac Liag their bishops were no doubt regarded as lower in rank than the *comarba*. One curious event during Flaithbertach's headship came in 1164 when a delegation from Iona came to Derry to offer him the ancient title *abb Iae*. The emissaries were led by senior figures from the old Hebridean monastery: the lector, the arch-priest, the chief hermit and the head of the Céli Dé. We might expect that a request from such high-level visitors to accept the abbacy of Iona would have been accepted with gratitude by a 'successor' of Columba. Besides, the invitation was undoubtedly a symbolic gesture rather than a serious attempt to entice the headship of the *familia* back across the sea. Needless to say, it was firmly rejected by Flaithbertach's powerful backers: Archbishop Gilla mac Liag and the king of Cenél nEógain. These two, no doubt, were suspicious of the motives behind it. They would have been aware, for instance, that Iona's secular patron was now the fearsome Somerled, one of the most famous warlords of the late Viking Age. As ruler of a large maritime domain encompassing much of the Hebridean zone, Somerled was a lurking menace in the seaways around Ireland. He already controlled the Isle of Man, having seized it by force. A link between his ambitions and the delegation from Iona to Derry in 1164 cannot be ruled out. The annalists seem to hint as much when they note that Iona's invitation to Flaithbertach came 'in accordance with the wishes of Somerled and the men of Argyll and the Isles'. The Cenél nEógain elite, together with their churchmen at Derry and Armagh, may have been deeply concerned. In rejecting the invitation they were perhaps sending a stern message to Somerled to keep his nose out of Irish affairs.

Such anxieties were soon eclipsed by events nearer home. The monastery at Derry suffered severe damage in a great fire in 1166. In the following year, the power of Cenél nEógain was broken in a battle with the king of Connacht who imposed his overlordship. Far more profound, however, was the impact of a military venture of a different kind: the Anglo-Norman invasion of Ireland in 1169. This dealt a mortal blow to the native political framework by disrupting the traditional alliances between royal dynasties and ecclesiastical elites. Churches and monasteries in districts seized by Anglo-Norman lords were detached from their ancient *paruchiae* to be redistributed among clerical friends of the conquerors. A broad swathe of territory centred on Dublin bore

The Normans

In 1166, the exiled Leinster king Diarmait mac Murchada, 'Dermot MacMurrough', asked King Henry II of England for military aid to regain his position in Ireland. Henry was a descendant of William I, 'The Conqueror', who had become the first Norman king of England a hundred years earlier. Henry granted Diarmait's request and allowed him to recruit a number of Anglo-Norman knights who invaded south-east Ireland in 1169. The invaders swiftly conquered Leinster and restored Diarmait before creating small Irish lordships of their own. Their leader Robert de Clare, known as 'Strongbow', married Diarmait's daughter and was adopted as his heir. In 1171, the year of Diarmait's death, King Henry himself landed in Waterford at the head of a large army. The kings of Ireland submitted to him before the end of the year. In 1172, the Irish ecclesiastical elite agreed to administer their monasteries and bishoprics in the way these institutions were administered in England. Henry's overlordship was subsequently rejected by native kings in Ulster and Munster, but a series of military campaigns mounted from Leinster eventually brought Ireland under the Anglo-Norman yoke. By c.1200 the conquest was all but complete.

the brunt of the initial assault and religious settlements in this region were among the first to be taken. Kells was attacked and plundered before becoming the site of a military stronghold. Other Columban sites such as Swords, Moone and Lambay Island were handed over to pro-Norman bishops. From his residence at Derry the *comarba* Flaithbertach could do little but watch in dismay as the federation was broken up. He could no longer rely on the support of strong protectors, for the ascendancy of Cenél nEógain was over and new patterns of power were developing in the wake of the Anglo-Norman onslaught. Flaithbertach's mentor Gilla mac Liag, archbishop of Armagh, died in 1174, pre-deceasing the *comarba* himself by one year. By then, the Columban *paruchia* had effectively ceased to exist in any real sense. A new *comarba* was appointed, but the title was now purely symbolic and his remit barely extended beyond the monastic estate of Derry.

The later history of Iona

Iona's abortive attempt to confer her vacant abbacy on the *comarba* at Derry in 1164 signalled the end of her direct involvement in Irish ecclesiastical affairs. It was not, however, the last act in her long relationship with Columba's homeland. In 1203, when Iona was headed by an abbot with the familiar name Cellach, it became an abbey of the Benedictine Order under the patronage of Ragnall, Lord of the Isles, a son of Somerled. Construction of the new buildings began at the end of the same year, but something about the work displeased the leaders of the former Columban churches in northern Ireland, even though the old federation was now a thing of the past. At Derry, an annalist voiced the outrage of his superiors in emotive words:

> A monastery was built by Cellach in the centre of the enclosure of Iona, without any right, in dishonour of the community of Iona, so that he wrecked the place greatly.[21]

Why the Irish felt such hostility towards Cellach's project is uncertain, for he had been granted the right to build an abbey by the Pope himself. Papal permission did not, however, grant sufficient protection from those who disapproved. In 1204, a formidable Irish quartet came to Iona at the head of an armed force and completely destroyed the new structure. One of the four was the abbot of Armagh, but the others represented former daughter-houses of Iona: Amalgaid, abbot of Derry, together with the bishops of Derry and Raphoe. Cellach was expelled and Amalgaid took his place as abbot. Nevertheless, the new abbey was completed and the Benedictines took charge. Amalgaid's period in office may have been short, for we hear no more of him. By then, in any case, the abbey was orientated towards Scotland rather than Ireland. In 1247, its primary dedication was referenced in a letter from the Pope who mentioned 'the monastery of St Columba of the order of Saint Benedict', but this was not so much a nod to the past as recognition of the reason why pilgrims still wanted to visit the island. Thus, although the abbey church had a separate dedication to the Virgin Mary, it housed a shrine containing Columba's relics, or rather those few relics that had not been removed from the island during earlier redistributions.

At some point in the thirteenth century a nunnery was built a little way south of the abbey. It had its own church and seems to have operated as a more or less independent institution. The chapel of St Ronan's was erected next to the nunnery to serve the lay population as a parish church. By then, the island was no longer exclusively clerical as it had been in former times. Abbey, nunnery and parish church were no doubt well established by c.1250, but a strange void appears in the documentary record after this time. We next hear of Iona in 1320 when the annals report the passing of Abbot Fionnlagh. He may have been responsible for some of the alterations to the abbey church that took place around 1300, these probably being necessary to accommodate increasing numbers of pilgrims and visitors.

During the Later Middle Ages, from c.1300 to the Reformation, Iona Abbey flourished under the patronage of the Lords of the Isles. A steady stream of pilgrims continued to visit the relics of St Columba. In fact, so great was this traffic that the abbey church had to be altered again, in the middle of the fifteenth century, under the direction of Abbot Dominic. Later in the same century, however, the abbey's fortunes begin to decline, the first major setback coming in 1493 when the Lordship of the Isles was absorbed into the kingdom of Scotland. Six years later, Iona became the seat of the new bishopric of the Isles, but the ecclesiastical autonomy and spiritual authority of former times were gone. The abbey church was refurbished again c.1500, but, by then, it was little more than an outpost on the western fringe of the kingdom of Scotland.

During the turmoil of the Reformation it was attacked by a destructive mob and never recovered. In the wake of the assault, which seems to have taken place in 1561, the abbey went the way of all Scottish monasteries. It was dissolved by the Protestant authorities and abandoned to dereliction. Within a hundred years it was a decaying ruin and remained so until the end of the nineteenth century when its owner, the Duke of Argyll, gave it to the Church of Scotland. Funds were raised for restoration and the work commenced in 1902. The twentieth century saw the costly, time-consuming project being completed in phases, the last of which was completed in 1965. Since then, the abbey has housed the Iona Community, an ecumenical religious organisation founded by the Reverend George MacLeod in 1938. Among the Community's many activities are residential courses involving education, worship and communal living, all of which maintain a strong sense of continuity with the island's past. The restored buildings, together with other features and structures nearby, continue to attract large numbers of tourists, many of whom find themselves drawn to the spiritual aura of Iona like the pilgrim travellers of old.

The fates of the daughter-houses

Other major centres of the erstwhile Columban federation endured their own tribulations in the later Middle Ages. At Derry, the era of Anglo-Norman rule turned the old monastery into a settlement of Augustinian monks under the authority of a bishop whose secular patrons were the kings of Cenél nEógain. In the late thirteenth century the latter lost much of their hegemony to the Norman earls of Ulster, the de Burgh family, who had risen to become the new power in northern Ireland. Derry soon fell under the sway of the de Burghs, but reverted to native control a hundred years later and remained so until the early 1600s when Protestant English forces seized the Augustinian monastery and its lands. This brought an end to a thousand years of religious settlement and ushered in a new phase in Derry's history. The place was turned into a city with a new population of English and Scottish colonists. These folk worshipped in St Columb's Cathedral, a Protestant foundation built in 1633, and their descendants still congregate there today. The cathedral's dedication to Derry's reputed founder preserves a measure of continuity with *Daire Calgach* of old.

Elsewhere in northern Ireland the former daughter-house at Raphoe in Donegal has enjoyed the longest period of continuity of any site within the old Columban *paruchia*. It continued as the seat of a bishopric throughout the medieval period and beyond, surviving even the depredations of the Reformation. Today, the site of the monastery reputedly founded by Adomnán is occupied by St Eunan's Cathedral, a Protestant church bearing a dedication in an Anglicised form of his name. The Catholic bishop of Raphoe now resides in a modern cathedral 8 miles to the north-west at Letterkenny. Further south, neither Durrow nor Kells enjoyed the same longevity as Derry or Raphoe. Durrow effectively ceased to be an ecclesiastical site after an Anglo-Norman warlord built a castle there in the late twelfth century. At around the same time the monastery at Kells was closed and its church downgraded to become the parish church of the district. What became of any bones or other relics of Columba that had been preserved by the monks is unknown. Only one relic, the famous Book of Kells, remained *in situ* at the church after the monks had gone. It stayed there for another four hundred years until the mid-seventeenth century when it passed into the care of Dublin's Trinity College.

In Scotland, the monastery at Dunkeld continued to benefit from royal patronage under the descendants of Cináed mac Ailpín. After the upheavals of the Viking Age it retained a position of importance despite relinquishing its claim to be the premier church of the kings of Alba. That mantle, as we have already noted, passed to St Andrews in the tenth century. After Alba became the core of the new kingdom of Scotland in the eleventh and twelfth centuries, Dunkeld maintained its role and was eventually given cathedral status. Its claim to still possess some of Columba's bones attracted pilgrims throughout the medieval period and, curiously, today's folklore asserts that the relics were secretly hidden in the grounds during the Reformation of the sixteenth century. In reality, whatever relics were still kept at Dunkeld at that time were probably taken to Ireland. The present-day cathedral is essentially a building of the fourteenth century with later additions. It suffered considerable damage during the Reformation, but was repaired soon after to be designated as the parish church of the town that had by then grown around it. It remains in use today for the same purpose.

CHAPTER 9
Legacy

Saints and cults

The history of the Columban *paruchia* begins with the foundation of Iona's first daughter-houses in the late sixth century and ends six hundred years later with the Anglo-Norman invasion of Ireland and the unravelling of the great monastic federations. Individual Columban churches on both sides of the Irish Sea thereafter continued in existence until, and in some cases beyond, the Reformation of the sixteenth and seventeenth centuries. We have noted long continuity at major sites such as Iona, Derry and Dunkeld throughout the Middle Ages and into modern times. Here, and at certain other places of lesser fame, the ancient connection with Columba was never forgotten. Devotion to the founder was maintained by clergy and congregation alike, in spite of the ever-widening gulf of years that lay between. Out of this devotion grew one of the most enduring saintly cults in the British Isles.

Veneration of holy men and women long after their passing from the world is a key characteristic of Christianity. Ancient pagan civilisations, such as the pre-Christian Roman Empire, did not accord such devotion to dead priests and priestesses. Deification of great rulers and the worship of ancestors were fairly common in paganism, but the Christian practice of praying to a saint was something new and different. Its origins lay in the third century, in the time of the persecutions at Rome and elsewhere, when places where early martyrs had been slain or buried were honoured by local Christians. At this stage, however, Christianity lacked any concept of sacred sites, deeming this to be linked to pagan worship of natural phenomena.[1] In early

Christian belief the physical world was distinct from the spiritual world and nothing within it was endowed with holiness. This mode of thinking remained unchanged until the fourth century when Christianity became the official religion of the Empire during the reign of Constantine the Great. Constantine erected churches in Palestine at places traditionally associated with significant events in the life and Resurrection of Christ. Pilgrims from all over the Empire came to visit these sites and soon the concept of the Christian holy place was born. This eventually extended beyond Palestine to encompass sites associated with the early martyrs who, as paragons of virtue, were seen as holding special status in Heaven. Martyrs' graves came to be seen as nodal points connecting the living pilgrim to the deceased. Prayers were offered in the hope that the spirit of the holy person or 'saint' (Latin: *sanctus*) would act as intermediary between the pilgrim and God. Out of this hope the idea of the saintly cult arose. The new development was not, however, a throwback to pagan practice, for Christianity held that a saint could not be worshipped in his or her own right. Christian worship was reserved solely for God, but a saint could be called upon – through prayer – to intercede on the supplicant's behalf. As time went on, sainthood came to be bestowed not only on martyrs but also on other holy folk. It was often applied in purely local contexts by communities wishing to remember an individual who had been active in developing Christianity in a specific district. The tombs of these minor saints were frequently enshrined in a church which then became the focus of a localised cult. A belief that miracles could happen at these shrines started to take shape, as did the idea that touching the tomb or other objects associated with the saint might be enough to cure illness or bring good fortune. Items used by the saint in life – such as clothing – and even bones from the grave were venerated at the shrine or taken elsewhere to bring the cult to a wider community. Some holy relics travelled great distances across Christendom, often being carried by missionaries despatched from a particular cult-centre. Relics of saints whose centres of devotion lay in Continental Europe were already circulating in Britain and Ireland in the sixth century when the first indigenous cults began to appear.[2]

It is not known which home-grown British or Irish saint was the first to acquire a cult of his or her own. Patrick, a Briton, lived in the fifth century and was certainly one of the earliest Insular saints. It is possible that an embryonic cult arose among his followers in Ireland immediately after his death, but, if so, we have no firm evidence for it. At the beginning of the sixth century St Ciarán of Clonmacnoise was active in the Irish midlands, but, again, we cannot be sure that a devotional cult grew around him at that time. Ciarán was a contemporary of St Brigid whose death in her monastery at Kildare was dated by the annalists to c.525. Although her cult is unlikely to have formed at so early a date, there are hints that both she and Patrick were being venerated in Ireland by c.600. A seventh-century *vita* of Brigid, written by Cogitosus, describes her tomb at Kildare as a focus of devotion for local people and as a place where prayers might be answered. Hagiography written about Patrick in the same century locates his grave at Downpatrick, but the main collection of his 'secondary' relics, including his bell, lay at Armagh which was already promoting itself as his primary cult-centre. Armagh may have justified its position by claiming special authority vested in possession of Apostolic relics supposedly brought to Ireland by Patrick himself.[3]

The cult of St Columba

In Chapter 1 we noted that stories of a legendary nature were being told about Columba from as early as the beginning of the seventh century, if not indeed while he was still alive in the final years of the sixth. There we observed that the praise-poem *Amra Coluim Chille* is the earliest known literary product of the cult that grew around him after his death. We also referred to the role played by Abbot Ségéne in gathering information from various informants, including the Bernician king Oswald, and to the ensuing collection of miracle-stories in Cumméne's book. Long before the publication of *Vita Columbae* at the end of the seventh century, Iona's founder had already achieved sainthood in the eyes of his disciples. It was, nevertheless, largely due to Adomnán that veneration of Columba was carried far beyond the places where it had begun. Before embarking on his great hagiographical project, Adomnán had already acknowledged the importance of cult-centres in an earlier work called *De Locis Sanctis*, 'On The Holy Places'. This was essentially an eyewitness report of sacred sites in Palestine and elsewhere. It was written by Adomnán from notes taken during conversations with Arculf, a Frankish bishop, who visited Iona sometime in the 680s.[4] Arculf told Adomnán of his nine-month sojourn in the Holy Land and described what he had seen there. What emerged from their discourse was a traveller's tale of journeys to exotic locations that few, if any, of Iona's inhabitants would ever see. As well as visiting iconic sites such as Jerusalem and Bethlehem, Arculf had also been to Alexandria, Constantinople, Damascus and Rome. His recollections as reported by Adomnán seem, at first glance, to provide a view of the origin-centres of Christianity through the eyes of a seventh-century Western clergyman. Bede was so impressed by *De Locis Sanctis* that he wrote his own abridged version from a copy presented to Jarrow by Adomnán himself.[5] Historians and archaeologists have long regarded Arculf's testimony as valuable contemporary information on the Holy Land during the earliest phase of Muslim rule. How much of *De Locis Sanctis* is actually based on Arculf's experiences rather than on Adomnán's input is a matter of debate that lies outside our present study. Of more relevance here is what the book might say about Adomnán's opinions on the veneration of sacred sites. It may reflect his preferred policy, as abbot of Iona and head of the Columban federation, towards sites and objects associated with Columba. That he did indeed regard certain objects as worthy of veneration is implied by his mention in *De Locis Sanctis* of a painted image of St George being a focus for prayer in Constantinople.[6]

It is in *Vita Columbae*, however, that Adomnán's literary promotion of Columba took shape. His description of the founder's grave on Iona suggests that he approved of the site's use in devotional rituals. Likewise, his allusions to the supernatural qualities of books written in Columba's own hand suggest that he regarded veneration of a saint's portable relics as appropriate. The role played by the *Vita* in spreading the cult of Columba cannot, in fact, be overstated. Not only did it become a well-known text throughout Britain and Ireland, but its influence spread to mainland Europe. Copies were circulating in the Frankish monasteries of Gaul and Germany before 800, having been carried there by Irish monks who came as pilgrims, scholars and missionaries.

An important aspect of the earliest manifestation of the cult of Columba was the protection granted by him in death to his living disciples in the monasteries of the *paruchia*. We see this protection being requested, through prayer, in seventh-century poetry attributed to Beccán of Rum. Like secular verses in which a king's power is highlighted by his ability to protect the bards of his court, so Beccán's two poems on Columba depict him as spiritual guardian of his followers.[7] Similar protection was granted by an apparition of the dead saint to King Oswald on the eve of his great battle against Cadwallon in 634. As we shall see below, the notion that Columba could be invoked as an aid to military victory persisted long after Oswald's time.

Relics and dedications

In medieval Scotland, Columba was elevated to the status of a patron saint on a par with St Andrew. Both were invoked as protectors of Scottish armies in wars against foreign foes, especially when the latter were invaders from England. Thus, in the fourteenth century, the monks of Inchcolm (Gaelic: *Innis Choluim*), 'Columba's isle' in the Firth of Forth, beseeched their eponymous patron to 'save the choir which sings your praise from the assaults of Englishmen and from the taunts of foes'.[8] A more direct participation by the saint in Scotland's wars came in 1314 when an object containing some of his relics – presumably bones – was carried into battle at Bannockburn. This was the mysterious *Breccbennach*, 'speckled peaked thing', traditionally identified as the Monymusk Reliquary, now held in the National Museums of Scotland. After Bannockburn, the abbot of Arbroath gave the Breccbennach to a keeper at Forglen in Aberdeenshire on condition that the object be borne in war to confer Columba's blessing on the Scottish army. The Monymusk Reliquary, a small wooden casket with an outer covering of metal, was made c.750 as a house-shaped shrine. Its claim to be the famous battle-talisman containing Columba's relics is based not only on its antiquity but on the characteristically Irish style of its decoration. What it once contained is unknown – it is now empty – but it long resided at Monymusk House, some 30 miles south of Forglen, before being purchased for the Museum of Scotland in 1933. Another object linking Columba to victory in war was the *Cathbuaid*, 'Battle Triumph', a crozier said to have been used by him in life. This was carried as a standard in the front rank of the Scottish army in 904, in an encounter with Viking marauders, its presence bringing victory as a reward for prayer and fasting on the eve of battle.[9] According to the annalists this was not the only occasion when the crozier brought military success, for in the late *Fragmentary Annals of Ireland*, it was said that the Scots 'have often won victory in battle with it'. Sadly, its present whereabouts are unknown, nor is there any other record of its use in battle. A third object with similar attributes shows that Columba's posthumous ability to influence the tides of war was not confined to Scotland. This was the *Cathach*, 'Battler', a psalter reputedly written in his own hand. It is preserved today among the collections of the Royal Irish Academy where it holds special status as possibly the oldest surviving manuscript written in Gaelic, its creation having been dated to the last quarter of the sixth century. For hundreds of years it resided in Donegal, in the lands of Tír Conaill, where descendants of Columba's royal kinsmen held power throughout the medieval period. In battle it conferred Columba's blessing and brought hope of victory to those who venerated him. Manus O'Donnell, himself a Tír Conaill chieftain, described the Cathach's powers in his sixteenth-century Life of Columba: 'and if it is borne three times sunwise around the army of Cenél Conaill when they go into battle, they will come back triumphant'.[10] It has the distinction of being the only one of this trio of martial talismans that we can today identify with certainty. Whether it really does preserve Columba's handwriting must be doubted. His primary relics were of course his mortal remains and these, too, were also credited with supernatural power. Both his native and adoptive homelands therefore benefited when his bones were divided between Kells in Ireland and Dunkeld in Scotland in the ninth century. At each site the relics were imbued with miraculous capabilities that did not fade through the ensuing centuries. As late as c.1500 the inhabitants of Dunkeld, threatened by plague, were given water into which one of the saint's reputed bones had been dipped.[11]

Saints were venerated not only at their primary cult-centres but also at sites with less tangible connections. Church dedications, regardless of date or location, fall into this category. Even a minor church bearing only the name of a particular saint but no other connection can be seen as participating in the cult. In Columba's case, a great many churches in Scotland and Ireland still acknowledge him as their patron, although only a few can claim any direct link with the saint himself or with the monastic *familia* overseen by his successors. Some church dedications show the common Anglicised form of his name (*Columba*), while others use the Gaelic *Colum Chille* or a variant such as *Columkill*. Unsurprisingly, the cathedrals of both Derry and Dunkeld are dedicated to him. The oldest dedications, however, seem to be those enshrined in place-names coined in early medieval times.

Examples include Kilmacolm in Renfrewshire and Kirkcolm in Galloway, both of which mean 'Church of Columba' in Gaelic and Old Norse respectively. Such names are not found in Ireland, in spite of a preponderance of *kil-* toponyms incorporating the names of numerous other saints. Nor do we find the names of Columba's successors attached to Irish place-names in the way they are commemorated in Scotland. The men who followed him in the abbacy of Iona appear in Scottish dedications and place-names that reflect not only devotion to them as individuals but also the expansion of the Columban *familia*. We find Adomnán commemorated in a dozen place-names in Perthshire alone, a distribution that seems to support the traditional view that he had dealings with Pictish communities. Even Baithéne, who held the abbacy of Iona for barely three years, is remembered today in the name of Abbey St Bathans, a village in East Lothian. What these place-names demonstrate is the power and influence of Iona across a broad swathe of northern Britain in the centuries after Columba's death. While it should be admitted that some names might relate to landholdings of the Benedictine abbey that replaced the old monastery in the beginning of the thirteenth century, these same lands might once have belonged to the abbots of earlier times. Thus, even where a dedication or place-name appears to be of post-1200 origin, it may simply denote an ancient possession of Iona taken over by the Benedictines.[12]

Perceptions of 'Celtic Christianity'

The Reformation of the sixteenth and seventeenth centuries disapproved of saintly cults but was unable to erase them. In Scotland, stories of Columba were handed down from one generation to the next and copies of old hagiographical texts were preserved. Reforming zeal was at its zenith when Stephen White rediscovered Dorbbéne's manuscript of *Vita Columbae* at Reichenau in 1621. On Iona at that time the islanders needed no written version of the saint's legend to help them recall his achievements. They possessed their own tales, preserved by word of mouth through generations of laymen in lands around the abbey. So, too, did the common people of Ireland who revered Colum Cille as a national saint alongside Patrick and Brigid. The publication of John Colgan's printed edition of *Vita Columbae* in

1647 made little impact on these ordinary folk, but did provide a small number of interested scholars with easy access – for the first time – to a definitive account of the saint's life. Scholarly fascination with Columba, although initially on a small scale, eventually broadened his appeal outside Scotland and Ireland and allowed him to be studied as a figure of history as well as venerated as a saint. Around this time, however, a different kind of interest began to appear. Scottish Protestant churchmen, fervent in their disdain for the papacy, sought to portray their 'Celtic' predecessors as untainted Christians making a brave stand against the corruption of Roman Catholicism. This huge distortion of the facts surrounding the Easter Controversy became popular in anti-Catholic quarters and has not entirely dissipated today. It was followed in the late eighteenth and early nineteenth centuries by an equally ill-informed trend to romanticise all things 'Celtic', a process that nurtured an extraordinarily idealised image of the indigenous peoples of the British Isles. This, too, is still with us. Together, these two movements produced the false notion that 'Celtic Christianity' was somehow different and separate from the mainstream Catholicism of pre-Reformation times. An offshoot from this type of thinking has given us the modern 'New Age' figure of the ascetic, nature-loving Celtic monk – essentially a druid or shaman – whose spiritual beliefs blend Christianity with the gentler aspects of paganism.

In company with other British and Irish saints, Columba has inevitably become a champion of 'Celtic Christianity'. The inverted commas are necessary to distinguish this modern term from the historical context with which it is all too frequently confused. There is, in fact, a fairly clear line between the two. On the one hand, we have the romanticised New Age perception of early medieval saints in which their beliefs and practices are seen to conform to present-day ideas about spirituality. On the other, we have historians and archaeologists seeking a genuine understanding of how Christianity developed in Britain and Ireland during what used to be called the 'Dark Ages'. Academic scholarship and New Age romanticism rarely coincide, the romantics generally preferring their own definitions of Celtic Christianity to the less esoteric ones offered by historians. Serious scholars rarely subscribe to the popular notion of a non-bureaucratic 'Celtic Church' organised along simple lines with an emphasis on Nature and little concern for wealth, power and status.[13] Ironically, this kind of skewed thinking brings Columba and his contemporaries closer to modern neo-paganism than to the Christianity that they valued so highly. Everything we know about the attitudes of these 'Celtic' monks suggests that they abhorred paganism. Moreover, by depicting them as simple ascetics who despised wealth and authority, the modernising stance denies them their true heritage as members of an elite social class, a position that enabled them to interact on equal terms with powerful contemporaries in the secular sphere. Ascetic lifestyles were certainly adopted by some monks and nuns in the Celtic lands, but the same can be said of their peers in Anglo-Saxon England and elsewhere in Western Christendom. Most religious communities in early medieval times were, in fact, hierarchical and tightly managed. The largest, as we have seen, held substantial economic interests via land ownership and agricultural production. All were places not only of prayer and contemplation but also of intensive labour. Few could afford to accommodate the kind of sentimentality sometimes imagined in modern visions of 'Celtic Christianity'. A monastery was a self-sufficient community whose inhabitants had to feed and clothe themselves through their own labours. Thus, although love and respect for the natural world created by God were integral to their beliefs, such values did not preclude, for example, the slaughter of animals for meat and leather. Even on Iona, a place revered by modern romantics as a Celtic spiritual paradise, we see few hints of what might now be called 'environmental awareness' among the monks of Columba's time. The saint's dismay at the seal-poaching antics of Erc moccu Druidi was directed at the act of theft, not at the fate of the helpless creatures slain by the thief's spear. Adomnán leaves us in no doubt that these same seals belonged to the monastery and were routinely culled by the monks.

Columba in the twenty-first century

In 1997, the 1,400th anniversary of Columba's death was marked by numerous events around the world. In Britain and Ireland the range of festivities included special programmes on radio and television, together with various pageants and exhibitions. Specially designed postage stamps were issued by the Royal Mint in London to commemorate not only Columba but also St Augustine of Canterbury whose arrival in Kent in 597 is seen by some as the true beginning of English

Christianity. On Mull a new heritage centre devoted to Columba was unveiled at Fionnphort, on the shore facing Iona, and the President of Ireland was guest of honour at the opening ceremony. A similar centre now stands in the saint's homeland at the traditional site of his birth near Lough Gartan in Donegal. In an effort to develop relationships between the Gaelic-speaking regions of Ireland and Scotland a 'Columba Initiative' (*Iomairt Chaluim Chille*) was also launched in 1997. Under its current name *Colmcille* this programme continues to support community-based cultural and educational projects in the two areas.[14]

Columba, like all saints, has a part to play in the modern world in whatever guise or role we choose to give him. As a respondent to prayer he offers a listening ear to those who call upon him. As a paragon of Christian virtue – the pious monk of *Vita Columbae* – he encapsulates an ideal to which people of faith might seek to aspire. Alongside Patrick and Brigid he represents, for the Irish, a link with the religious beliefs of their ancestors. Likewise in Scotland he stands only a few paces behind Andrew in the panoply of national saints as a Gaelic companion of the Apostle. On a purely commercial level Columba is a useful 'brand' in the promotional activities of a number of business sectors. Of these, the most obvious is tourism in both Scotland and Ireland, but others include craftworking of objects with Celtic or early Christian themes. Columba and Iona are also popular topics in a steady output of literature dealing with 'Celtic Christianity' in its various aspects. It is in this latter role that we see him as an idealised, almost mythologised figure somewhat removed from the image presented by Adomnán. This modern Columba is a softer, gentler person than the dynamic individual remembered on seventh-century Iona. Both are virtuous Christians who care deeply for their fellow human beings, but the former seems too perfect, too comfortable, to be a three-dimensional character.[15] In other words, the edges of his personality are too smooth. Adomnán's Columba, by contrast, has a robustness, at times almost a brashness, that makes him not only more believable but also more accessible. We see him confronting ruthless pirates and hostile heathen priests; we hear him openly pouring scorn on those whom he felt deserved it. Notwithstanding the elements from his own time that Adomnán introduced into *Vita Columbae* we can probably conclude that he has brought us as close as we are likely to get to the Columba of history.

Notes

ABBREVIATIONS

AC *Annales Cambriae* (Welsh Annals)
AT *Annals of Tigernach*
AU *Annals of Ulster*
HE Bede's *Ecclesiastical History*
VC Adomnán's *Vita Columbae*

CHAPTER 1: THE SOURCES

1 Sharpe 1995, 57; Herbert 1988, 138.
2 Anderson and Anderson 1991, 23.
3 Picard 1985, 75–7.
4 Gregory the Great, *Dialogues*, ii; Charles-Edwards 2010, 215.
5 Sharpe 1995, 242.
6 Sulpicius; Sharpe 1995, 245.
7 Sulpicius; Sharpe 1995, 248.
8 *VC*, i, 1.
9 Charles-Edwards 2010, 215.
10 e.g. at *VC*, ii, 4, where he observes that the miracle combines both prophecy and power. On this point see Charles-Edwards 2010, 208.
11 Charles-Edwards 2010, 209.
12 *VC*, iii, Introduction.
13 Herbert 1988, 13. See also Picard 1984.
14 As in *VC*, ii, 6 and iii, 4.
15 Herbert 1988, 140.
16 *VC*, 2nd Preface.
17 *VC*, iii, 23.
18 Herbert 1988, 18.
19 *VC*, iii, 5. On Cumméne's book see also Fraser 2003/04. On the scribe Dorbbéne mac Altaine see further below.
20 Herbert 1988, 25.
21 *VC*, ii, 4.
22 Ernéne mac Craseni: *VC*, i, 3; Oswald: *VC*, i, 1.
23 *VC*, iii, 23.
24 Herbert 1988, 139.
25 McClure and Collins 1994, xxii.
26 *AU* 713; Picard 1982, 216–17, n. 2; see also Anderson and Anderson 1991, lxi–ii
27 Sharpe 1995, 235.
28 Anderson and Anderson 1991, lviii–lx.
29 On Dallán see Charles-Edwards 2004.
30 Herbert 1988, 10.
31 Bodleian Library Rawlinson B502.
32 Bannerman 1968; Herbert 1988, 23. Some scholars prefer a date in the late seventh century for the beginning of annal-writing on Iona, e.g. Hughes 1972, 118.
33 Fraser 2009, 94–5; Herbert 1988, 22–3.
34 Hughes 1972, 235.
35 Herbert 1988, 184.
36 Herbert 1988, 189.
37 On the date see Hughes 1972, 236.
38 Irish Life, ch. 38.
39 Herbert 1988, 190–2, 199.
40 Anderson and Anderson 1991, lxii.
41 Stokes 1905; Dumville 2002.

CHAPTER 2: FROM IRELAND TO IONA

1 Charles-Edwards 2000, 212.
2 Hood 1978.
3 Charles-Edwards 2000, 239.
4 On Irish monasticism see Ryan 1992.
5 The Uí Néill ancestry of Cenél Conaill has been questioned. See Lacey 2006, 145–66.
6 *VC*, 2nd preface; Sharpe 1995, 247–8; Mac Niocaill 1972, 39.
7 Irish Life, ch. 20.

8 Sharpe 1995, 10.
9 Finlay 1979, 53.
10 Irish Life, ch. 23 (Cruithnechan's resurrection); ch. 21 (loaf).
11 Clancy 2001, 69.
12 *VC*, ii, 1.
13 *VC*, ii, 25.
14 Smyth 1984, 92. On the *Lex Innocentium* of 697 see Chapter 7 below.
15 On Clonard see Hughes 1954.
16 *Martyrology of Oengus*, 11 February (Stokes 1905, 72–3).
17 *AC* 547; *AU* 549=546.
18 Sharpe 1995, 255–6.
19 *VC*, 2nd preface.
20 *VC*, iii, 3.
21 Sharpe 1995, 13.
22 *VC*, 2nd preface and i, 7.
23 *VC*, iii, 3.
24 Binchy 1958, 122–3.
25 Herbert 1988.
26 Herbert 1988, 28.
27 *VC*, iii, 3.
28 *VC*, iii, 3.
29 Watson 1926, 87–8.
30 *AU*/*AT* 574=576; Macquarrie 1997, 87; Fraser 2009, 97; Anderson 1922, 75.
31 *VC*, i, 7.
32 Finlay 1979, 143.
33 On the name Alba see Woolf 2007, 125–6.
34 Finlay 1979, 143.
35 *AU*/*AT* 568=570.
36 Fraser 2009, 97.

CHAPTER 3: KING ÁEDÁN

1 *AU*/*AT* 576=578.
2 *VC*, iii, 5; Meckler 1990.
3 Fraser 2009, 122.
4 Binchy 1958.
5 Enright 1985a, 86–90.
6 Macquarrie 1997, 77.
7 See Nieke and Duncan 1988, 11–12, 16, on the Dunaverty footprint, 11–12, 16. A second footprint was carved in the nineteenth century, the two being known today as 'St Columba's Footprints'.
8 *VC*, i, 9.
9 I Samuel 16:1–13; Enright 1985b, 15–19.
10 *VC*, i, 28; On Dunadd see Lane and Campbell 2000.
11 *AU* 575. It has been suggested that *contio* might be a contraction of *conventio*, 'convention', or *condictio*, 'conference', but *contio*, 'public assembly', would fit the context well enough. See Sharpe 1995, 312; Fraser 2007, 318 n.8.
12 Herbert 1988.
13 *do sidugad etir firv Herenn Alban im Dál Riaddai*. The English translation is from Ryan 1946, 42.
14 Anderson 1922, 83–4.
15 Herbert 1988, 215, 217 and (for the text) 265.
16 *VC*, i, 11.
17 Sharpe 1995, 272.
18 Meckler 1997, but see Jaski 1998 for the counter-argument.
19 Fraser 2009, 139.
20 *VC*, i, 50.
21 On the possibility that the account of the Convention in *Vita Columbae* reflects seventh-century rather than sixth-century politics see Fraser 2007.
22 *VC*, i, 8.
23 Watson 1926.
24 Fraser 2009, 16.
25 *AU* 582=584.
26 See Macquarrie 1997, 107, for arguments against equating *bellum Miathorum* with the Battle of Circhind.
27 Aitchison 2003, 32–3.
28 Clarkson 2010, 44.
29 Bromwich 1961.
30 *Red Book of Hergest* see Bromwich 1961.
31 Fraser 2009, 133.
32 *AU*/*AT* 590=592.
33 Macquarrie 1997, 109.
34 *HE*, i, 34.
35 This chapter has not made reference to the late and evidently spurious traditions of Áedán's submission to Báetán mac Cairill. For discussion, see Macquarrie 1997, 106, 112–13, and Fraser 2009, 122–3.

CHAPTER 4: ABBOT

1 *VC*, ii, 29.
2 O'Sullivan 1999, 231; McCormick 1993.
3 Sharpe 1995, 375.
4 RCAHMS 1982, 31–48; Redknap 1977; O'Sullivan 1999, 220–1.
5 MacDonald 1984, 287–8.
6 MacDonald 1984, 284–9; McCormick 1997.
7 O'Sullivan 1999, 222.
8 O'Sullivan 1999, 236; Barber 1981.
9 *VC*, i, 25. On the archaeological remains see Thomas 1971 and Fowler and Fowler 1988.
10 O'Sullivan 1999, 236.

11 Markus 1999, 121–2.
12 Sharpe 1995, 354.
13 Sharpe 1995, 19.
14 Sharpe 1995, 20.
15 Taran: *VC*, ii, 23. On the possibility that Taran belongs to a later period see Fraser 2009, 5–6, 246–8; Oengus: *VC*, i, 13.
16 *VC*, i, 16.
17 *VC*, i, 4; On the Life of Cainnech see Sharpe 1995, 262–3.
18 *VC*, i, 2. This was St Fintan, also known as Munnu, founder of the monastery at Taghmon in County Wexford.
19 *VC*, i, 21.
20 *VC*, ii, 39.
21 *VC*, i, 22.
22 *VC*, iii, 12.
23 *VC*, i, 44; Reeves 1857, 85n.
24 *VC*, iii, 17; Sharpe 1995, 368.
25 *VC*, i, 37; Purser 1992.
26 *VC*, ii, 9.
27 *VC*, i, 26.
28 bell-ringing: *VC*, i, 8; ii, 42, iii, 23.
29 Columba: *VC*, i, 24; Luigbe: *VC*, i, 35.
30 *VC*, i, 23.
31 *VC*, iii, 23 (psalter); ii, 8–9 (book of hymns). On the Cathach see Herity and Breen 2002.
32 *VC*, ii, 29.
33 Markus 2010.
34 *VC*, ii, 8; see Waterer 1968 on Irish book-satchels.
35 *VC*, iii, 23. On agriculture in general see Kelly 1997.
36 *VC*, i, 45; Sharpe 1995, 308–9.
37 *VC*, iii, 10.
38 *VC*, ii, 3.
39 *VC*, i, 37.
40 Sharpe 1995, 298.
41 Sharpe 1995, 298–9.
42 *VC*, i, 41; Sharpe 1995, 303.
43 *VC*, ii, 38.
44 *VC*, ii, 16.
45 *VC*, ii, 16; *bocetum*: *VC*, iii, 23; Sharpe 1995, 375.
46 *VC*, ii, 28; MacDonald 1984, 281; Sharpe 1995, 331.
47 Reece 1973, 44.
48 *VC*, ii, 29.
49 *VC*, i, 41.
50 *VC*, ii, 23.
51 *VC*, ii, 37.
52 *VC*, ii, 19.
53 *VC*, i, 19.
54 Bieler 1963, 160.
55 *VC*, i, 21. Bieler 1963, 160; Sharpe 1995, 282.
56 Barber 1981, 318–28. On the type and style of shoes probably worn by the monks see Lucas 1956.
57 *VC*, ii, 29.
58 *VC*, ii, 45.
59 *VC*, iii, 23. On chariots in early Ireland see Greene 1972.
60 Lugaid: *VC*, i, 38; Reeves 1857,75n.
61 Sharpe 1995, 73.
62 *VC*, i, 4.
63 On St Brendan and his voyages see Burgess 2002. On Eileach an Naoimh see Pallister 2005.
64 *VC*, ii, 42.
65 *VC*, i, 20.
66 *VC*, ii, 45.
67 On the early medieval currach see Hornell 1977.
68 Sharpe 1995, 335–6.
69 Sharpe 1995, 70.
70 Columba's death and burial are discussed further in Chapter 7.

CHAPTER 5: IONA AND HER NEIGHBOURS

1 See Macquarrie 1997, 91–102, for a useful study of Hinba.
2 *VC*, iii, 17.
3 Ernán: *VC*, i, 45; penitents: *VC*, i, 21.
4 *VC*, iii, 18.
5 *VC*, ii, 24.
6 Colonsay: Clark 1845; Oronsay: Reeves 1857; Uist: Innes 1853; Canna: Reeves 1857; Jura: Watson 1926; Gunna: Lamont 1978; Eileach an Naoimh: Skene 1874.
7 *VC*, iii, 23.
8 Sharpe 1995, 275, n. 93.
9 Sharpe 1995, 308; Macquarrie 1997, 99–100.
10 *VC*, i, 26.
11 Reeves 1857, 59n.; Watson 1926, 92.
12 *VC*, ii, 18.
13 *VC*, i, 31.
14 *VC*, iii, 18. On the monastery of Eigg see MacDonald 1973.
15 On St Moluag and Lismore see MacDonald 1973.
16 Kilkerran: the tradition appears in John of Fordun's *Chronica Gentis Scotorum* of the late fourteenth century.
17 On the hagiography surrounding St Blane see Macquarrie 2001. On Kingarth see Fraser 2005.
18 On Inchmarnock see Lowe 2008.
19 For the theory that Tiree belonged to Cenél Loairn see Bannerman 1974, 113–14.

20 *VC*, ii, 22.
21 *VC*, ii, 24.
22 Sharpe 1995, 329.
23 *VC*, ii, 23.
24 *VC*, ii, 20.
25 *VC*, i, 46.
26 Watson 1926, 94.
27 Watson 1926, 78; Sharpe 1995, 310.
28 Anderson and Anderson 1991, xxxii.
29 *VC*, i, 3.
30 *VC*, i, 29.
31 *VC*, ii, 2.
32 *AT* 620; Charles-Edwards 2000, 282.
33 *VC*, iii, 23; Herbert 1988, 31–2.
34 Herbert 1988, 255–6.
35 Lacey 1998.
36 See Lacey 2010, 28, on Drumhome as a re-foundation by Áed.
37 Drumhome: *VC*, i, 20; Sharpe 1995, 29. Lathreg inden: *VC*, i, 20; Sharpe 1995, 281; MacDonald 1984, 277, on the identification with Larragharril. Cell Mór Dithruib: *VC*, i, 50; Sharpe 1995, 317.

CHAPTER 6: THE PICTS

1 Bede, HE iii 4.
2 Bede, HE iii 4.
3 *VC*, i, 33. Adomnán renders the place-name in Latin as *Dobur Artbranani.*
4 Fraser 2004.
5 Dumville 1981.
6 *VC*, ii, 46.
7 Sharpe 1995, 336.
8 *VC*, iii, 14.
9 Watson 1926, 95.
10 *VC*, ii, 32.
11 *VC*, ii, 11.
12 *VC*, ii, 27.
13 Although Ó Riain 1983 suggested that Luigne moccu Min and his near-namesake Luigbe moccu Min were one and the same, this is not a necessary deduction. See Sharpe 1995, 289.
14 On the Ness episode see Borsje 1994.
15 *VC*, ii, 4.
16 *VC*, ii, 33.
17 Sharpe 1995, 335.
18 *VC*, ii, 35.
19 *VC*, ii, 42.
20 *AU*/*AT*.
21 *VC*, ii, 33.
22 *VC*, ii, 34.
23 *VC*, ii, 23.
24 *VC*, ii, 46.
25 Carver 2004.
26 For a detailed assessment of Columba's Pictish mission and its wider context see Fraser 2009, 97–115.

CHAPTER 7: SAINT

1 The account of Columba's death and funeral appears in *VC*, iii, 23. On his final visit to the machair see *VC*, ii, 28 and, on the similarity with Evagrius (*Vita Antonii*, 56) see Sharpe 1995, 331.
2 Walahfrid Strabo, Life of Blathmac (c.840). See Anderson 1922, 264, for an English translation of the relevant passage.
3 Herbert 1988, 11.
4 Herbert 1988, 14.
5 Herbert 1988, 21, 24.
6 *Vita Baithéne*, ed. W. Heist, 1965.
7 Lamlash: Watson 1926, 305–6; Taylor 1999, 52.
8 See Lacey 2010, 30, for a suggestion that Fergna belonged to the Cenél mBogaine of western Donegal.
9 *VC*, iii, 19.
10 *VC*, i, 1.
11 *HE*, iii, 1.
12 *HE*, iii, 3.
13 *HE*, ii, 19.
14 On the different styles of tonsure see James 1984.
15 See Charles-Edwards 2000, 251, on the location of Mag Lene.
16 On Cummian see: Walsh and Ó Cróinín 1988, 74–5; Charles-Edwards 2000, 402; Bracken 2007.
17 This and the following quotations are from *HE*, iii, 25. English translations in McClure and Collins 1994, 157–9.
18 *HE*, iv, 4.
19 Herbert and Ó Riain 1988, 41.
20 Herbert 1988, 168.
21 *VC*, iii, 23.
22 Lacey 2010, 33.
23 Herbert 1988, 48.
24 *HE*, v, 15. For discussion of Adomnán's views on Easter see Stancliffe 2010.
25 Herbert 1988, 54.
26 On Armagh's position at this time see Charles-Edwards 2000, 435.
27 Ni Dhonnchadha 1982; Markus 1997.
28 Clancy 1999, 11.
29 *HE*, v, 15.
30 *HE*, v, 22.
31 On Naiton (Nechtan) see Clancy 2004.

CHAPTER 8: *PARUCHIA* AND *FAMILIA*

1 Herbert 1988, 60.
2 Gwynn 1915.
3 Herbert 1988, 61.
4 On the Law of Patrick see O'Keeffe 1904, and Charles-Edwards 2000, 564.
5 Charles-Edwards 2000, 501.
6 Herbert 1988, 65.
7 Bannerman 1999. On the Viking threat see also Etchingham 1996.
8 Herbert 1988, 69.
9 *AU* 849.
10 Lapidge 1982.
11 Book of Leinster ('Comarbada Patraic'): *Mael Brigti mac Tornain .xxxix. comarba Patraic & Coluim Chille de Chlaind Chonaill .i. na hoentad*
12 *AU* 938
13 *AU* 986. On the Norse graves on Iona see Sharpe 1995, 84.
14 *AU*/*AT* 1055
15 Herbert 1988, 100.
16 Herbert 1988, 92.
17 Kenney 1929, 470–1; Herbert 1988, 103.
18 Herbert 1988, 106. On monastic towns see Swan 1985 and Doherty 1985.
19 On the Synod of Rath Breasail see Herbert 1988, 109–10, and Candon 1984. For the wider context see Gwynn 1968.
20 *Annals of the Four Masters* 1150; Herbert 1988, 113–14.
21 *AU* 1158.

CHAPTER 9: LEGACY

1 Clancy 1999, 3.
2 Davies 2010, 1–3.
3 Clancy 1999, 8–9. The traditions of Downpatrick assert that all three of Ireland's national saints – Patrick, Columba and Brigid – are buried there.
4 On *De Locis Sanctis* see Aist 2010 and O' Loughlin 1996.
5 *HE*, v, 15–17.
6 *De Locis Sanctis*, iii, 4; Clancy 1999, 20.
7 Clancy and Markus 1995, 129–34; Clancy 1999, 22–3.
8 English translation by Gilbert Markus in Clancy 1998, 318.
9 See Bourke 1997, on the crozier.
10 *Betha Coluim Chille*, 182–5.
11 Clancy 1999, 29 n78.
12 Taylor 1999, 39–40.
13 Meek 1999, 263. For an accurate study of 'Celtic' Christianity see Corning 2006.
14 On the 1997 anniversary celebrations see MacArthur 1999, 245–51.
15 Meek 1999, 269.

Bibiography

Aist, R. (2010) 'Adomnán, Arculf and the Source Material of *De Locis Sanctis*', pp.162–80 in J.M. Wooding (ed.) *Adomnán of Iona: Theologian, Lawmaker, Peacemaker* (Dublin)

Aitchison, N. (2003) *The Picts and the Scots at War* (Stroud)

Anderson, A.O. (1922) *Early Sources of Scottish History, AD 500 to 1286*. Vol. 1 (Edinburgh)

Anderson, A.O. and Anderson, M.O. (eds) (1991) *Adomnán's Life of Columba*. Revised edition (Oxford)

Bannerman, J. (1968) 'Notes on the Scottish Entries in the Early Irish Annals', *Scottish Gaelic Studies* 11: 149–70

Bannerman, J. (1974) *Studies in the History of Dalriada* (Edinburgh)

Bannerman, J. (1999) 'The Scottish Takeover of Pictland and the Relics of Columba', pp.71–94 in D. Broun and T.O. Clancy (eds) *Spes Scotorum, Hope of Scots: Saint Columba, Iona and Scotland* (Edinburgh)

Barber, J. (1981) 'Excavations on Iona, 1979', *Proceedings of the Society of Antiquaries of Scotland* 111: 282–380

Bieler, L. (1963) *The Irish Penitentials* (Dublin)

Binchy, D.A. (1958) 'The Fair of Tailtiu and the Feast of Tara', *Eriu* 18: 113–38

Borsje, J. (1994) 'The Monster in the River Ness in *Vita Sancti Columbae*: a Study of a Miracle', *Peritia* 8: 27–34

Bourke, C. (1997) '*Insignia Columbae* II', pp. 162–83 in C. Bourke (ed.) *Studies in the Cult of Saint Columba* (Dublin)

Bracken, D. (2007) 'Juniors Teaching Elders: Columbanus, Rome and Spiritual Authority', pp. 253–75 in E.O Carragain and C. Neuman de Vegvar (eds) *Roma Felix: Formation and Reflections of Medieval Rome* (Aldershot)

Bromwich, R. (ed.) (1961) *Trioedd Ynys Prydein: the Welsh Triads* (Cardiff)

Burgess, G. (2002) *The Voyage of St Brendan* (Exeter)

Candon, A. (1984) 'Ráith Bressail: a Suggested Identification', *Peritia* 3: 326–9

Carver, M.O.H. (2004) 'An Iona of the East: the Early Medieval Monastery at Portmahomack, Tarbat Ness', *Medieval Archaeology* 48: 1–30

Charles-Edwards, T.M. (2000) *Early Christian Ireland* (Cambridge)

Charles-Edwards, T.M. (2004) 'Dallán Forgaill (fl. 597)' in *Oxford Dictionary of National Biography* (Oxford)

Charles-Edwards, T.M. (2010) 'The Structure and Purpose of Adomnán's *Vita Columbae*', pp. 205–18 in J.M. Wooding (ed.) *Adomnán of Iona: Theologian, Lawmaker, Peacemaker* (Dublin)

Clancy, T. O. (ed.) (1998) *The Triumph Tree: Scotland's Earliest Poetry, 550–1350* (Edinburgh)

Clancy, T.O. (1999) 'Columba, Adomnán and the Cult of Saints in Scotland', pp. 3–34 in D. Broun and T.O. Clancy (eds) *Spes Scotorum, Hope of Scots: Saint Columba, Iona and Scotland* (Edinburgh)

Clancy, T.O. (2001) 'The Real St Ninian', *Innes Review* 52: 1–28
Clancy, T.O. (2004) 'Philosopher-King: Nechtan mac Der-Ilei', *Scottish Historical Review* 83: 125–49
Clancy, T.O. and Markus, G. (1995) *Iona: the Earliest Poetry of a Celtic Monastery* (Edinburgh)
Clark, F.W. (1845) 'United Parish of Kilfinichen and Kilviceuen, Iona', pp.312–39 in *The New Statistical Account of Scotland*. Vol. 7.ii (Edinburgh)
Clarkson, T. (2010) *The Men of the North: the Britons of Southern Scotland* (Edinburgh)
Corning, C. (2006) *The Celtic and Roman Traditions: Conflict and Consensus in the Early Medieval Church* (London)
Davies, J.R. (2010) *The Cult of Saint Constantine* (Govan)
Doherty, C. (1985) 'The Monastic Town in Early Medieval Ireland', pp.45–75 in H.B. Clarke and A. Simms (eds) *The Comparative History of Urban Origins in Non-Roman Europe*. Vol. 1 (Oxford)
Dumville, D.N. (1981) '*Primarius Cohortis* in Adomnán's Life of Columba', *Scottish Gaelic Studies* 13: 130–1
Dumville, D.N. (2002) '*Félire Óengusso*: Problems of Dating a Monument of Old Irish', *Éigse* 33: 19–34
Enright, M.J. (1985a) 'Royal Succession and Abbatial Prerogative in Adomnán's Vita Columbae', *Peritia* 4: 83–103
Enright, M.J. (1985b) *Iona, Tara and Soissons: the Origins of the Royal Anointing Ritual* (Berlin)
Etchingham, C. (1996) *Viking Raids on Irish Church Settlements in the Ninth Century* (Maynooth)
Finlay, I. (1979) *Columba* (London)
Fowler, E. and Fowler, P.J. (1988) 'Excavations on Torr an Aba, Iona', *Proceedings of the Society of Antiquaries of Scotland* 118: 181–201
Fowler, J.T. (ed.) (1894) *Adamnani Vita S. Columbae* (Oxford)
Fraser, J.E. (2003/04) 'Adomnán, Cumméne Ailbe and the Picts', *Peritia* 17–18: 183–98
Fraser, J.E. (2004) 'The Iona Chronicle, the Descendants of Áedán mac Gabráin and the Principal Kindreds of Dál Riata', *Northern Studies* 38: 77–96
Fraser, J.E. (2005) 'Strangers on the Clyde: Cenél Comgaill, Clyde Rock and the Bishops of Kingarth', *Innes Review* 56: 102–20
Fraser, J.E. (2007) 'St Columba and the Convention at Druimm Cete: Peace and Politics at Seventh-Century Iona', *Early Medieval Europe* 15: 315–34
Fraser, J.E. (2009) *From Caledonia to Pictland: Scotland to 795* (Edinburgh)
Greene, D. (1972) 'The Chariot as Described in Irish Literature', pp.59–73 in C. Thomas (ed.) *The Iron Age in the Irish Sea Province* (London)
Gwynn, A. (1968) *The Twelfth-Century Reform* (Dublin)
Gwynn, L. (1915) 'The Reliquary of Adomnán', *Archivum Hibernicum* 4: 199–214
Herbert, M. (1988) *Iona, Kells and Derry: the History and Hagiography of the Monastic Familia of Columba* (Oxford)
Herbert, M. and Ó Riain, P. (eds) (1988) *Betha Adamnáin: the Irish Life of Adamnán* (London)
Herity, M. and Breen, A. (2002) *The Cathach of Colum Cille: an Introduction* (Dublin)
Hood, A.B.E. (ed.) (1978) *St Patrick: his Writings and Muirchu's Life* (London)
Hornell, J. (1977) *British Coracles and Irish Curraghs* (New York)
Hughes, K. (1954) 'The Cult of St Finnian of Clonard from the Eighth to the Eleventh Century', *Irish Historical Studies* 9: 13–27
Hughes, K. (1972) *Early Christian Ireland: Introduction to the Sources* (London)
Innes, T. (1853) *Civil and Ecclesiastical History of Scotland*. Edited by G. Grub (Aberdeen)
James, E. (1984) 'Bede and the Tonsure Question', *Peritia* 3: 85–98
Jaski, B. (1998) 'Druim Cett Revisited', *Peritia* 12: 340–50
Kelly, F. (1997) *Early Irish Farming* (Dublin)
Kenney, J.F. (1929) *Sources for the Early History of Ireland: Ecclesiastical* (New York)
Lacey, B. (1998) '"Columba, Founder of the Monastery of Derry?" – *Mihi Manet Incertus*', *Journal of the Royal Society of Antiquaries of Ireland* 128: 35–47
Lacey, B. (2006) *Cenél Conaill and the Donegal Kingdoms* (Dublin)
Lacey, B. (2010) 'Adomnán and Donegal', pp.20–35 in J.M. Wooding (ed.) *Adomnán of Iona: Theologian, Lawmaker, Peacemaker* (Dublin)

Lamont, W. D. (1978) 'Where is Adomnán's Hinba?', *Notes and Queries of the Society of West Highland and Island Historical Research* 7: 3–6
Lane, A. and Campbell, E. (2000) *Dunadd: an Early Dalriadic Capital* (Oxford)
Lapidge, M. (1982) 'The Cult of St Indract at Glastonbury', pp. 179–212 in D. Whitelock, R. McKitterick and D. Dumville (eds) *Ireland in Early Medieval Europe: Studies in Memory of Kathleen Hughes* (Cambridge)
Lowe, C. (2008) *Inchmarnock: An Early Historic Island Monastery and its Archaeological Landscape* (Edinburgh)
Lucas, A.T. (1956) 'Footwear in Ireland', *Journal of the County Louth Archaeological and Historical Society* 13: 309–94
MacArthur, E.M. (1999) 'Celebrating Columba on Iona, 1897 and 1997', pp.245–52 in D. Broun and T.O. Clancy (eds) *Spes Scotorum, Hope of Scots: Saint Columba, Iona and Scotland* (Edinburgh)
McClure, J. and Collins, R. (eds) (1994), Bede: *The Ecclesiastical History of the English People* (Oxford)
McCormick, F. (1993) 'Excavations on Iona in 1988', *Ulster Journal of Archaeology* 56: 78–108
McCormick, F. (1997) 'Iona: the Archaeology of an Early Monastery', pp.45–68 in C. Bourke (ed.) *Studies in the Cult of Saint Columba* (Dublin)
MacDonald, A.D.S. (1973) 'Two Major Early Monasteries', *Scottish Archaeological Forum* 5: 57–64
MacDonald, A.D.S. (1984) 'Aspects of the Monastery and Monastic Life in Adomnán's Life of Columba', *Peritia* 3: 271–302
Mac Niocaill, G. (1972) *Ireland Before the Vikings* (Dublin)
Macquarrie, A. (1997) *The Saints of Scotland: Essays in Scottish Church History,* AD *450–1093* (Edinburgh)
Macquarrie, A. (2001) 'The Office for St Blane (10 August) in the Aberdeen Breviary', *Innes Review* 52: 111–35
Markus, G. (1997) *Adomnán's 'Law of the Innocents'* (Glasgow)
Markus, G. (1999) 'Iona: Monks, Pastors and Missionaries', pp.115–38 in D. Broun and T.O. Clancy (eds) *Spes Scotorum, Hope of Scots: Saint Columba, Iona and Scotland* (Edinburgh)
Markus, G. (2010) '*Adiutor Laborantium* – a Poem by Adomnán?', pp.145–61 in J.M. Wooding (ed.) *Adomnán of Iona: Theologian, Lawmaker, Peacemaker* (Dublin)
Meckler, M. (1990) 'Colum Cille's Ordination of Áedán mac Gabráin', *Innes Review* 41: 139–50
Meckler, M. (1997) 'The Annals of Ulster and the Date of the Meeting at Druim Cett' *Peritia* 11: 44–52
Meek, D. (1999) 'Between Faith and Folklore: Twentieth-Century Interpretations and Images of Columba', pp.253–70 in D. Broun and T.O. Clancy (eds) *Spes Scotorum, Hope of Scots: Saint Columba, Iona and Scotland* (Edinburgh)
Ni Dhonnchadha, M. (1982) 'The Guarantor List of *Cain Adomnain*', *Peritia* 1: 178–215
Nieke, M.R. and Duncan, H.B. (1988) 'Dalriada: the Establishment and Maintenance of an Early Historic Kingdom in Northern Britain', pp.6–21 in S.T. Driscoll and M.R. Nieke (eds) *Power and Politics in Early Medieval Britain and Ireland* (Edinburgh)
O'Keeffe, J.G. (1904) 'The Rule of Patrick', *Ériu* 1: 216–24
O'Loughlin, T. (1996) 'The View from Iona: Adomnán's Mental Maps', *Peritia* 10: 98–122.
Ó Riain, P. (1983) 'Cainnech alias Colum Cille, Patron of Ossory', pp.20–35 in P. de Brun *et al.* (eds) *Folia Gadelica* (Cork)
O'Sullivan, J. (1999) 'Iona: Archaeological Investigations, 1875–1996, pp.215–44 in D. Broun and T.O. Clancy (eds) *Spes Scotorum, Hope of Scots: Saint Columba, Iona and Scotland* (Edinburgh)
Pallister, M. (2005) *Lost Argyll: Argyll's Lost Heritage* (Edinburgh)
Picard, J-M. (1982) 'The Purpose of Adomnán's *Vita Columbae*', *Peritia* 1: 160–77
Picard, J.-M. (1984) 'Bede, Adomnán and the Writing of History', *Peritia* 3: 50–70
Picard, J.-M. (1985) 'Structural Patterns in Hiberno-Latin Hagiography', *Peritia* 4: 67–82
Purser, J. (1992) *Scotland's Music: a History of the Traditional and Classical Music of Scotland From Earliest Times to the Present Day* (Edinburgh)
RCAHMS (1982) *Argyll IV: Iona* (Edinburgh)

Redknap, M. (1977) 'Excavations at Iona Abbey, 1976', *Proceedings of the Society of Antiquaries of Scotland* 108: 228–53

Reece, R. (1973) 'Recent Work on Iona', *Scottish Archaeological Forum* 5: 36–46

Reeves, W. (ed.) (1857) *Saint Adamnan, Abbot of Hy, Life of St Columba, Founder of Hy* (Edinburgh)

Ryan, J. (1946) 'The Convention of Druim Cett', *Journal of the Royal Society of Antiquaries of Ireland* 76: 35–52

Ryan, J. (1992) *Irish Monasticism: Origins and Early Development*, 2nd edn (Dublin)

Sharpe, R. (ed.) (1995) *Adomnán of Iona: Life of St Columba* (London)

Skene, W.F. (ed.) (1874) *Life of St Columba, Founder of Hy, Written by Adomnán*. Transl. A.P. Forbes (Edinburgh)

Smyth, A.P. (1984) *Warlords and Holy Men: Scotland, AD 80–1000* (London)

Stancliffe, C. (2010) 'Charity With Peace: Adomnán and the Easter Question', pp.51–68 in J.M. Wooding (ed.) *Adomnán of Iona: Theologian, Lawmaker, Peacemaker* (Dublin)

Stokes, W. (ed.) (1905) *Felire Oengusso: the Martyrology of Oengus the Culdee* (London)

Swan, L. (1985) 'Monastic Proto-Towns in Early Medieval Ireland: the Evidence of Aerial Photography, Plan Analysis and Survey', pp.77–102 in H.B. Clarke and A. Simms (eds) *The Comparative History of Urban Origins in Non-Roman Europe*. Vol. 1 (Oxford)

Taylor, S. (1999) 'Seventh-Century Iona Abbots in Scottish Place-Names', pp.35–70 in D. Broun and T.O. Clancy (eds) *Spes Scotorum, Hope of Scots: Saint Columba, Iona and Scotland* (Edinburgh)

Thomas, C. (1971) *The Early Christian Archaeology of North Britain* (Oxford)

Walsh, M. and Ó Cróinín, D. (1988) *Cummian's Letter* De Controversia Paschali *and the* De Ratione Conputandi (Toronto)

Waterer, J.W. (1968) 'Irish Book-satchels or Budgets', *Medieval Archaeology* 12: 70–82

Watson, W.J. (1926) *A History of the Celtic Place-Names of Scotland* (Edinburgh)

Woolf, A. (2007) *From Pictland to Alba, 789–1070* (Edinburgh)

Index